W9-BNX-564

The Everyday Sexism Project was founded by writer and activist Laura Bates in April 2012. It began life as a Web site where people could share their experiences of daily, normalized sexism, from street harassment to workplace discrimination, to sexual assault and rape.

The Project became a viral sensation, attracting international press attention from *The New York Times* to *Glamour* (France), from *Grazia South Africa* to the *The Times of India,* and support from celebrities such as Rose McGowan, Amanda Palmer, Mara Wilson, Ashley Judd, James Corden, and Simon Pegg. The Project has now collected more than one hundred thousand testimonies from people around the world and has launched new branches in twenty-five countries worldwide. The Project has been credited with helping to spark a new wave of feminism.

From a social media following of a quarter of a million, the impact of the Project has spread offline. Laura regularly briefs government ministers on specific issues from the gender pay gap to sex and relationships education, using real women's testimonies she has collected to lobby for meaningful policy change. She visits schools and universities to talk to young people about gender equality, body image, and consent, using real entries from young people to open up discussion and debate.

In March 2014 an event about Everyday Sexism was held at the United Nations in New York, where Laura spoke alongside Ministers from the UK and Danish governments, sharing the Project's findings and strategies for combating gender inequality with delegates from countries around the world.

Laura writes regularly for *The Guardian*, the *Independent*, and *TIME* magazine, among others. She was named on the Woman's Hour Power List of Top 10 Game Changers and has been named a Woman of the Year by *Cosmopolitan* (UK), *Red* magazine, and *The Sunday Times* (UK). She won the Women in Journalism Georgina Henry Award at the 2015 British Press Awards and was awarded a British Empire Medal by the Queen in the 2015 Birthday Honours List.

everyday sexism

LAURA BATES

THOMAS DUNNE BOOKS
ST. MARTIN'S GRIFFIN
NEW YORK

THOMAS DUNNE BOOKS.
An imprint of St. Martin's Press.

www.thomasdunnebooks.com
www.stmartins.com

The Library of Congress Cataloging-in-Publication Data is available upon request.

ISBN 978-1-250-10018-4 (trade paperback)
ISBN 978-1-250-06793-7 (hardcover)
ISBN 978-1-4668-7666-8 (e-book)

A different version of this book was published in Great Britain in 2014 by Simon & Schuster UK, Ltd., a CBS Company.

First U.S. Edition: April 2016

10 9 8 7 6 5 4 3 2 1

This book is dedicated to every single person who raised her voice and made the world listen.

Contents

Introduction	Everybody Has a Tipping Point	1
Chapter 1	Silenced Women: The Invisible Problem	13
Chapter 2	Women in Politics	43
Chapter 3	Girls	77
Chapter 4	Young Women Learning	123
Chapter 5	Women in Public Spaces	159
Chapter 6	Women in the Media	189
Chapter 7	Women in the Workplace	221
Chapter 8	Motherhood	253
Chapter 9	Double Discrimination	289
Chapter 10	What About the Men?	319
Chapter 11	Women Under Threat	349
Chapter 12	People Standing Up	377
	A Note on Statistics	401
	Resources	402
	Acknowledgments	405

everyday sexism

Introduction

Everybody Has a Tipping Point

The funny thing is that when mine came, in March 2012, it wasn't something dramatic or extreme, or even particularly out of the ordinary. It was just another week of little pinpricks: the man who appeared as I sat outside a café, seized my hand, and refused to let go; the guy who followed me off the bus and lewdly propositioned me all the way to my front door; the man who made a sexual gesture and shouted, "I'm looking for a wife," from his car as I walked wearily home after a long day. I shouted back, "Keep looking!" but as I trudged home, I started for the first time really thinking about how many of these little incidents I was putting up with from day to day.

I remembered the university supervisor who was rumored to wear a black armband once a year to mourn the anniversary of my college admitting women. I thought about the night that a group of teenage boys had casually walked up behind me in the street and then one of them grabbed me, hard, between the legs, forcing his fingers upward against my jeans. I recalled the boss who'd sent me strange e-mails about his sexual fantasies and mysteriously terminated my freelance contract with no explanation almost immediately after learning I had a boyfriend. The university supervisor whose e-mail suggesting we meet for our first tutorial said, "I'll bring a red rose and you bring a copy of yesterday's *Telegraph* . . ." The senior colleague who, on my first day working as an admin temp—age just seventeen—propositioned me via the company's internal e-mail system. The guy who sat next to me on the bus and started running his hand up and down my leg—and the other one who sat opposite me and began masturbating under his coat, his confident eyes boring into mine. I remembered the men who cornered me late one night in a Cambridge street, shouting,

"We're going to part those legs and f*ck that c*nt!" and left me cowering against the wall as they strolled away cackling.

And the more these incidents came back to me, the more I wondered why I'd played them down at the time—why I'd never complained, or even particularly remembered them, until I sat down and really thought about it.

The answer was that these events were normal. They hadn't seemed exceptional enough for me to object to them because they weren't out of the ordinary. Because this kind of thing was just part of life—or, rather, part of being a woman. Simply, I was used to it.

And I started to wonder how many other women had had similar experiences and, like me, had just accepted them and rationalized them and got on with it without stopping to protest or ask why.

So I started asking around—among friends and family, at parties, even in the supermarket. Over the course of a few weeks, I asked every woman I met whether she'd ever encountered this sort of problem. I honestly thought that if I asked twenty or thirty women, one or two would remember something significant from the past—a bad experience they'd had at university, perhaps, or in a previous job.

What actually happened took me completely by surprise. Every single woman I spoke to had a story. But not from five years ago, or ten. From last week, or yesterday, or "on my way here today." And they weren't just random one-time events but reams and reams of tiny pinpricks—just like my own experiences—so niggling and normalized that to protest each one felt petty. Yet put them together and the picture created by this mosaic of miniatures was strikingly clear. This inequality, this pattern of casual intrusion whereby women could be leered at, touched, harassed, and abused without a second thought, was sexism: implicit, explicit, commonplace, and deep-rooted, pretty much everywhere you'd care to look. And if sexism means prejudice, stereotyping, or discriminating against people purely because of their sex, then women were experiencing it on a near-daily basis.

The more stories I heard, the more I tried to talk about the problem. And yet time and time again I found myself coming up against the same response: Sexism doesn't exist anymore. Women are equal now, more or less. You career girls these days have the best of all worlds—what more do you want? Think about the women in other countries dealing with real problems, people told me—you women in the West have no idea how lucky you are. You have "gilded lives"! You're making a fuss about nothing. You're overreacting. You're uptight, or frigid. You need to learn to take a joke, get a sense of humor, lighten up . . .

You really need to learn to take a compliment.

How, I wondered, was it possible for there to be so much evidence of sexism alongside so much protest to the contrary? Gradually, as I became more aware of the sheer scale of the problem, I also began to understand that it was an invisible one. People didn't want to acknowledge it, or talk about it—in fact, they often simply refused, point-blank, to believe it still existed. And it wasn't just men who took this view; it was women, too—telling me I was getting worked up about nothing, or being oversensitive, or simply looking for problems where there weren't any.

At first, I wondered if they were right. People weren't exactly falling over themselves to share my "Eureka!" moment. This could be like my ill-fated but utter conviction, at age eleven, that it was actually "helicockter," not "helicopter," and everybody else was pronouncing it wrong. Perhaps I was just overreacting and women really were equal now, more or less. I thought I'd take a look at the statistics, to see if we had in fact finally reached a level playing field.

At first, being UK-based, I looked at the statistics there. I found that at the time, in early 2012, in this supposedly "equal" society, with nothing left for women to want or fight for, they held less than a quarter of the seats in Parliament, and only 4 out of 23 cabinet positions. That just 4 out of 35 lord justices of appeal and 18 out of 108 high court judges were female. That it had been more than thirteen years since a female choreographer had been commissioned to create a piece for the main stage at our Royal Opera House. That in 2010 it was reported that the National Gallery's collection of some 2,300 works, contained paintings by only 10 women. That our Royal Society had never had a female president, and just 5 percent of its fellowship was made up of women. That women wrote only a fifth of front-page newspaper articles and that 84 percent of those articles were dominated by male subjects or experts. That women directed just 5 percent of the 250 major films of 2011, down by nearly half from a paltry 9 percent in 1998. That a Home Office survey as recently as 2009 had showed that 20 percent of those polled thought it "acceptable" in some circumstances "for a man to hit or slap his wife or girlfriend in response to her being dressed in sexy or revealing clothes in public."

Then I looked at the crime statistics. I found that on average, more than 2 women were killed every week by a current or former partner, that there was a call to the police every minute about domestic violence, and that a woman was raped every six minutes—adding up to more than eighty-five thousand rapes and four hundred thousand sexual assaults per year. That one in five women was the victim of a sexual offense and one in four a victim of domestic violence.

In the few years since I completed that eye-opening research, very little has changed. And the comparable stats for the United States are broadly similar: At the time of writing, women hold one-fifth or less of seats in the Senate and the House of Representatives. Only 35 women in history have ever served as governor, compared to more than 2,300 men. Just 4 of the 112 justices ever to serve on the Supreme Court have been women. *The New York Times* reported in 2014 that women run a quarter of the biggest art museums in the United States (but only five of the thirty-three with the largest budgets) and earn about a third less than their male counterparts for doing so. Eighty percent of the reviewers and authors of reviewed books in the *New York Review of Books* in 2013 were men, as were almost 80 percent of the "notable deaths" reported in *The New York Times* in 2012. Data from the U.S. National Science Foundation reveals that women make up just 20 percent of architects, 17 percent of economists, and 11 percent of engineers. Only 5 percent of CEOs at Fortune 500 companies are women. The full-time pay gap is around 20 percent overall. Around one in five women in the United States has experienced rape or attempted rape at some time in her life, and more than one in three have experienced intimate partner violence. On average, more than three women every day are killed by a current or former partner.

And worldwide, one in three women on the planet will be raped or beaten in her lifetime.

Those stats did very little to convince me that everything was okay and I shouldn't be worrying my pretty little head about it. In fact, they had the opposite effect. I started wondering whether there might not be a connection between ours being a society in which so many women become so accustomed to experiencing gender-based prejudice that they almost fail to even register it anymore, and the fact that men dominate political and economic spheres and so many women suffer some form of sexual violence. The figures certainly didn't allay my fears and convince me I was making a mountain out of a molehill—far from it. They suggested an urgent and essential need to pay attention to the "minor" incidents—each and every one of them—in order to start connecting the dots and build up a proper picture of what was going on.

I didn't for a moment think that the problem of sexism could be solved overnight. But neither did I see how we could possibly even begin to tackle it while so many people continued to refuse to acknowledge that it even existed. I thought if I could somehow bring together all those women's stories in one place, testifying to the sheer scale and breadth of the problem, then perhaps people would be convinced that there was, in fact, a problem to be solved.

At least that would be a start.

So in April 2012, I started a very simple Web site where people could upload their stories—from the niggling and normalized to the outrageously offensive and violent—and those who hadn't experienced the problem firsthand could read them and, I hoped, begin to realize what was really happening on a daily basis.

Without any funding, or means to publicize the project beyond my own Facebook wall, I thought perhaps fifty or sixty women would add their stories, or that I might be able to persuade a hundred or so of my own friends to add theirs.

Stories began to trickle in during the first few days. Within a week, hundreds of people had added their voices. A week later, the number had doubled, then trebled and quadrupled. I started a Twitter account, @EverydaySexism, and found that people were keen to discuss the phenomenon there too. In exactly the same way that raising the subject in a roomful of people led to more and more women chipping in with their own examples, the idea spread through social media like wildfire, snowballing and gathering momentum as it traveled.

Suddenly stories began to appear from America and Canada, Germany and France, Saudi Arabia and Pakistan. Tens of thousands of people started viewing the Web site each month. Before two months had passed, the site contained more than one thousand entries.

There were people who said I might be making it all up, or that it didn't prove anything because the stories couldn't be independently verified. And that's true (the verification part, not the making it up) and applies to the project entries quoted in this book. This is important, so while we're here, let's clear it up. The project was only ever intended to be used as a qualitative source, just like many other highly respected social studies and research projects that rely on reported evidence. Yes, we should be aware of the possibility that an entry has been fabricated. But really there's no incentive for anybody to make things up. First, the project consists of so many accounts that there's no fame or attention to be gained from adding a false story—each one is just a drop in the ocean. Second, because IP addresses are automatically submitted with the entries, we're immediately alerted when anyone submits more than one story. On the few occasions when trolls have posted a small batch of sarcastic and exaggerated entries, it has been easy to spot and remove them. More important, though, now that tens of thousands of women have added their experiences, the stories are corroborated by each other—they're repeated and echoed by those of other women, of different ages and backgrounds and from different countries, with the same themes arising again and again. These accounts are also supported by the thousands of girls and women I have met at schools and events over the past few years, by women who have contacted me in confidence, and women I have interviewed for this book. They're all saying very similar things. It would have to be an awfully big coincidence for so many of them to be making up the same story.

The stories kept coming. Then one day a journalist contacted me, asking about running a feature on the project. Other papers and magazines swiftly followed, then radio and television programs. I began to write regularly for the national and then international press, chronicling the accounts as they streamed in and highlighting common themes. Articles about the project appeared around the world, from *Grazia South Africa* to the *Times of India,* French *Glamour* to *Gulf News,* the *Los Angeles Times* to the *Toronto Standard.* Every time the project was featured in the foreign press, I'd receive e-mails from women in those countries asking if we could start a version of the project for their country too. Within eighteen months, we had expanded to eighteen countries worldwide.

Hundreds of women and girls wrote to me about their experiences, describing not only what had happened to them but also how they'd felt guilty or unable to protest, how they'd been made to feel that whatever had happened was their fault, or that they shouldn't make a fuss. The first time the true scale of what I had started to uncover really hit me was when one woman wrote to me saying, "I'm 58 so I have too much to say in a small box. Here are some highlights arranged in decades."

The stories came from women of all ages, races and ethnicities, social backgrounds, gender identities and sexual orientations, disabled and nondisabled, religious and nonreligious, employed and unemployed. Stories from the workplace to the pavement, from clubs and bars to buses and trains. Of verbal harassment and "jokes," of touching and groping and grabbing and kissing and being followed and sworn at and shouted at and belittled and assaulted and raped.

This is why the project, which initially set out to record daily instances of sexism, quickly came to document cases of serious harassment and assault, abuse and rape. In the early days, as the first stories of this kind were recorded, I wondered why people were coming to us, why they weren't sharing and being supported elsewhere. And then I started to realize that there wasn't anywhere else. Thousands of these stories had never been told. Thousands of these women had grown up in the confident assumption that these violations were their fault, that their stories were shameful, that they should never tell anybody. Yet their experiences weren't "out of place" among the tales of daily, niggling, normalized sexism any more than the violets "don't belong" in the same spectrum of colors as the oranges and greens. You can't separate one out and look at it without the others, because together they create a full picture. Our experiences of all forms of gender prejudice—from daily sexism to distressing harassment to sexual violence—are part of a continuum that impacts all of us, all the time, shaping ourselves and our ideas about the world. To include stories of assault and rape within a project documenting everyday experiences of gender imbalance is simply to extend its boundaries to the most extreme manifestations of that prejudice. To see how great the damage can be when the minor, "unimportant" issues are allowed to pass without comment. To prove how the steady drip-drip-drip of sexism and sexualization and objectification is connected to the assumption of ownership and control over women's bodies, and how the background noise of harassment and disrespect connects to the assertion of power that is violence and rape.

And so we accepted all these stories, and more, until in April 2015—exactly three years after the project was launched—one hundred thousand entries had poured in. This is their story. This is the sound of a hundred thousand voices. This is what they're telling us.

Chapter 1

Silenced Women: The Invisible Problem

Even though I am an experienced businesswoman, I feel I can't say anything. It's my choice: tell him to please not touch me and create a fuss, making things awkward with my clients, or stay quiet. I stay quiet.

Everyday Sexism Project entry

Vital Statistics

65 percent of rape and sexual assault victimizations go unreported to the police.
-U.S. Department of Justice, Bureau of Justice Statistics, National Crime Victimization Survey, 2013

Only around 3 out of every 100 rapes results in the rapist spending a single day in prison.
-Rape Abuse and Incest National Network (RAINN), 2014

In 2005-2010, only 24 percent of rapes or sexual assaults were committed by strangers.
-U.S. Department of Justice, National Crime Victimization Survey, 2012

80 percent of rape and sexual assault victimizations of students age eighteen to twenty-four go unreported to the police.
-Bureau of Justice Statistics, National Crime Victimization Survey, 1995-2013

28 percent of women who are the victims of the most serious sexual offenses never tell anybody about it.
-UK Ministry of Justice, Home Office, Office for National Statistics, 2013

It's something I just always accepted as a reality since I was young. No one told me that it wasn't my fault or that I could/should speak up. I was told to be passive and not to stir things up.

Being told I have no sense of humor when comments are made about my breasts, vagina or behind.

I joined a dating site. Got one message instantly. "I'd pay to ram you up the ass." And guess what his excuse was when I argued with him? "Chill out love, it's just banter." It really isn't.

Dismissal of arguments or thoughts because "she's just pms-ing" or hormonal.

I was raped by 2 men at the age of 14 and my family normalized it by ignoring it . . . I was confused . . . I was sure it was wrong.

Called a prude for objecting to Porn Fridays where female colleagues' faces were photo-shopped onto porn pics.

Sexism is often an invisible problem. This is partly because it's so frequently manifest in situations where the only witnesses present are victim and perpetrator. When you're shouted at in a deserted street late at night. When a senior colleague with wandering hands corners you in the empty copy room. When a man presses his erection into your back on a subway so crowded nobody could possibly see what's going on. When a car slows down as you walk home from school and the driver asks you for a blow job, then pulls away as smoothly and silently as he arrived. When your boss casually mentions as she passes you on the stairs that you need to arrive with a lower-cut top and more makeup on tomorrow if you want to keep your job. When a pair of hands moves you aside in the queue for the bar and slides down to grope you. Moments that slip like beads onto an endless string to form a necklace that only you can feel the weight of. It can drag you down without another person ever witnessing a single thing.

It's not easy to take something invisible and make people start to talk about it. There's a lot of wariness and caution at first—people sneakily giving each other a sideways look because they don't want to be the one to admit they see it if everyone else is going to carry on pretending not to. So at best the person who's experienced the sexism is left jumping up and down with her arms in the air pointing out the patently obvious, while everybody else scratches her chin and gazes earnestly into the middle distance.

At worst, the victim doesn't say anything either.

In this, sexism is a bit like climate change. Human beings tend to cling to convenient obliviousness—"I haven't seen it, so it can't really exist!"—in spite of embarrassing, burgeoning bodies of evidence to the contrary. In order for this comfortable bliss of ignorance to be maintained, it follows that any mention of the problem will be met with denial, so naturally you get accusations of lying, or exaggeration. These aren't always intentionally unkind—I think they're as often motivated by a horrified inability to accept the severity of the problem as by a deliberate attempt at dismissal.

But whatever the motive, such reactions come as a secondary blow on top of the initial injurious experience.

As girls grow up, these responses start to skew their own judgment of situations—they learn not to trust themselves and not to make a fuss. Society teaches them that they don't have the right to complain. One way or another, women are silenced.

One girl who wrote to the Everyday Sexism Project described just such a "learning experience":

> When walking to a friend's house on Saturday at about 6:30 pm, two drunk men started following me. One grabbed my hair and said "you are too pretty to be out alone" . . . I felt violated and arrived shaking. I told my boyfriend the next day; he said my "story" was unlikely as I was just being attention seeking. I began to feel like I myself was exaggerating and should just remain quiet. We are both 15.

Disbelief is the first great silencer.

The incidents that go unwitnessed definitely help to keep sexism off the radar, an unacknowledged problem we don't discuss. But so too do the regular occurrences that hide in plain sight, within a society that has normalized sexism and allowed it to become so ingrained that we no longer notice or object to it. Sexism is a socially acceptable prejudice and everybody is getting in on the act.

The past couple of years alone have given us some amazingly high-profile examples. During this time the Russian conductor Vasily Petrenko helpfully announced that in his profession men will always be superior because orchestras are distracted by a "cute girl on a podium," and the German artist Georg Baselitz declared, "Women don't paint very well. It's a fact." Meanwhile

London mayor Boris Johnson "joked" that women go to university only because "they've got to find men to marry" (hilarious, no?), and the Canadian literature professor and author David Gilmour blithely revealed that he's simply "not interested in teaching books by women." (I expect Zadie Smith, Toni Morrison, Maya Angelou, and Margaret Atwood could set him straight, were they not so busy winning more awards than Gilmour has ever managed to scrape up nominations for.)

In the UK, in November 2012, Labour MP Austin Mitchell directed a sexist tirade at his former colleague Louise Mensch after she disagreed in an interview with something her husband had said. In a message that appeared on his Facebook and Twitter pages as well as his official Web site, Mitchell wrote, "Shut up Menschkin. A good wife doesn't disagree with her master in public and a good little girl doesn't lie about why she quit politics." He later showed his great amusement at the ensuing public anger, first telling those who protested, "Calm down, dears," and later asking, "Has the all-clear siren gone? Has the Menschivick bombardment stopped?"

Such swaggering pride in misogyny will not be unfamiliar to listeners of U.S. radio host Rush Limbaugh, who not only gleefully launches sexist tirades against women at every opportunity but also seems to delight in mocking subsequent criticism. From calling female journalists "info babes" and decrying the "chickification" of the media, to describing the National Organization for Women as "a bunch of whores to liberalism," Limbaugh knows he is being misogynistic and plows happily on regardless.

Clearly none of these men fear repercussions. In fact,

Mitchell's "Calm down, dears" couched his "prejudiced and proud" stance firmly within the political context of a British prime minister who publicly silenced a female MP with the same words the previous year.

Against such a backdrop, it's little wonder other politicians feel so confident wearing their bigotry like a badge of honor.

In the same week as Mitchell's outburst, and with the earnest air of a radio consumer phone-in about synthetic versus feather duvets, BBC Radio Cumbria produced a segment that managed to combine both sexism and racism, asking, "If you could have a Filipino woman, why would you want a Cumbrian one?"

In 2012, Limbaugh was able to keep his job and his show despite launching a misogynistic barrage of abuse at law student Sandra Fluke, whose only "crime" was to be invited to testify to Congress on the importance of including contraceptive coverage in health-insurance plans. Limbaugh attacked her repeatedly on air, labeling her a "slut" and a "prostitute," suggesting that her parents should be ashamed of her and saying she was "having so much sex, it's amazing she can still walk." With all the unimaginative persistence of a dog with a chew toy, he seemed unable to drop the subject, later adding, "If we are going to pay for your contraceptives, and thus pay for you to have sex, we want something for it, and I'll tell you what it is. We want you to post the videos online so we can all watch."

Over in Hollywood, the actor Seth MacFarlane decided that the best possible way to celebrate the combined talents of actresses attending the 2013 Oscars ceremony was to sing a song titled "We Saw Your Boobs." (No prizes for guessing what it was about.) Apparently the fact that several of the breast-baring scenes he gleefully referenced explored rape or abuse passed MacFarlane by. (As did, it seems, the abilities and, you know, *humanity* of the women themselves.) That this was presented as a hilarious piece of entertainment at one of the most widely watched media events of the year speaks volumes.

Back in the UK, the television critic (and noted sex bomb) A. A. Gill was busy veering into wildly irrelevant sexism in his review of *Meet the Romans,* a series presented by the Cambridge Classics professor Mary Beard. Rather than critiquing Beard's (considerable) credentials or presenting skills, he chose to condemn her looks and style, branding her "too ugly for TV" and suggesting that she "should be kept away from cameras altogether." In a column for the *Daily Mail,* Beard responded with the dry observation that Gill had "mistaken prejudice for being witty"—which excellent riposte frustratingly gave rise to the common excuse that sexism isn't a problem because "women can handle it." Yes, some can, but the point is that they shouldn't have to! (In this instance, who knows what incisive historical revelations would have occupied that week's column had Beard not been forced to waste her time responding to Gill's puerile snot-flicking?)

During the London Olympics, the *Telegraph*'s Andrew Brown pronounced a breathtakingly patronizing and pompous censure on the female athletes daring to represent their country in the martial arts. "I realize this will probably sound appallingly sexist," he wrote, and then carried on regardless. "It's disturbing to watch these girls beat each other up." His condescension was spectacularly misplaced when you consider how easily the "soft limbs" he was wringing his hands over could have taught him a swift lesson about respect for equal rights had he strayed into the Olympic arena.

In each of these situations—which together represent just a tiny sample from an extensive daily stream—we have women being openly lambasted, dismissed, or objectified on the simple basis of their gender. Nothing more. From our politicians to our broadcasting corporations, from the biggest media event in the world to the most famous sporting contest, sexism seems to occupy a stubbornly acceptable position when it comes to public discourse, with a general willingness to laugh at and ignore it rather than define it as the prejudice it is. And this makes it particularly difficult to fight, allowing objectors to be ridiculed and dismissed as "overreacting" while perpetrators like Mitchell can take up cowardly defenses behind the poor shield of "humor" or "irony."

So women are silenced both by the invisibility and the acceptability of the problem. And perhaps the most powerful evidence of all for the public acceptance of sexism is the growing number of major daytime television programs taking issues around women's safety and assault as topics for "debate."

The very fact that it is necessary in the twenty-first century to explain why it's not okay to publicly debate whether or not women are "asking" for sexual assault is mind-boggling. Yet the refrain has become so common that it seems difficult to open a newspaper or turn on the television without hearing the issue being discussed, as if it is a perfectly valid question with interesting points to be made both for and against.

In February 2013, the UK morning TV show *Daybreak,* with an average of eight hundred thousand viewers, ran a segment asking, "Are women who get drunk and flirt to blame if they get attacked?" The discussion was introduced with: "Some of you think so . . . others vehemently disagree." Then: "Keep your thoughts coming in—it's really interesting to hear what you think."

The words "horrifying," "depressing," or "painful" would have better described what it was like to hear what some of the *Daybreak* viewers thought. Comments were aired from interviewees on both sides of the debate, including one young man who said that "if you want to be treated with respect, you've got to dress with respect" and a studio panelist who—when discussing *sexual assault!*—used the phrase "It takes two to make a decision about something." The presenters later announced the results: "One in six people in the *Daybreak* poll think sexual-assault victims are to blame if they're drunk or flirtatious with the offender." No comment was passed on this statistic as it was presented.

In the same week, the BBC 3 current-affairs program *Free Speech* ran a segment posing the question: "Are young women in this country putting themselves at risk of being abused by going out clubbing and wearing provocative clothing?" Once again, the ensuing debate showcased points made for and against. One panelist put herself firmly in the camp of agreement: "Absolutely . . . You should not be going out dressed like a hussy, quite frankly. There's no other word for it . . . You are putting yourself at risk. And, as women, we need to understand we are vulnerable."

Yes, for the love of God, young women, come along—*learn your limits*. Or, rather, know society's limits. How dare you think you have the right to go out wearing whatever you like, how *foolish* and *ignorant* of you to expect not to be assaulted, you *brazen hussies*! What do you think this is? A free country?

Meanwhile, the online community Debate.org is running an ongoing poll on the topic "Are rape victims who dress provocatively 'asking for it'?" (21 percent say yes, at the time of writing).

There has been a long string of similar public declarations in all corners of the media. In June 2014, the *Washington Post* columnist George Will penned a column suggesting that the problem of sexual assault on campus had been exaggerated because "victimhood" had become a "coveted status that confers privileges," causing victims to "proliferate" (and thus implying a lack of belief in such victims' testimony).

And after a shocking video emerged showing NFL player Ray Rice knocking his fiancée Janay Palmer unconscious, many media outlets focused their outrage and surprise on Palmer, demanding why she had gone on to marry Rice after the attack. After denouncing the attack, Fox News commentator *Fox and Friends* host Steve Doocy went on to say, "We should also point out . . . she still married him!" Cohost Brian Kilmeade took this as his cue to jump in with some more victim blaming: "Rihanna went back to Chris Brown right after; a lot of people thought that was a terrible message." Good old Limbaugh also quickly chimed in (he's nothing if not reliable), asking, "Now the obvious question behind the question. Why did she marry the guy, right? If she got decked like that." And CNN contributor Ana Navarro tweeted, "Woman in video married Ray Rice AFTER he punched & dragged her? RICE IS DISGUSTING. But as women, we need to love & respect ourselves 1st."

Such comments show a breathtaking lack of awareness of

the complex psychological and coercive elements of domestic abuse. But they also serve the same old purpose of shifting some of the blame away from the perpetrator and onto the victim instead.

Meanwhile in the UK, the actress Joanna Lumley has been busy urging young women to behave properly: "Don't be sick in the gutter at midnight in a silly dress with no money to get a taxi home, because somebody will take advantage of you, either they'll rape you, or they'll knock you on the head or they'll rob you." In an interview soon afterward, Conservative MP Richard Graham appeared to support her, saying, "If you are a young woman on her own trying to walk back home through Gloucester Park, early in the morning in a tight, short skirt and high shoes and there's a predator and if you are blind drunk and wearing those clothes how able are you to get away?" (Actually, as one young woman shrewdly pointed out to me, you're generally much more able to run in a short skirt than in a long one.) It is in this focus on women's behavior while utterly failing to analyze the actions and impact of the society around them that we encounter the greatest silencing method of all: the blaming of victims.

Let me immediately make two important points. First, the idea that women's dress or behavior is in any way to blame for sexual assault or rape is *nonsense.* Second, to publicly debate such a notion is to give it credence and to spread the idea, it is to send perpetrators the message that they can act with impunity and to remind victims they may be blamed if they speak up. It creates a world in which people feel more justified in questioning and shaming victims who do come forward, creating an atmosphere in which even fewer are likely to take their case to the authorities. The victim is *never* to blame.

According to the U.S. Department of Justice, in 2005–2010, only 24 percent of rapes or sexual assaults were committed by strangers. The 2013 UK government figures on sexual offenses state that the vast majority of rapists are known to their victims: "Around 90 percent of victims of the most serious sexual offences in the previous year knew the perpetrator." According to Rape Crisis (England and Wales), "Women and girls of all ages, classes, culture, ability, sexuality, race and faith are raped. Attractiveness has little significance. Reports show that there is a great diversity in the way targeted women act or dress." Rape is *not* a sexual act; it is not the result of a sudden uncontrollable attraction to a woman in a skimpy dress. It is an act of power and violence. To suggest otherwise is deeply insulting both to victims and to the vast majority of men, who are perfectly able to control their sexual desires.

Where, in the narrative of careless, oversexualized young victims foolishly luring their attackers with short skirts, does the story of the one-hundred-year-old woman raped during a home invasion in Wichita in October 2014 sit? What about the baby against whom Lostprophets singer Ian Watkins recently admitted a count of attempted rape?

Perhaps most important of all, this insistent focus on the victim prevents us from ever coming close to solving the problem, which can be achieved only by preventing perpetrators from acting in the first place. Yet rather than educate boys about consent, or focus on the act and the criminal when it happens, we pour time, money, and research into reactive rather than preventative remedies. It's how we end up with antirape underwear and antirape alarms and antirape self-defense classes and even, more recently, antirape nail polish.

That's right—a group of students at North Carolina State University invented a nail polish that will change color if it comes into contact with so-called date rape drugs such as Rohypnol. The product, Undercover Colors, allows women to test their drinks by dipping a finger in, swirling it around, and checking to see if the polish changes color.

Like the antirape underwear before it, any product that claims to enable a woman to protect herself from being raped can't help but contribute to the suggestion that it is partly a victim's responsibility to take precautions against attack. The more we focus on victim actions, the more the very concept at hand becomes an abstract danger: "sexual assault," rather than a person—an individual rapist—making a decision to rape. When we suggest victims can stop rape, we also (however unintentionally) imply that rape is an inevitable aspect of life rather than an action deliberately carried out by a perpetrator.

Not to mention the fact that a woman shouldn't have to remember to go out armed with the equivalent of a chemistry lab litmus test to ensure freedom from being drugged and assaulted in 2016. That we have arrived at this frankly absurd point only demonstrates the lengths to which we will go to avoid focusing on stopping rape in the first place.

More important, the focus of the product on social situations such as bars and clubs reinforces our cultural misconception that such scenarios, and the shadowy strangers therein, present the highest risk of rape. Nail polish is of little use to the women who are raped in their homes and workplaces, by husbands and partners.

And hey, if we're so focused on parties and bars, and finding ways for women to keep themselves safe there, why not go one step farther? If you forget your antirape nail polish one night, perhaps it's best to avoid having any drinks, just in case. In fact, why not advise women against going out at all?

These arguments might seem exaggerated, but they are all part of the same spectrum, which looks at ways women can take responsibility to stop themselves from being raped instead of focusing time, energy, and resources on programs to prevent rape.

It may come from a well-meaning place, but that doesn't stop it from being damaging. On their Facebook page, the students behind Undercover Colors proudly wrote that their product was about "Empowering women to prevent sexual assault." Doesn't the word "empowering" in this context set your teeth a little on edge? Is it really "empowering" to live in a world where you have to swirl your fingers around in your margarita just to be sure you aren't at risk of assault? Are we supposed to be grateful?

Sorry, it doesn't sound like empowerment to me. But I can think of another slogan, and campaign, that might be more successful: "Educating men to prevent sexual assault." Now that might make some real headway. Or hey, here's a crazy idea: punishing more rapists with actual jail time!

The whole thing is at risk of becoming an absurd spiral. When a woman in Sydney was raped in autumn 2014 after meeting a man using the dating app Tinder, the *Sydney Morning Herald* reported, "Police are warning online daters to be careful of meeting with strangers." Why not, "Police are warning online daters their profiles will be used to trace and arrest them if they perpetrate illegal sex crimes"? or "Police are asking urgent questions of Tinder about its safety and vetting mechanisms"? Where does this line of logic end?

What if women meet rapists in bars without having first connected online? "Police are warning women not to go to bars." What if women are raped in their homes or workplaces? "Police are warning women to avoid work and their own houses at all costs." What if "Police are advising women to remain inside a large, padlocked box at all times"?

The same inverted approach is taken in relation to pretty much every form of assault and harassment you can think of. During a discussion about sexual harassment in his eponymous television show in September 2014, Alan Titchmarsh used the phrase "asking for it" to describe thirteen-year-old girls who walk past building sites wearing crop tops or short skirts. In 2012, the popular television show *The Wright Stuff* (where female viewers are frequently addressed as "you girls," making me want to claw my own eyes out—but that's beside the point) ran a jaunty segment asking whether men pinching women's bottoms in nightclubs was "just a bit of fun." This time the healthy side order of "they're asking for it" was thrown in by panelist Lynda Bellingham. "Oh, for God's sake, it's just a bit of fun," she opined. "Have you seen what women wear in clubs these days? If they bend over you could see their knickers." So once again a direct line of causation is drawn between women's dress and sexual assault.

Setting apart the euphemistic description of groping and physical assault as a cheeky "ass pinch," the fact that such efforts are immediately met by cries of "Aren't you making a fuss about nothing?" from such high-profile platforms shows the uphill battle women are fighting to even *begin* to object to sexism and harassment. What we are really hearing is the suggestion that if women dare to leave the house, they must expect to be manhandled and touched by strangers against their will. If something happens to a woman when she's in a club, or when she has dared to dress up (in the way, incidentally, dictated and demanded by the media with which she is constantly bombarded), then she certainly shouldn't have the audacity to complain.

These three powerful silencing factors—the invisibility of the problem, the social acceptance of it, and the blaming of victims—are corroborated loud and clear by the testimonies shared with Everyday Sexism, particularly from young women who are learning such lessons hard and early. They said they felt unable to complain about incidents, either because they wouldn't be taken seriously or, sometimes, because they didn't even think they'd be believed.

I tried to tell family about harassment or assault, but they'd almost always imply I'd done something to make it happen.

Pretty much told it was my problem or that I was "too sensitive."

One woman described how her family's attitudes toward victims in the public eye spilled over into their indictment of her:

Just watching BBC Look North. Story about a woman who was raped in a park at night. My mother: "Stupid woman, what on earth was she doing walking in a park?"

Incidentally, when I came home and told Mum I'd been raped by my boyfriend, she replied: "That's what you get if you behave like a slut."

Often the social acceptability of sexism and harassment is so ingrained that the abuse itself appears to come second in importance to the family's desire to avoid a scene. One girl explained:

▸ When I was about 13, a friend of the family used to grab my bum or my breasts whenever we saw him (which sadly, was quite a lot). He would do it right in front of my mum, sister and his WIFE and nobody ever said anything. It made me feel really uncomfortable (obviously), but at the time I was far too young to understand what was going on and it's only very recently that I've come to understand that he was actually assaulting me. I have felt so confused and unhappy about this for years, I'm so angry that his wife and my own family never questioned the fact I was being inappropriately touched right in front of them. I want to bring up the subject with my mum and sister, but I'm afraid that they won't take it seriously.

We've received countless accounts reflecting this theme of young girls learning early, and even from their parents, that responsibility for sexual harassment falls on their own shoulders.

Harassed in the street aged 12 (by an adult man), told by my mum it was my own fault for wearing a short skirt.

It is significant that the silencing starts early. One woman's entry highlights how the impact of learning such "truths" from the people you trust the most can cause them to become deeply ingrained—making it much harder for women to realize that what is happening to them is wrong, or to speak up about it later on:

My father told me it's impossible to rape a girl, it's the girls fault. I was 16 & a virgin when I was raped several times—I was 30 when I realized it was rape thanks to dad.

I am sad to report that many women describe similarly belittling comments from their own partners:

Had a frightening experience with a drunk man muttering threats while sitting across from me on a train, and then following me off and throughout the station, until I literally had to run and hide to lose him. When I later told my boyfriend what happened he said: "well I'm glad you're home safe now" and completely dismissed it.

I told my husband [about a sexual assault] but he didn't believe me and said it must have been a mistake.

Such dismissal is not limited to an "out-of-touch" older generation; it is reported just as frequently by young people. After somebody she knew had been sexually assaulted, one young woman heard her acquaintances discussing the case, saying, "She's an attention whore; she should have seen it coming." Young people repeatedly reported their peer groups silencing and policing victims who tried to speak out:

▸ At a nightclub at my uni a guy walked past me and put his hand right up my dress, at the front, very violently, and then walked past. I was SO shocked, furious and confused. Went back over to my group of friends and told them what happened; general apathy and no surprise. One male in the group said, "Well, you are wearing a really nice dress tonight."

The crucial thing to understand is that dismissive patterns learned at an early age become internalized, which in turn begins to prevent women from even trying to speak out if the need subsequently arises. One young woman describes an experience that took place at a house party when she was just sixteen. The end of her account starkly reveals how strongly society had already programmed her not to report what happened:

▸ One guy kept calling me a bitch . . . "excuse me bitch," "oi bitch, what's your name?" I thought he was a bit weird—and had a terrible sense of humor. I kept away from him and chatted to my friends for the rest of the night.

Later on I was so drunk I went upstairs to sleep in a spare bedroom of my friend's house.

I woke up later, it was quiet and it sounded like everyone had gone home—except that guy from earlier who was on top of me, having sex with me, one hand covering my mouth and the other round my throat. I knew that, being drunk, no one would believe me.

Another young woman reported that a man who harassed her went on to sexually assault another girl. Her description of the public reaction to the case perfectly illustrates why so many girls believe they will not be taken seriously from the outset:

▸ I was waiting at a bus stop late at night and a drunk, leering man was also waiting for the same bus. He intimidated me into a conversation with him. I tried to be polite as I was scared not to talk to him. He said he'd get off at the same stop as me, which filled me with fear.

Once the bus arrived I let him get on first to not sit near him. I rang my Dad who thankfully met me a few stops early. Sadly, a few months later I was reading our local newspaper online and saw the photo of the same man and an article—he was convicted of sexually assaulting a 14-year-old girl on the same bus by groping her bottom. I can imagine how frightening this was for her after encountering him myself. The worst thing was the comments people left regarding the 14-year-old girl—saying she had "over reacted" was a "drama queen" and "had been wearing a short skirt," and that "it was harmless touching—a bit of fun." How must she feel reading that? What must she make of our society, and her place as a young woman in it? So many people dismissed what he had done.

Even for those who do find the courage to speak out, often after a long period, being dismissed, disbelieved, or silenced by their own family or friends can be a devastating experience. The refusal to believe that something has happened—from minor sexist incidents all the way up the scale to more serious harassment, assault, or violence—is revictimization. It silences the victims and often prevents them from reaching out for help. For one woman, the response she got from a friend was as much of a blow as the horrendous experience of domestic violence she had survived:

▸ A friend of mine who I told my story to decided to tell everyone. And then he had the nerve to tell me that he didn't believe me. That I just wanted attention. That I just wanted people to feel sorry for me. And that something like that couldn't have happened to me because I have a family and a house and I go to a good school. I guess the worst part of the whole thing isn't even the betrayal, but the desperation that I felt. Not only had I experienced the abuse, but when I tried to trust someone with my feelings, they were dismissed as a lie.

There is a triple bind here. Media coverage in which victims are blamed sends insidious messages to young people, causing them to criticize and doubt themselves; the dismissive responses of those closest to them make them question their own experience; and the abject normalization of it all makes them wonder what the point is in speaking out anyway. In short, society, the media, and those close to the victim collaboratively demonstrate such extensive doubt that they simply stop trusting themselves.

▸ Once at a party when I was 16 I was lying half-asleep and drunk on a sofa when I felt a boy I barely knew put his hand up my skirt and touch me. I was too embarrassed to confront him when I realized what he was doing, I just moved away. I told my boyfriend and he didn't believe me. I had been sleepy and drunk so I decided not to tell anybody else because I thought it seemed implausible although I was certain it had happened.

The impact of these multiple methods of silencing is immense. Heartbreakingly, the women who have finally shared their stories with the Everyday Sexism Project have often already suffered the effects of keeping their stories to themselves for months or years.

▸ I haven't told anyone else about it six years later. I still feel ashamed and dirty, and some part of me resents myself for not doing anything—I still feel like it's my fault.

▸ Once I found the Everyday Sexism Project, I felt (in a bizarre way) relieved to see other women with stories similar to mine. It also made me realize that these and other incidents in my life was sexual harassment, not just me overreacting.

▸ Reading through the stories on this site has been both painful and healing. I have admitted more here than I have to my dearest friends.

One of the saddest things about the silencing of women through shame, normalization, dismissal, disbelief, and blame is that it has become so common that it is used as a controlling tool by abusers themselves.

▸ My neighbor raped me when I was 16—he said I was a slut and was asking for it and no one would believe me if I told anyone.

As long as we as a society continue to belittle and dismiss women's accounts, disbelieve and question their stories, and blame them for their own assaults,we are playing right into the hands of those who silence victims by asking: “who would believe you anyway?”.

▸ In hindsight, I probably should have reported him but due to previous experience I felt like no one would have done anything about it.

This is an all-too-common refrain.

There is another, final and widespread silencing tool: the defense of “humor.” The backlash against feminism has played a significant role here, in its portrayal of all criticism as “humorlessness” and its veiling of harassment and abuse under the protective shield of “banter.”

▸ Colleague just used the term "lady logic." Another colleague then said "Oooh heads down chaps" meaning that I was about to kick off. My attempts to halt the sexist banter have become part of the joke for them now. I'm being silenced.

▸ My twenty-year-old brother recently revealed to me that he didn't see the point of my university education, as I am "only a baby machine" anyway. Hurt, I tried to protest, while he and his friends loudly laughed at me, told me to get back into the kitchen and to stop being so publicly "menstrual."

▸ In a club a group of guys watched me and my then-boyfriend for a few minutes before coming over to me and putting their arms round my waist and asking for a blowjob the second my boyfriend left me to go to the toilet. I told them to have some respect for both me and my boyfriend, a bouncer overheard the whole thing, burst out laughing and told me to lighten up "because it's only banter."

▸ Two weeks ago at work my manager came up behind me and slapped me very hard on my bottom. I spun around and confronted him, then reported the incident to a manager in a higher position. The man in question phoned me the following day . . . he said "I didn't realize you couldn't take a joke."

Since starting the Everyday Sexism Project, I've become painfully aware that the correlation between humorlessness and people trying to talk about sexism is strong in the public consciousness. There's an almost absurd lack of questioning on this subject: People who have known me for years have suddenly refused to tell jokes in front of me in case I'm "offended"; others have expressed sympathy with my partner because he probably now has to "watch what he says."

The irony is that I've never needed my sense of humor *more* than when facing the daily barrage of sexist incidents reported through the project and the constant stream of online insults and attacks. It's often the strongest line of defense—and frankly the only way I've held on to my sanity. When people write to me on Twitter, for example, telling me that writing about these issues is a pathetic waste of time when I could be concentrating on more important things, I find some light relief in replying that while they may be right, I'm quietly confident it's a better use of time than writing to other people to tell them what they shouldn't be wasting their time on! It's the wry smile that keeps me going when I receive an e-mail like the recent ironic missive that began, "Sexism doesn't exist . . ." but ended, "so why don't you get off your high horse and change your tampon?" Or the tweet from a man who felt I was misguidedly barking up the wrong tree in trying to expose sexism where it didn't exist.

Obligingly, he helped to solve the problem by writing, "Still not seeing the sexism, you daft cunts. Go back to the kitchen, you slags."

You have to laugh.

Over the last year or so, I've come up against this insistence on equating feminism with humorlessness a lot. Perhaps the most revealing example, though, was when I took part in a televised debate alongside a glamour model on the issue of the *Sun*'s Page 3. (Yes, the *Sun*, one of Britain's most widely read "family" newspapers, still, in 2014, printed a picture of a topless young woman almost daily on its third page.) The driver taking me to the studio was kind, welcoming, and loquacious, chatting away and cracking jokes. We had a great time until I incidentally revealed which side of the debate I was on. He stammered, stuttered, and stopped talking—he apologetically explained that he'd assumed I was the "Page 3 girl." The stream of conversation quickly died away after that. It really brought home to me how firmly cemented in the public consciousness is the idea that a young blond woman couldn't possibly be talking about feminism and women's rights—particularly not if she also had a sense of humor and the ability to chat happily away about frivolous topics! It was as if I had morphed terrifyingly before his startled eyes into a green-skinned, horn-sprouting monster FEMINIST with not only a capital F but all shouty letters after it too. This idea of the humorless feminist is an incredibly potent and effective silencer. It is used to isolate and alienate young girls, to ridicule and dismiss older women, to force women in the workplace to "join in the joke" and, in the media, to castigate protest to the point of obliteration. Former News International employee Neil

Wallis's weak attempts to discredit the No More Page 3 campaigners by branding them whining "wimmin" is a classic recent example, where the ridiculing of the women as out-of-touch harpies was used as a smoke screen to cover the fact that he had not a single actual argument to make to counter their cause. It's a pernicious and cowardly silencing tool, which uses baseless bullying as an excuse to avoid engaging intellectually with the issues at hand, and it has been used to shut down feminist campaigners for decades. Most troubling of all is the impact it has on really young girls, who are faced with a barrage of objectification and abuse yet told to lighten up and find their sense of humor just for voicing tentative objections.

▸ I'm 16 and in my last year of school. Constantly the guys (and girls) in my friendship circle make sexist remarks. Most of the time they don't realize they're being offensive, most of the time it's just "banter." For example, the other day my male friend said to me if I wear shorts to this Halloween party he will "rape me, oh but it won't be rape because I will like it." I responded telling him you shouldn't say things like that and I got called uptight . . . What is wrong with the world so that this is deemed OK? I am scared of going to university when I am older. Not because of exam stress but because of the horror stories I have heard from friends and family. The horror stories of girls that have been subjected to assault for "banter." I am scared. I am actually scared of being a female.

Obviously there's a lot to overcome if we're going to start talking properly about sexism, sexual harassment, and assault: the invisibility; the social acceptability and normalization; the dismissal, disbelief, and blaming of victims; and the accusations

Chapter 2

Women in Politics

I think if you're going to lead a country you've got to be powerful and have a loud voice.

Eleven-year-old schoolgirl interviewee

Vital Statistics

Women hold only 20 percent of U.S. Senate seats and 18.3 percent of seats in the House of Representatives.
-Center for American Women and Politics, 2014

Women hold 22.6 percent of statewide elective executive offices.
-Center for American Women and Politics, 2014

Only 35 women in history have ever served as governor, compared to more than 2,300 men.
-Center for American Women and Politics, 2014

Worldwide, women make up 21.8 percent of total parliamentarians and 14.7 percent of presiding officers of Parliament.
-Inter-Parliamentary Union, 2014

The UK comes 65th and the U.S. joint 85th in the world for gender equality in Parliament.
-Inter-Parliamentary Union, 2014

At the current rate of progress, it will be 2121 before gender parity is achieved in Congress.
-Institute for Women's Policy Research, 2013

I love her, but when I first told mum I wanted to go into politics, she said "Oh yes! You'd make a WONDERFUL politician's wife."

Guy in my politics class told the teacher he didn't think women had the right to vote. His reason: "it doesn't seem right."

I was on a busy train reading my Comparative Government textbook (I'm a politics student) when the man opposite me commented "That looks a bit complicated for you love, why don't you try something a bit simpler?"

At school, a teacher said it was good that "masculine" girls like me wanted to go into politics because most women were only there because men let them, to "shut up the feminists for a bit."

I was told "if you want to be in Politics, you could be an MP's secretary."

Recently told by stranger I'm "too pretty to be involved in politics." Reply: "Good thing I was blessed with a brain, then."

In the heat of the Paris summer, the minister for housing takes the floor in France's National Assembly to begin an address. A deafening chorus of hooting and catcalls drowns out the words. She is wearing a dress. Her male colleagues—her fellow politicians—are sexually harassing her, publicly, openly, in Parliament. For wearing a dress.

Does this sound like an exaggeration? Like a bad film? It was the experience of Cécile Duflot in July 2012.

Bishkek, Kyrgyzstan. A packed audience eagerly hangs on

every word of the woman onstage, the U.S. secretary of state. This is a once-in-a-lifetime opportunity for students of the University of Central Asia to put their questions to her, and for the Kyrgyzstan Public TV and Radio to grill her on her foreign policy. "Which designers do you prefer?" asks the moderator. "What designers of clothes?" the secretary of state replies. "Yes," the moderator confirms. "Would you ever ask a man that question?" she responds. The moderator pauses to reflect. "Probably not. Probably not."

This was a question asked of Hillary Clinton during a "townterview" in Bishkek in 2010.

The House of Commons, London. The Labour and Co-operative MP for Walthamstow steps into an elevator with a female colleague. Suddenly they are confronted by a Conservative MP demanding to know what they're doing there. Obviously, he says, they must be unable to read, "because this is a lift for MPs or disabled people and you're clearly neither." When the young blond woman informs him that she is indeed an MP, *as well as* a woman, he remains incredulous enough to demand to see her Commons pass as proof. This was 2011, and one of Stella Creasy's early experiences of Westminster.

Giving a stump speech as a mayoral candidate and being interrupted to be asked, "Just what are your measurements?" —Siobhan Bennett, Pennsylvania, 2001. Trying to speak in Parliament as male MPs made breast-jiggling gestures.—Jackie Ballard, Liberal Democrat MP, 1997. Described in media headlines on her death as "a better politician than wife and mother."—Margaret Thatcher, former prime minister, 2013.

Sarah Palin: branded "Caribou Barbie." Wendy Davis:

"Abortion Barbie." Rosy Bindi: sarcastically described by Silvio Berlusconi as "more beautiful than intelligent." Lindiwe Mazibuko: dismissed as a "tea girl" by the ANC youth leader who refused to debate with her.

The list could go on and on. Again and again, female politicians the world over are subjected to ridicule, criticism, and dismissal on the basis of their sex—from their colleagues, the media, and the general public alike. It is a catalog of prejudice that takes many subtle forms, and its impacts are enormous—on individual women in office, on the political aspirations of younger women, on the gender balance of government, and on political outcomes that affect women everywhere. Even when it doesn't outright prevent women from achieving political success, they still are unable to operate free of ongoing and pernicious discrimination.

First, there's the irrational obsession with political women's appearance, despite this being immaterial to their job performance . . .

Angela Merkel, chancellor of Germany, is one of the most influential and authoritative world leaders, named by *Forbes* magazine as the most powerful woman in the world. But that didn't stop the very same magazine running an article on her "silly pageboy haircut" and "ill-fitting suits."

Failing to consider that one of the leaders of the free world might have a few things on her mind other than leafing through the latest copy of *Vogue* for fashion tips, they went on to deal her possibly the most condescending backhanded compliment ever given: "Merkel's frumpy style," they said, may in fact have "proved an asset to her career." The author draws this brilliant conclusion from the observation that "the dull outfits for which she became famous demonstrated consistency and prudence, two qualities generally prized in German politics."

Merkel has been consistent and prudent in her policies. Isn't *that* (rather than, say, the tailoring of her trousers) more likely to be the reason that German voters have so far reelected her *twice*?

"Oh yes, Merkel's leadership is exemplary—she's effectively led Europe through the recent financial crisis while keeping domestic policy on an even keel with outstanding results and continues to head one of the strongest economies in the world, completely bucking the local trend, but somehow I'm still just not . . . WAIT, A FRUMPY SUIT?! Where do I vote?!"

In the UK, from "Hollande's Honeys" to "Blair's Babes" and "Cameron's Cuties" (a cringeworthy attempt by the *Telegraph* in 2010 to coin the painful "Brown Sugars" thankfully failed), the advent of a new Parliament has long been the cue to examine the political stance and voting history of male politicians while analyzing the heels and hairstyles of their female colleagues. Witness the *Sun*'s feature comparing the cleavage of various MPs, under the headline "The Best of Breastminster," the *Mirror*'s piece on the fashion faux pas of "Cameron's Cuties," and countless column inches devoted to Theresa May's shoes (I mean actually countless; I tried).

When the cabinet reshuffle was announced in July 2014, the *Daily Mail* dedicated a double-page spread to images of the female members, dissecting their hair, fashion, body shapes, and makeup under the headline "Esther, the Queen of the Downing Street Catwalk." Esther McVey was described as "sashaying" and wearing a dress that "emphasized her bust." The piece also described the cabinet members as "new girls," just for good, infantilizing, measure.

Next, there's the scrutiny of female politicians' "femininity" . . .

Hillary Clinton's experience shows that women in politics are fair game for an arbitrary lambasting purely on the basis that they are either *too* feminine or not feminine *enough*. Her "unfeminine" laugh has been commented on so many times it has been dubbed "the Clinton cackle."

Yet in 2007, the *Washington Post,* in a piece whose title was phrased to sound uncannily like an actual piece of political commentary—"Hillary Clinton's Tentative Dip into New Neckline Territory"—condemned Clinton for daring to let slip the awful secret that she had female anatomy. Straining desperately to spin an entire eight-hundred-word article out of an irrelevant observation, the *Post* resorted to phrasing the revelation in bulletinlike sentences as if it were the latest breaking news in a tensely unfolding political situation:

She was wearing a rose-colored blazer over a black top. The neckline sat low on her chest and had a subtle V-shape. The cleavage registered after only a quick glance. No scrunch-faced scrutiny was necessary . . . there it was. Undeniable.

That five sentences were required to confirm that Clinton does in fact have cleavage is less surprising when you see the pictures and realize that she was smartly dressed, with less than one inch of visible cleavage on display.

Sarah Palin was repeatedly attacked for being "Too Sexy for Vice President," "Too Sexy for the Left," "Too Sexy for the White House," "Too Sexy to Be President," "Too Sexy for National Office," and even, bizarrely, "Too Sexy for Her Feet." She was eventually immortalized as a blow-up doll.

When the American actress Ashley Judd considered running for office in 2013, media outlets exploded with consternation at the fact that she had previously performed *outraged stage whisper* *nude* scenes in movies. Would Judd be "the first potential senator who has—literally—nothing left to show us?" they fretted. Eventually, citing her responsibility to her family, Judd chose not to run. (Meanwhile Anthony Weiner blithely continued his run for New York City mayor, blissfully unconcerned that his junk had been pinged around the Internet more times than a Grumpy Cat video.)

Then there are the sexist tropes (mother, virgin, whore, harpy, ballbreaker, bitch) into which political women are neatly and arbitrarily pigeonholed, and from which their wherewithal as candidates is irrationally extrapolated . . .

When Sarah Palin's vice presidential candidacy was announced in August 2008, CNN debated the breaking news under the headline "VP Pick: Teen Daughter Pregnant." One pundit loudly declared that "the facts are this: what kind of mother is she? Is she prepared to be the vice president? Is she going to be totally focused on the issues?"

(None of which, it's worth noting, were actually facts.)

These hollow sexist labels also have another major impact—they help to create the artificial idea that any two women in conflict with one another must be hormonal bitches having a gendered scrap.

When male politicians disagree, it's described as just that—a disagreement. But when UK MPs Nadine Dorries and Louise Mensch failed to see eye to eye on policy, the papers dubbed it the "catfight" of the Tory "blondes," playing on negative stereotypes of bickering women and raking Mensch for being "undignified."

That same tired "catfight" narrative also dogged Sarah Palin and Michele Bachmann, with commentators drawing comparisons to the movie *Bridesmaids* and declaring them "best political frenemies." Even Bachmann's own strategist, Ed Rollins, told *Politico*, "People are going to say, 'I gotta make a choice and go with the intelligent woman who's every bit as attractive.'" (He later described it as "one comment . . . I shouldn't have made.")

In Canada, when British Columbia's premier Christy Clark clashed with Alberta's premier Alison Redford over the Northern Gateway Pipeline in 2012, it was described by the media as a "catfight" and a "spat." Throwing both subtlety and punctuation to the wind, one journalist even described some of Clark's comments on the issue as "akin to a cat hissing, raising it's [*sic*] hackles and baring its teeth."

In reporting on several high-profile disagreements between female Indian politicians, the *Times of India* went farther still, not only proclaiming "Catfights: The New Politics" but also berating female politicians for failing to use their womanly ways to provide some magical new soft and gentle politics. "Whatever happened to the notion that women could provide an alternative model of politics—sensitive, caring and for the greater common good?" it moaned. I don't know, *Times of India*. Maybe the reality of women's multifaceted and nonhomogenous personalities got in the way?

When Australian prime minister Julia Gillard was accused of being a hard-hearted harpy for not having a husband and children, the suspicion of her "unwomanliness" somehow carried over into an irrational questioning of her political ability.

New South Wales senator Bill Heffernan famously accused her of being unfit to lead the country specifically because she was "deliberately barren"—not a charge likely to be leveled against any male politician.

And when UK home secretary Theresa May made a mistake in timing in the case of the deportation of Abu Qatada in 2012, the *Metro* newspaper headline screamed "It Only Takes a Minute, Girl" above a photo of her and Qatada captioned "Dating game." Gleefully invoking the archetype of a befuddled old dear, they branded her "Muddled May"—destroying any fears of subtlety with a cartoon portraying her, complete with head scarf and tortoiseshell glasses, clutching her handbag and saying, "I'm having one of those days."

Of course all politicians should face media criticism and scrutiny. But here the focus was not on May's disorganization or error, where it should have been; it was on her gender and age—or rather the implication that she had a feeble, unreliable woman's mind. And with this single lazy, sexist stereotype they attempted to call into doubt her entire suitability for political office.

This combination of ageism and sexism was also blatant in the *Boston Herald*'s treatment of sixty-three-year-old Elizabeth Warren, whose 2012 Senate bid it sought to undermine by repeatedly dubbing her "Granny" in its pages, as if to imply that an older woman could not possibly be trusted with political responsibility.

It was the same nonsensical prejudice that saw right-wing commentators try to tarnish Hillary Clinton's race for president on the grounds of both her age and sex. Good old Limbaugh (who else?) got in early on the action, way back in 2007, when he asked, "Will this country want to actually watch a woman get older before their eyes on a daily basis?" (Presumably as opposed to all those male leaders who have Dorian Gray portraits stashed away somewhere in the bowels of the White House and don't age a day in office.) As ridiculous as this criticism sounds, and even though he was eight years ahead of the game, Limbaugh still managed to set the tone for the abuse that dogged Clinton's presidential bid from the outset.

A message from Donald Trump's Twitter account (quickly deleted) took the trophy for sheer snide irrelevance, asking, "If Hillary Clinton can't satisfy her husband, what makes her think she can satisfy America?" One Republican strategist declared, "I don't need her to drown me in estrogen every time she opens her mouth." Another pundit explained that Clinton could never be president, in part because she is too "profoundly ugly." (Elsewhere in his deeply nuanced political analysis, he referred to her as a "damned bimbo.") Milwaukee county supervisor Deanna Alexander decided to cut to the chase and just start referring to Clinton as "Ovary" when discussing her presidential bid on Twitter. Because once you reach that level of searing political commentary, why not just go all in?

Time published an online article dealing Clinton the supreme backhanded compliment of declaring her "The Perfect Age to Be President," before going into great detail about the "hormonal ebbing" she might be experiencing as a postmenopausal woman. A *Los Angeles Times* columnist wrote at length about her surprise that Clinton would even *consider* running for the presidency without first having Botox or plastic surgery. And in a *New York Times* op-ed titled "Granny Get Your Gun," Clinton was accused of "basking in estrogen" because she discussed her granddaughter's birth on the campaign trail.

Basking! Because that kind of brief anecdote really is the only proof you need that a woman without much else on her mind is just WALLOWING in hormones.

One bright spark even started a #HowOldIsHillary hashtag, posting unflattering pictures of Clinton alongside images of rusting cars and dilapidated drive-thrus with imaginative captions like "Hillary Clinton is older than this."

Naturally, despite coming under heavy fire for being a grandmother, Clinton was also accused of exploiting the very status she was criticized for—one *Washington Free Beacon* writer even penned the extraordinary line, "Clinton's flaunting of her grandchild is one of the most transparently cynical and sentimental acts of a major American politician that I can recall."

Remember, these commentators are referring to a woman who, during her relatively recent term as secretary of state, traveled almost a million miles and visited 112 countries in the space of four years.

It is worth mentioning, of course, that several other White House occupants have been grandparents, both before and during their term in office. Jeb Bush is also a grandfather, as it happens, but as of the time of writing not a peep has been spoken about the potential this might have to derail his chances of making a bid for the Oval Office.

For Clinton, on the other hand, the question has been considered so overwhelmingly critical that it started to surface even before she announced her intention to run in the first place. That's right, we were freaking out so hard about the idea of a grandmother in the White House that we started fretting about it before we even knew if she'd be in the race, *and* before the baby had even been born!

It all started in April 2014 with the earth-shattering news that Chelsea Clinton was pregnant, leading, naturally, to the most obvious question in the world: How could Hillary possibly expect to run for office now?

Confused? I'm not surprised. What possible impact could her daughter's offspring have on Clinton's (as yet not even declared) presidential prospects? Luckily, the media was around to explain. "President or grandmother?" fretted Charlie Rose, while NBC's David Gregory asked whether a new grandchild would "factor into" Clinton's decision about whether or not to run.

The bizarre non-question proliferated, with *USA Today* reporting, "It's unclear how Chelsea's pregnancy will affect Hillary Clinton, who is considering a race for president in 2016," and the *Christian Science Monitor* trumpeting, "Chelsea Clinton baby: Will Hillary Clinton be less likely to run in 2016?" ("Perhaps it's sexist even to ask the question," it mused . . . before going right ahead anyway.) Its sharp political conclusion? "If we had to guess, we'd say that Hillary Clinton will be a tad less interested in running for president now that she's about to be a grandmother." Incisive, guys. Guess you were wrong.

The gist of the hand-wringing seemed to center around the idea that Clinton's grandma hormones would go wild, preventing her from being able even to consider concentrating on anything other than her daughter's baby for one. Single. Second. Again, similar accusations haven't been leveled at male political candidates, who are assumed to have mastered the incredible feat of willpower required to both hold down a job and enjoy the occasional weekend with their grandchildren.

In fact, women face age-related prejudice at both ends of the spectrum, with younger women also likely to be taken less seriously and considered less suitable for political office. But the issue of older women being seen as somehow less reliable is likely to have a more insidious impact, because of the fact that an unequal balance in domestic labor means women are likely to come later to politics than their male peers. When Nancy Pelosi was asked at a press conference if she felt her decision to continue as House minority leader was preventing "a younger leadership" from progressing, she pointed out that she was able to start her political career only when her youngest child was eighteen, meaning that many of her male colleagues "had a jump on me." But, as she rightly added, it is a short-sighted mistake to consider that age gap a weakness in female political candidates, as the time spent bringing up a family gave her "the best experience in diplomacy and interpersonal skills."

These stereotypical and restrictive female tropes are used as the justification to find female politicians wanting—whether because they will be too authoritative or not firm enough, too stylish or too unfashionable, distracted by partners and children or hard-hearted for lack of them.

The idea that women can't be good politicians is worryingly persistent. I asked Labour MP Stella Creasy how she felt sexist typecasting affected women in political life. She told me, "Too often women aren't being considered as capable leaders because our concept of what leadership is, is defined by our history rather than our future. So it's defined by a sense of people gone past and the role they played."

So, she concludes, since historically so many more men than women have been leaders, we tend toward the assumption that leadership is an inherently "male" role, requiring "male" qualities and attributes.

It's not hard to see where she's coming from. On a recent school visit, talking to a mixed class of eleven-year-olds, I asked the pupils to guess how many out of just under two hundred countries in the world had a female leader. I assumed they'd make a guess of around sixty or seventy, allowing me to shock them with the actual figure (then just nineteen). But the real shocker turned out to be the guesses themselves—"less than 10 percent," "about 9," "3 percent" . . . The first estimate was almost exactly on the money. Intrigued, I asked them why they thought so few women were political leaders.

"I think men have more leadership than women," replied one boy—not rudely or antagonistically, but as if it was a simple, noncontentious statement of fact. And in a group where the girls had angrily and vocally responded to an earlier claim that "sports is for boys" with cries of "No, it's not!" not one person contradicted him. In fact, the girls seemed to agree.

"I think if you're going to lead a country you've got to be powerful and have a loud voice, and men are associated more with that and girls are usually more quiet," said one. Another articulated Creasy's fears almost to the letter: "I think it's because they think men have more leadership and men can be more controlling—they just don't think it's a woman's thing."

Sitting at her desk under a large banner reading WELL-BEHAVED WOMEN RARELY MAKE HISTORY, Caroline Lucas, MP for Brighton Pavilion, voices almost identical concerns: "Most people's concept of what a leader is has been a male stereotype of somebody who is having power *over* rather than empowering people."

Both she and Creasy agreed that female leaders are treated differently from their male peers by the press. Creasy cited the media analysis in the wake of Margaret Thatcher's death as an example of tired sexist stereotypes being applied to female leaders: "Last week on *Question Time,* they were talking about Baroness Thatcher. You had a panel of four men and one woman talking about women in politics and how they should behave and what was 'a good temperament' or a 'bad temperament.' "

She was tired, she said, of "seeing mainly men defining what is acceptable for women . . . Too often, women in public life are caricatured—you've got to be a harridan, or a bitch, or somebody's mother."

If you take each example individually, it might be difficult to gauge the negative impact of media sexism on female politicians. There are articles written about male politicians' appearance, children, and family lives too, of course. But (setting aside the fact that the incidence of such coverage is vastly less frequent) there is a simple way to appreciate the absurdity and definite difference in tone of the commentary faced by their female peers. Simply pluck some lines at random from the press female politicians receive and try to imagine the same quotes being included in articles about David Cameron, Barack Obama, or any other high-profile male political figure:

A White House Counsel known for her shoes . . . Ruemmler first attracted attention for her glam heels as a Justice Department prosecutor trying Enron executives.

—*The Washington Post,* on White House Counsel Kathryn Ruemmler

183 centimetres tall, with long, dark hair, a taste for leopard print and a collection of elegant size-11 stilettos. The term "glamazon" might have been invented for her.
—*Sydney Morning Herald,* on Peta Credlin, chief of staff to Tony Abbott

As she expounded her tough stance on immigration she stood in shoes worthy of the front row at Paris fashion week.
—*Guardian,* on Home Secretary Theresa May

Though aged 60 (and counting), she teeters up to the Despatch Box in high heels, grinning girlishly at the Opposition benches before hesitantly lisping a few opening apologies for losing her place or some such calamity.
—*Daily Mail,* on Equalities Minister Lynne Featherstone

Who's hotter: Janet Yellen or Miley Cyrus? [SLIDESHOW]
—The *Dailey Caller,* on Federal Reserve Chair Janet Yellen

What's worse is that this sexism doesn't come from the media alone. Often political women find that their male colleagues exacerbate such prejudice, or try to use it as political capital. Examples are many and can be drawn from all levels of politics.

Congressman Jim Sensenbrenner attacked Michelle Obama's dietary initiatives by complaining, "She lectures us on eating right while she has a large posterior herself." Senate Majority Leader Harry Reid announced at a New York fund-raiser that "we in the Senate refer to Senator Gillibrand as the hottest member."

Indeed, Senator Kirstin Gillibrand has described a litany of such inappropriate comments from her male colleagues in Congress, including: "Good thing you're working out, because you wouldn't want to get porky!" (Her reply: "Thanks, asshole.") Another member of Congress held her arm and said, "You know, Kirstin, you're even pretty when you're fat." Yet another squeezed her waist, saying, "Don't lose too much weight now. I like my girls chubby."

When seventy-six-year-old MP Glenda Jackson spoke passionately about Thatcherism during a debate in the House of Commons, another Conservative councilor publicly branded her a "rotting pork chop on a stick." When former Liberal leader Lord Steel's wife voiced differing views from his on the topic of Scottish independence, MSP Murdo Fraser tweeted, "Is he not master in his own house?" When photographs emerged of Nigella Lawson seemingly being throttled by her then husband, Charles Saatchi, member of the European Parliament Nick Griffin tweeted, "If I had the opportunity to squeeze Nigella Lawson, her throat wouldn't be my first choice."

When thirty-five-year-old Tokyo assembly member Ayaka Shiomura spoke in a debate on support for child rearing, male politicians shouted and heckled her, one crying, "You should get married," and another demanding, "Can't you even bear a child?"

And so on.

Like Austin Mitchell's vitriolic outpouring about "good little girls" obeying their "masters," each of these instances serves as a painful and weighty reminder of how steeply sloped the political playing field is—and how willing some male politicians are to use gendered prejudice to attack and debase their female peers.

You might think—given these and other extreme examples of sexism in politics—that it should be relatively easy for female leaders to fight back. It isn't. One of the cleverest and most insidious twists in the whole sorry tale is the way women are double bound by a gender-biased definition of professionalism and the threat of being labeled "whining." For an archaic method of silencing, it remains depressingly successful in preventing complaint. A perfect example of this phenomenon emerged in 2012, when Australian prime minister Julia Gillard stopped the international press with a passionate, eloquent skewering of the opposition party's open misogyny toward her in Parliament and elsewhere. The video of Gillard's speech quickly went viral. In it she ran through a whole catalog of sexist tripe thrown her way by the leader of the opposition, Tony Abbott (this included photographs showing him alongside signs saying DITCH THE WITCH and branding her a "man's bitch"). She declared that he had subjected her to "misogyny" and "sexism"—"every day, in every way."

And yet—despite international public acclaim for Gillard's strength in standing up against the abuse to which she'd been subjected—media commentators and politicians alike were quick to brand her melodramatic and oversensitive. In the UK, one *Telegraph* writer accused her of "gratuitously" betraying her "emotional sensitivity" and (perhaps oblivious of the irony in the statement) suggested that she simply needed to "man up." Opposition politicians similarly sought to shame Gillard into silence. One described her pithy, intelligent refutation of months of misogyny as "playing the gender card" and claimed that she had "demeaned every woman in this Parliament." (Ah, so *she* was the real threat to women in politics? Of course!) Finally he came to his illogical and unoriginal conclusion: "If you can't stand the heat, get out of the kitchen."

This unimaginative attempt to silence Gillard (with a kitchen-related metaphor, no less!) perfectly illustrates the irrationality of sexism in politics. She's the victim of a vast range of misogynistic abuse so she chooses to confront it, clearly and deliberately, sending a firm message that she won't tolerate such prejudice. And then this very response is cited as proof of her unsuitability for the political environment. Thus the power remains firmly in the hands of the perpetrators, for whom gender prejudice serves both to underpin the initial line of attack and to undermine any subsequent rebuttal.

These patterns are so hard to break because they are self-perpetuating. When the basis of the prejudice itself makes protest near impossible without facing a backlash almost greater than the initial injury, female politicians are left, once again, between a rock and a hard place.

So why does all this matter?

It matters because, around the world, women are enormously underrepresented in politics. According to information compiled by the Inter-Parliamentary Union in February 2013, just 21.8 percent of parliamentary seats in the world are held by women. Figures from the Center for American Women and Politics reveal that in the United States, women hold only 20 percent of Senate seats and 18.3 percent of seats in the House of Representatives. Four states (Delaware, Iowa, Mississippi, and Vermont) have never sent a woman to either the Senate or the House. Only two women of color have ever served in the U.S. Senate and only forty-nine in the House of Representatives. Just 24 percent of state legislators are women, and only five out of fifty states have a female governor. Only thirty-five women in history have ever served as governor, compared to more than twenty-three hundred men.

In the UK, women hold less than a third of seats in the House of Commons. The House of Lords was barred to women until as recently as 1958, so it doesn't come as much of a surprise that women hold only a fifth of the seats there too. Bishops also sit in the House of Lords, creating an extra twenty-six places which, until 2015, could not be occupied by women, since the Church of England refused to allow women to reach those lofty heights. (When the issue was recently debated, one wry tweeter succinctly summarized the issue: "This week the Church of England General Synod will be discussing 'women Bishops,' or as I call them, 'Bishops.' ")

The UK figure for political representation is only very slightly above the international average at 22.5 percent, bringing it in at an underwhelming sixty-fifth in the world for gender parity. The United States comes joint eighty-fifth. This means that, in terms of achieving gender equality in politics, the United States trails behind, among other countries, Saudi Arabia, Iraq, Afghanistan, and Pakistan.

At the time of writing, only 22 of the world's 196 countries have female leaders. (There are disagreements about the number of countries in the world depending on how the word is defined, but of the 5 disputed countries, only one—Kosovo—has a woman president, which hardly makes a difference in the percentage. We're still struggling to make it far beyond 10 percent.)

So while we're still fighting for equal representation, the issues of sexism in politics and in the media portrayal of politicians are hugely important—because they play a major role in creating and maintaining that gender gap.

Accounts sent into the Everyday Sexism Project certainly suggest that these attitudes about the "unsuitability" of women for political roles are trickling down from the media and political environments to impact strongly on girls' ambitions from a very young age.

▸ I took A-level politics . . . I had worked hard to prepare for a debate in which I was the only female in my team. While providing a counter-argument my teacher stopped me and asked the males in my team whether they were going to let a woman do all the talking.

▸ Told I should be a "porn star" and that I look like a "prostitute" when talking about what we wanted to do when older, after I said that I wanted to get involved in politics.

A little later on, when girls start to consider the possibility of studying politics at university, they are frequently met with the assertion that it isn't a "suitable" subject for women, or that they don't have a natural aptitude for it.

One student recalls being told:

▸ Oh, you're doing a politics course? You must be very smart, things like that are really hard for girls!

Another writes:

▸ I thought I was part of a fairly liberal and progressive Sixth Form College until I attended debate club. Our first motion was to discuss whether a woman's place was in the home. A stupid motion to begin with, but I was told that it was a question that could come up in competitions.

▸ I was shocked to find that my own Government and Politics teacher felt that women were somehow "Genetically" better at housework and cooking. He later made another ridiculous claim that men were just simply better at economics and politics. Backing up all his points with pseudo-psychology. Obviously I was fuming by this point, when I later tried to question his ideas he simply told me to "Calm Down."

Unfortunately, these ideas sometimes come from the least likely sources.

▸ Went on a trip to the Houses of Parliament as part of our Government & Political Studies A-Level . . . We were given a tour . . . The guide said, "There is a book shop over there, there are recipe books for the girls."

▸ During a tour of the Houses of Parliament this week an official male guide commented that MPs were not allowed to change their minds once they had entered the voting lobby and he added "surprisingly the rule was not changed . . . even when women became MPs."

Everywhere you look, the idea that women aren't suited to politics seems to be deeply ingrained, with even direct evidence of strong female leaders being twisted to fit the stereotype instead of debunking it.

▸ I was discussing politics with a guy I know who began to say how much he admired Margaret Thatcher . . . This guy later told me, in the same conversation, that women shouldn't ever be leaders. I said, "Well what about Thatcher?"

He then told me "she was basically a man anyway . . . she had a male brain." So obviously women don't owe their success to hard work and have to hope they have masculine qualities to make up for it.

One frustrating consequence of women being underrepresented in politics is that often *any* woman is seen first and foremost to represent *all* women, as if she speaks and advocates for them, and can be judged as if all womankind stands or falls by her actions. MP Stella Creasy says, "The notion that I could represent all women: that's a thing that really annoys me. As though women aren't very diverse—as though we're quite homogenous really in what we care about. Somehow, men are multifaceted and talented and represent all sorts of different things, but women? The prime minister can have *a* woman to advise on women—job done!"

This is particularly pertinent when you consider the enormous political underrepresentation of women of color, disabled women, and LBGT women—none of whom are miraculously "included" in the debate simply by the introduction of a white, middle-class female voice.

And just as in business, the visibility of women lower down the rungs of political power is often used as a veneer of equality, to ignore even greater gender imbalance higher up. Even the aforementioned eleven-year-olds seemed satisfied by it, commenting, "There are quite a few women in politics but they're not like the president or prime minister, because men rule."

Within such an environment, can it be a coincidence that the policies coming out of these governments often seem to hit women particularly hard?

In 2011 *alone,* the Guttmacher Institute for sexual and reproductive health and rights reported that legislators in American states introduced more than 1,100 provisions relating to reproductive health and rights. Of those that were enacted, 68 percent restricted access to abortion services.

In the UK, women comprise around two-thirds of public-sector workers, so the huge cuts made in this area by our majority male government as a result of the recession have a disproportionate impact on women's jobs. The *Guardian* reported that unemployment among women age fifty to sixty-four rose by 39 percent from 2010 to 2012, and unemployment among all women by 11 percent, compared to an overall increase of just 5 percent among all those over sixteen. And according to the Fawcett Society, with the majority of caretakers for children, disabled people, and the elderly being women, around three-quarters of all cuts to benefits come out of women's pockets. Finally, because public services such as child care and social services tend to be used more frequently by women than by men, budget cuts here also impact disproportionately. The Fawcett Society has dubbed this combination of disadvantages "Triple Jeopardy."

A comparable relationship could also be drawn between the gender imbalance of other important power structures and the impact of their actions. In the 2014 decision of the U.S. Supreme Court, for example, to allow closely held corporations such as Hobby Lobby to refuse to provide contraceptive coverage to female employees, the five justices in the majority were men; the dissenting justices were three women and one man. The split along gender lines on this issue, which directly affects women, was perhaps one of the most blatant examples yet of the way underrepresentation of women in the echelons of power can have a clear and direct negative impact on female citizens.

Of course it can be argued that the men in question are capable of rationally debating the pros and cons of the argument without requiring lived experience of not wanting to get pregnant. Except that apparently most of them couldn't. So distanced were those five men from the experience of a woman's choice to have sex without choosing to bear a child, to take control over the financial and emotional planning of her own life, to go through the physical experience of pregnancy and childbirth, that they were able to make a ruling that effectively allowed corporations to wield the right of religious belief—a right traditionally accorded to people—while denying women what many consider a basic right of humanity—thus reducing them to a status lower than personhood.

Discussing another recent concrete example of the negative impact on women of men's dominance in positions of power, Stella Creasy told me, "I certainly think that there are connections. I'll give you a very practical example of what I mean on a day-to-day level of making policy. I was talking to some of my colleagues here, who were involved in the debates around tax credits. When tax credits were first proposed there was a suggestion that they would also go to the main earner in the household. And it was women in the treasury, women in government, saying, 'Hold on a minute: have you realized the different lives that women lead and the implications that that would have in terms of tackling child poverty, in terms of social justice?' That meant they went to the main carer. It is frightening to me that [we can] fast forward twelve, thirteen years and we're having exactly the same debate around universal credit—where again that's going to go to the main earner in a household, which potentially sees 300,000 women losing what is their basic income."

While it's vital to consider the negative impact media sexism may have on voters' impressions of political candidates, it is as important to look through the other end of the telescope, at the impact sexism might have on male politicians' ideas about female constituents and voters.

If you need further convincing that some political men might not have the firmest grasp of women's best interests or needs, look no farther than the attempts made by many male politicians and political groups to engage with female voters.

Consider, for example, the 2014 self-described "culturally relevant" ad campaign by the College Republican National Committee to woo young women to vote for Republican candidate Rick Scott for governor of Florida instead of Democrat Charlie Crist. Did they harness the power of social media, you may be wondering, to appeal to the young female demographic using eye-catching infographics packed with relevant statistics?

Er, no.

They produced a schmaltzy, reality TV–esque wedding dress

scene, in which a young woman tries on a beautiful dress, declaring, "The Rick Scott is perfect!" before her fussy mother attempts—unsuccessfully—to force her into choosing the outdated, frumpy "Charlie Crist" instead: "It's expensive and a little outdated, but I know best." (As we all know, those pesky overbearing moms do *literally* use phrases like "I know best" in real life.)

I know it'll be tricky for you to work out the subtext of an ad this subtle, so let me help you out . . .

DON'T WORRY YOUR TINY LADY BRAINS ABOUT THE DETAILS OF POLITICS—JUST THINK OF VOTING AS IF IT WAS THE ONLY OTHER IMPORTANT CHOICE YOUR ESTROGEN-ADDLED BRAINS COULD POSSIBLY COMPARE IT TO: WEDDING DRESS SHOPPING! YAY!

Did I mention there's typical female woohooing and squealing at the end? Oh, yeah, ladies, the CRNC has you pegged.

That CRNC national chair Alex Smith described the ads as "culturally relevant" can demand only one follow-up question: To what, the 1950s? "It might appear to be silly on the surface," she continued, "but there's absolutely a deeper meaning that will resonate with young voters." I agree with her there.

The deeper meaning (she was referring to blatant sexism, right?) is certainly likely to "resonate" with young women—leading them, I'd imagine, to look for another candidate who doesn't have such an incredibly low opinion of their mental capacity.

It strikes me that, for all its archaic quirks and elitism, politics in many ways serves as a kind of microcosm, demonstrating the impact of so many of the wider issues described within the Everyday Sexism Project—stereotypical notions of gender, sexual harassment, the portrayal of women in the media, the objectification of women, workplace imbalance—and demonstrating how they combine to create the perfect storm.

One of the clearest messages to emerge from the Everyday Sexism Project has been that everything is connected: Inequality is a continuum, with the minor and major incidents irrevocably related to one another as the attitudes and ideas that underlie one allow the other to flourish. This isn't to say that one directly leads to another; rather, the culture created and sustained by each incident is part of the fertile ground from which the others spring. Perhaps this is particularly pertinent in politics, where a barbed sentence in a newspaper article, or the simple insertion of the qualifier "mother of two," or the "lighthearted" sniggering of a male MP, or an inappropriate "slip of the tongue" on the part of our prime minister can all add to the subtle, insidious ideas that prevent female politicians from being taken seriously and succeeding both among their peers and with the public.

It's a catch-22: It seems inevitable that politics must both lead and benefit from the charge against sexism—we need political change to ensure practical change, from flexible working hours and parental leave to more comprehensive education on the subjects of sex and relationships. But, equally, a cultural shift in attitudes toward women is desperately needed to give younger women traction in gaining political positions in the first place, and established politicians the opportunity, like men, to be judged on their work, not their womanhood, and to operate free of discrimination, objectification, and prejudice.

So how do we achieve this? Just as the problem manifests

itself at many different points along the journey of a political woman's career, so the solution needs to be multifaceted.

As the Representation Project has so brilliantly illustrated, you can't be what you can't see. We need to tackle gender stereotypes at an early age and take a careful look at career advice so no girl grows up believing politics is "just for men." We should bring greater pressure to bear on sexist media outlets to apply the same standards to reporting on political women as on their male colleagues, and we must continue vocally to point out the double standard when they fail.

We need to see concrete, decisive action from political leaders when members of their party express sexist views, just as we should expect in the case of any other form of prejudice. When Austin Mitchell tweeted about good little girls obeying their masters, he faced no consequences—leaving him free to go on, in 2014, to pen an article about how women make "gentler" politicians who are "more amenable and leadable . . . preoccupied with . . . small problems rather than big ideas and issues." Yet in contrast, Andrew Mitchell was forced to resign from his position as chief whip at around the same time for voicing offensive class prejudice after he allegedly called policemen "plebs."

There are also concrete structural adjustments that could be made to our political institutions. Archaic late voting hours and unpredictable timetables (maintained, it seems, almost as a matter of macho, historic pride) mean that Westminster lags far behind most other modern workplaces in its amenability to working mothers. (Unlike the Scottish Parliament, for example, whose more sociable hours are enjoyed by a membership consisting of 35 percent women, a proportion far higher than its London counterpart.)

These measures would encourage meaningful change. But things aren't changing fast enough. In America, the Institute for Women's Policy Research estimates it will be 2121 before Congress achieves gender parity at the current rate of progress. Doesn't there come a point at which we should at least be having a conversation about quotas?

For a long time I felt torn about quotas. To advocate for them feels somewhat defeatist, as if admitting that the underlying prejudice and discrimination that currently prevent equally qualified women from reaching the top is so ingrained and unchallengeable that action must be taken to work around it, rather than tackling the problem itself at the root.

To give women a leg up feels like an admission of their need for extra help, when in fact the excellence so clearly displayed by many serving female politicians demonstrates that such a notion is an insult—nothing could be further from the truth. And given the enormous underrepresentation of other groups, including disabled and black and minority ethnic candidates, it also seems arbitrary to choose to instigate positive discrimination to right some forms of inequality but not others.

But as I've listened to the debate playing out over and over, I've come to feel that the strongest point in favor of quotas is the main argument against them. I've heard men argue passionately that a quota system would disenfranchise them, putting unqualified women in jobs they don't deserve and failing to select the best candidate.

But this is to suggest that the current playing field is even, and that quotas would tilt it in women's favor. In reality, of course, the playing field has for hundreds of years been steeply sloped against women as a result of societal and structural prejudice, tradition, and both overt discrimination and subconscious bias. The use of quotas would merely temporarily rectify the existing imbalance.

To suggest that quotas would put underqualified women in office is to imply that the current system is based entirely on merit or, in plain terms, that only around one-fifth of women are as politically capable or talented as men. While attitudes as preposterous as these prevail, and while so little political will seems to exist to tackle the problem with any urgency (a 2013 poll by ABC News–Fusion revealed that just 23 percent of Republicans surveyed agreed "It would be a good thing if more women were elected to Congress"), quotas may prove a necessary short-term measure to jump-start progress.

The phrase "positive action" or "affirmative action" suggests something artificially added on, over and above the existing norm, but this is misleading. In reality, it is a necessary adjustment to compensate for existing bias and inequalities within the status quo.

It is hardly a wildly outrageous suggestion—more than one hundred countries worldwide have used political gender quotas with great success, many of them ranking higher than the United States and UK in the leaderboard for equality in political representation. The United Nations Convention on the Elimination of All Forms of Discrimination against Women specifies that the "adoption by States Parties of temporary special measures aimed at accelerating de facto equality between men and women shall not be considered discrimination."

And research by Anisa A. Somani, published in 2013 in the *William and Mary Law Review,* argues that the adoption of voluntary party quotas (relating to the nomination, not the selection of candidates) as a mechanism to increase women's participation in Congress would not be unconstitutional.

Quotas are not the best answer for anybody. One of the things I tend to find most amusing about the outraged men protesting their disenfranchisement is the implication that positive action is some kind of special prize women will be thrilled to win. In reality, of course, quotas are about as appealing to women as flu shots.

Don't think of this as some great "victory" for us—what we'd really like is not to need them. Men, in that respect, remain very much the victors.

Quotas won't be successful on their own. Helping women to overcome bias and barriers won't prevent them from being made to feel unqualified to pursue a political career in the first place, or from continuing to face the negative effects of discrimination once in office, unless we continue to tackle the underlying problem as well.

But change is coming too slowly. If there are tools available to us that could help to rectify that, what on earth are we waiting for?

If you don't have a thigh gap you NEED to get a thigh gap.

Fourteen-year-old schoolgirl interviewee

Vital Statistics

31 percent of girls age thirteen to seventeen admit to starving themselves or refusing to eat as a strategy to lose weight.
-Girl Scouts of the USA/Girl Scout Research Institute, 2010

60 percent of girls age thirteen to seventeen say they compare their bodies to fashion models.
-Girl Scouts of the USA/Girl Scout Research Institute, 2010

21 percent of high school girls were electronically bullied in the last twelve months.
-Centers for Disease Control and Prevention, High School Youth Risk Behavior Survey, 2013

10 percent of high school girls were physically forced to have intercourse against their will in the last twelve months.
-High School Youth Risk Behavior Survey, 2013

14 percent of high school girls experienced sexual dating violence in the last twelve months.
-High School Youth Risk Behavior Survey, 2013

Only 37 percent of high school girls were not trying to lose weight at the time of the survey.
-High School Youth Risk Behavior Survey, 2013

My father's reaction when he learned I was a baby girl: "They are twins, and GIRLS to boot?!"

My 2-year-old daughter given toys/books all based on beauty and getting her prince. My son given cars and trains.

My mom told me repeatedly that men won't like me because I was too opinionated . . . it started when I was 3.

We were asked what we wanted to be. I wanted to say a doctor but didn't because I thought girls couldn't be doctors. I was 4 years old.

Aged 5, man leaned over the garden wall where I was playing, asked me to twirl so he could see my knickers.

6 years old, as a bridesmaid, took my cardigan off at the reception and got WOLF WHISTLES from adult men nearby. Straight back on.

In Brownies (age 7) sang songs about potential careers. One verse I remember went: "typing letters, sitting on the boss's knee."

Got told by a friend of mine to suck his cock, in the street. We were both 8, and his dad laughed.

Being told by age 9 that getting catcalled, whistled, honked at were to be taken as compliments.

When I was 10, my 50-year-old neighbor telling me he wanted to be the first person to know when my breasts started to develop.

When I was in 1st year (age 11), my form teacher held a beauty contest—asked the boys to vote for the girls, ranked us on blackboard.

Age 12, at KFC, some guy hands me a note with crap handwriting, but reads pretty much as "I want to fook you."

13 years, told teachers I wanted to be an engineer: "Too complicated, women don't do that usually." I was the best pupil in my maths class.

Told I was pretty and then asked my age. Said I was 14 and he asked me to sit on his lap.

Men shouted at me from their car "get your tits out you fucking slag." I was 15.

When I was 16, a boy forced me into closet, said he "wanted to get to know me" and wouldn't let me go. I fought my way out, was called a tease.

At my careers interview aged 18 I said I wanted to be a barrister. She laughed in my face. I was a straight A student.

Working in a bar aged 18, collecting glasses, man waits until both my hands are full then grabs my boobs from behind.

You can trace an entire childhood in sexism through the entries sent in to the Everyday Sexism Project. The flashes of realization and first, painful moments of learning a woman's place. Often the memories are so vivid women carry and are shaped by them for the rest of their lives.

I've been asked in countless interviews what has shocked me the most since starting the project. I think journalists expect me to tell them that it's the stories of rape or the appalling accounts of violence. Those stories have certainly angered and devastated me, but nothing has shocked me more than the thousands and thousands of entries from girls under the age of eighteen. When I started the project, I thought adult women would share their stories. The torrent of harassment, abuse, violence, and assault being faced by children was a horribly unexpected surprise.

We often talk about the terrible struggles faced by children in other countries around the world. Meanwhile we are ignoring the increasingly desperate situation faced by girls right under our smug noses.

One day, in the very early months of the project, I read several entries in a single week from girls who had been subjected to leering and shouting from men in the street while walking home from school in their uniforms. Dismayed, I posted a question on Twitter: Surely, I asked, this couldn't be a common occurrence? By the end of the day, a deluge of hundreds of tweets had confirmed that the experience was not only common but almost ubiquitous.

Some were memories recounted by older women, but many came from current pupils and have been borne out since by painful conversations with girls in schools, who describe the phenomenon as simply the norm. One entry read:

▸ At the age of 15 I was recently greeted with "hello sexy" on the street by a creepy man . . . it was only about 5 in the evening. I have also had men say things like "hello darling" and "sexy lady" whilst walking home from school IN MY UNIFORM.

As the weeks went by, the problem was reported so frequently that it became rare for a day to go by without a "schoolgirl harassment" entry.

I learned that I had a sexy body when I was in elementary school because that's when grown men started staring at me and making sexual comments to me.

Age 14, walking to school, in uniform, man on a motorbike reaches out and grabs my breast as he passes me.

Between the age of 12 and 14 me and all of my friends have been followed home at least once. I'm told it's because of what I wear, but I have had people talking to me when I'm wearing my school uniform with a below the knee dress. Whose right is it?

I am only a teen, and I was in my school uniform walking home from school, and even then men in a car drove past me, yelled obscene things and whistled and called me sexy bitch and stuff! I mean, I'm only 15!

I was with my two cousins walking home from the convenience store. We were walking in front of an elementary school on the other side of the street and some guy shouts from his vehicle to my male cousin, "hey, you their pimp?" He was thirteen, I was eleven, and his seven year old sister was with us.

▸ When I was partway through high school I was walking my younger sister and our neighbor home (both in elementary school). Some guy and his friend stopped his car beside us on the street, opened up the driver side door and displayed his erect penis to us shouting something like "want to suck my dick."

There were several occasions during those early days when something like this stunned me almost into denial. A great sadness of running the project is that almost nothing surprises me anymore. Gradually, as time went on, I started to build up a picture of what children are facing—from their first experiences of toys and tantrums ("Don't cry like a girl") through elementary and middle school and into their early teens, with all the incumbent pressures and bombardment of sexualization, and finally to near adulthood—all the while learning, learning. But rather than acquiring the skills and knowledge that would open up the world to them, girls appeared to be seeing it close down at every turn, constantly being taught harsh lessons about all the restrictions and insults and petty categorization that being a woman brings. It starts so young, and once it has started, it never stops . . .

One of the earliest manifestations of childhood sexism is in the segregation of children's toys. The absolute separation along color, type, and aesthetic lines has now become so complete that the briefest glance around almost any children's toy store reveals a bizarre battleground. Bright hothouse pinks face off against defiant blues across a strip of notably empty no-man's-land. Soft and cuddly on one side; sporty and energetic on the other. Cooking and domesticity here; science and exploration there.

No toy so neutral as to defy categorization. The outright lack of gender neutrality gives pause when imagining the contortions of the poor shelving staff—where best for a purple tractor, one can't help but wonder, or a gun that fires bubbles?

With the overt segregation of our children's playthings, as with sexism in many other forms, we become so accustomed to the norms that it can take a shock to jolt us into realizing how ridiculous they are. A good case in point was the infamous hijacking of hundreds of talking Barbies and G.I. Joes by the Barbie Liberation Organization, which switched the dolls' voice boxes and took them back to the shelves. Barbie lisping, "Vengeance is mine!" while the macho action figures proclaimed, "The beach is the place for the summer!" forced us to acknowledge the absurdity of such exaggerated lines.

It has been suggested that to protest against the categorization of "boys'" and "girls'" toys is an over-the-top feminist reaction to a harmless marketing decision. Yet when you actually look at the divide—with science, exploration, construction, engineering, discovery, adventure—for all intents and purposes, creativity itself—cordoned off as "boys' only," you start to realize what an impact these apparently arbitrary definitions could be having on children's skill development and aspirations. As one woman wrote on Twitter:

Each time a girl sees science toys under a "boys" sign, she is told science is not suitable for her.

Similarly, of course, this absurdly exaggerated separation sends the message to boys, loud and clear, that cooking, shopping, and playhouses are not for them, nor is the "girly" compassion of caring for dolls—and that theirs is the domain of aggression, sport, and technology.

> My daughter was never keen on playing with dolls—she had one baby doll, and a little pushchair, but never really played with them. My son, however, loved pushing the doll around in the pushchair.
>
> I lost count of how many negative comments this received—from my mother, other kids' mums, etc. I always simply said, "He's playing at being a Daddy." How odd that we're comfortable for a girl to "play Mummy," and even think it odd if she doesn't, and yet society is freaked out by a little boy playing Daddy.

But while it is true that both boys and girls are denied access to much of the contents of the others' toy chests, the breadth of choice available to boys, from building sets to sporty games, LEGO to woodwork, remains markedly wider than that presented in pink. Girls are not only being denied access to scientific and adventurous toys, they're also presented with such a narrow range of options that domesticity and stereotypically "female" duties are shoved down their throats before they've even reached the age of five.

> When I was 2 years old I had a toy vacuum cleaner, at 3 I had a toy iron and ironing board and at 4 a toy oven.

Or, as one woman wryly remembered:

> In primary school we had a playground wedding. I was the "bride" and my wedding present from my "groom" was a saucepan.

Oh, the romance!

It's clever, this childhood gender imbalance, because it hides in the things we take for granted and consider most innocuous and integral to infanthood.

Take, for example, children's films and television. Although there have been laudable attempts to subvert the stereotypes in recent years, with films like *Frozen, Tangled,* and *Brave* showcasing strong female heroines rather than the typical "damsel-in-distress" formula, most remain stubbornly problematic in other ways. The heroines are still unrealistically thin and overwhelmingly white, for a start. Meanwhile Rapunzel's power comes from her glossy long blond hair—and, although she spunkily knocks out the male hero with a frying pan on their first meeting, her story still ends with the "happily ever after" of marriage.

Elsewhere, just the briefest glance at the shelves of any newsagent carrying children's magazines is enough to reveal the bombardment of media messages bulldozing young girls toward pretty pink pliancy. I'm not talking about teen magazines, like *Seventeen* and *J-14,* but titles explicitly targeted at *children.*

For boys, a wide variety of activities and interests are represented, from Doctor Who to building, dinosaurs to architecture. There is choice, and with it a platform on which boys can build their own identities. But for girls the shelves overflow with pink and all that pink represents.

Magazine options include *Tinker Bell, Princess Kingdom, Fairy Princess, Princess Friends, Pretty Princess,* and *Disney Princess.* Judging by the type of activities included ("What color is the princess's dress?" "Point to your favorite color fish!"), it's pretty clear these mags are aimed at young children. Of the eleven titles I buy (the man behind the counter looks at me like I've taken leave of my senses), only one doesn't include free jewelry or makeup (the most common choice being a pink lipstick).

Among them, these eleven magazines offer six separate stories or articles about weddings—from Princess Aurora, who "dreamed many times that a handsome prince would find her," to Ariel and Cinderella, who had "perfect wedding days." Among just *seven* titles, there are thirty-seven images of a princess embracing, kissing, dancing with, or otherwise striking a loving pose with her handsome prince. Almost every princess is white with long blond hair and blue eyes. Their waists are smaller than their heads, their legs matchstick thin. When they're not busy planning their weddings, they engage in such other engrossing activities as dressing up, finding their missing lip gloss, counting their lipsticks, trying on new lipsticks, getting their lipsticks muddled up, searching through mazes to find hidden lipsticks . . . You get the picture.

There is a smattering of stories in which the princesses are allowed to be active, but even here the "weakness" of their sex seems to let them down—whether losing races to boys because they are too "busy bickering," or dropping their tiaras while swinging in the trees.

It feels a bit like a punch in the stomach every time I read an Everyday Sexism entry about girls being told, unequivocally, at such a young age that they are somehow by definition inferior to their male peers. Marked out—sometimes even at their very moment of success—as if they're somehow defective on the basis of sex alone. One mother tweeted to tell me:

My 11 yr old just won a cross country race. As she passed the boys, a teacher shouted "Come on, don't be beaten by a girl!

And while these magazines push the idea of feminine allure and makeup as the ultimate achievement to their young readers, the parameters of the "beauty" they present are stiflingly narrow. While interviewing two young mixed-race girls, I ask them what they think of the magazines. They tell me:

It's a bit weird because they're all white skinned . . . none of them have black skin—I think that means if people are looking at this and they're dark skinned, they'll think, "Oh my gosh, I really wish I looked like this."

There is one, the Frog Princess, but all the most famous ones are like Cinderella . . . a typical princess—blonde hair, white skin, blue eyes, pink lipstick—perfect girls. It makes it seem like black people aren't as popular. You don't see a punk princess, you don't see a princess with tattoos, you don't see a black princess, or a Goth princess . . . It'd be really fun if you saw a princess with baggy jeans on and a normal jumper and normal weight, but then people would say that's not a princess!

Fast-forward a couple of years, and the older girls' magazines segue into a similarly narrow fixation with real-life male idols and female beauty.

On the *Twist* magazine Web site, front covers with slogans like "Let's end the pressure to look perfect" (September 2014) sit uncomfortably alongside others blaring "Be Irresistible"

(July 2014) and articles with titles like "19 things your hair says about you" and "Shocking: Sel's Fashion Fail." An entire category of articles is dedicated to "Guys we love!" and headlines include "25 ways to make him like you" and "10 reasons why you should love Harry Styles."

Seventeen magazine's Web site showcases similar priorities, with categories on fashion, beauty, celebrities, and love life ("Which Twilight guy is right for you?" "25 ways to roll out of bed looking amazing"). Even the game that pops up alongside the article I'm reading is heavily skewed toward looks ("It's hard for a girl to keep looking beautiful all day long . . . help Penny look awesome all day long").

Top Model magazine—aimed at girls—features waiflike cartoon "models" with torsos barely the width of their heads, prominent collarbones, and enormous eyes with dilated pupils. A cartoon titled "The Perfect Girl" describes the trials and tribulations of a top model unable to attract the attention of a cute guy, despite trying all the *obvious* methods ("I've tried everything: colorful outfits, basic look, curly hair, straightened hair . . . he ignores me").

"Mascara alone is not enough!" wails an article on the magazine's Web site. "You need more to achieve a radiant look . . ."

Another online section, titled "Fight against cellulite," offers this pearl of girlhood wisdom: "Have you tried pinching?" Great news, girls: "Pinching yourself with a twisting hand movement . . . every day for 5 minutes will prevent cellulite from forming."

Hallelujah! You no longer have to wait to hit your teens

before you can start inflicting pain on your own body because it doesn't match the pictures in a magazine!

Enter Monster High, a new franchise aimed at tweens, based on a world inhabited by makeup-caked, miniskirt-clad ghosts and skeletons who provide the perfect excuse for a litany of (literally) bone-thin characters.

(You almost wonder if there was a meeting where the producers were scratching their heads over how to promote utterly unrealistic and unattainable body shapes to children without attracting criticism—answer: skeletons!) The character descriptions on the Web site quickly reveal their deepest concerns:

Clawdeen Wolf is a "fierce fashionista . . . gorgeous, intimidating." Her major "flaw" is her hairy legs, but though "plucking and shaving is definitely a full-time job . . . that's a small price to pay for being scarily fabulous." Her favorite activities are "shopping and flirting with the boys." Meanwhile, Draculaura has the terrible defect of not being able to "see my reflection in the mirror" so "I have to leave the house not knowing if my clothes and makeup are just right." Monster High is supposed to be a horror story. I'm not sure its creators realize just how well they've succeeded.

One parent summed it up when she wrote:

My 7-year-old daughter told me "Barbie is fat" when she compared it to her Monster High doll.

Of course, in isolation none of these things is a disaster. There's nothing wrong with girls taking an interest in fashion or beauty or boys. But the sheer saturation of tween culture with these characters and images creates a powerfully dictatorial consensus about who girls should be (princesses, fashionistas, girlfriends), what they should be interested in (boys, makeup, clothes), and how they should look (thin, white, made-up). And these influential cultural mores are having a profound effect on the way our daughters see themselves and the shape of their futures.

In the words of one ten-year-old interviewee:

It's more important for girls to be pretty. Girls are meant to be used as models, but boys are more clever so they don't have to worry about their looks because they can get a different job.

As I struggle to find words, her older sister, age twelve, agrees:

Men are more powerful; they are firmer and stricter and people think that will be better for being a boss—because they'll put their foot down.

If we think we've cracked this equality thing—that we're bringing up our sons and daughters to believe they can be whatever they want to be—we need to take a reality check.

▸ **When I was a small child and thought about what I wanted to be when I grew up, I always thought, I want to be a man. It was just not possible in my mind to be a woman and a scientist, or a politician, or basically anything other than a pretty, silent girl on the hero's arm.**

Despite women's gains in the job market, girls appear to be growing up with incredibly restrictive ideas about what career paths are open to them. Ironically, their visions of the future resemble the past far more closely than they do the present. One ten-year-old interviewee tells me:

Girls think of more feminine jobs, like fashion designer. I think most girls think if they want to do something in medicine that they can't be doctors—because mostly a doctor is a man and a nurse is a girl.

The truth is that these ideas are not just coming from TV and fairy-princess magazines. They are also shamefully reinforced, day after day, by the adults in the children's lives—from their teachers and neighbors to their own parents and families. We're forcing our girls into gendered straightjackets, and they're suffocating.

Got better marks at school than my 2 older brothers. Dad was livid about it and told me I'm not clever, I just try too hard.

A friend of mine was told by her dad that "It's better to be dumb than to look un-pretty."

As a young Indian woman, being told at age 12 that I should walk with my eyes down. Girls walking with their chin up gives the wrong impression.

From their first hobbies to early tentative academic and career ambitions, girls are taught again and again that only certain appropriate, approved paths are available to them.

They're even bombarded with messages suggesting that just being a girl is in itself an immediate handicap.

In elementary school, unfortunately, "You throw like a girl" and "You were beaten by a girl" are still common insults among boys.

I told teachers at school that I wanted to be an airline pilot. They told me I was suited to be a nursery nurse.

All through elementary school, we had a gym teacher who would spend every class period denigrating and insulting the girls while cheering the boys on, saying things like, "Come on, show the girls how sports are really played!"

That was the same year that the band teacher refused to teach me to play drums because I was female (I got to play the bells instead) and the boys started grabbing our barely developing chests and shouting, "Pinchy titties!" The school didn't do anything about that either.

I was told by my Chemistry Professor that I was "too pretty to do science."

The way that the obsessive focus on girls' looks plays into the dialogue around what they can and can't do is particularly poisonous. It inserts the self-consciousness of the watched, objectified woman into girls' internal narratives before they would ever have noticed it themselves. (One girl noted her bemusement at having her legs commented on, age just ten: "I'd never thought much about my legs before, they were just something I walked on.") And it teaches them lessons about their own value being measured by their bodies and faces—lessons that will stay with them for the rest of their lives.

When I was about 9 years old, my dad started calling me "thunder thighs." I've never felt comfortable in shorts ever since.

The T-shirt labeled "Future Fox" when I was 6 . . . I could do anything when I grew up, as long as I was also pretty.

As girls hit the age of ten or eleven, this obsession with their appearance takes a distinctly sexualized turn. Suddenly they are defined not only by their looks but also, more specifically, by what boys and men think of them.

And in a culture that bombards us daily with overwhelming messages about the precise attributes that make a woman "sexy," this often translates into a single all-encompassing quest for thinness.

When I'm asked to point to a single project entry that has most moved me, it isn't a difficult question to answer. It is this one, the first that ever made me cry:

I'm fifteen and feel like girls my age are under a lot of pressure that boys are not under. I know I am smart, I know I am kind and funny, and I know that everybody around me keeps telling me that I can be whatever I want to be. I know all this but I just don't feel that way. I always feel like if I don't look a certain way, if boys don't think I'm "sexy" or "hot" then I've failed and it doesn't even matter if I am a doctor or writer, I'll still feel like nothing. I hate that I feel like that because it makes me seem shallow, but I know all my friends feel like

that, and even my little sister. I feel like successful women are only considered a success if they are successful AND hot, and I worry constantly that I won't be. What if my boobs don't grow, what if I don't have the perfect body, what if my hips don't widen and give me a little waist, if none of that happens I feel like what's the point of doing anything because I'll just be the "fat ugly girl" regardless of whether I do become a doctor or not.

I wish people would think about what pressures they are putting on everyone, not just teenage girls, but even older people—I watch my mum tear herself apart every day because her boobs are sagging and her skin is wrinkling, she feels like she is ugly even though she is amazing, but then I feel like I can't judge because I do the same to myself.

I wish the people who had real power and control the images and messages we get fed all day actually thought about what they did for once.

I know the girls in adverts are airbrushed. I know beauty is on the inside. But I still feel like I'm not good enough.

The results from the 2013 U.S. High School Youth Risk Behavior Survey are striking. Around two-thirds of girls (63 percent) were actively trying to lose weight at the time of the survey. Nearly one-fifth of them (19 percent) said they had fasted for twenty-four hours in the past month to lose weight or keep from gaining weight, and 7 percent had taken diet pills, powders, or liquids without a doctor's advice in the same period. Saddest of all, even though the same percentage of girls and boys were overweight (17 percent) and girls were significantly less likely than boys to be obese (11 percent compared to 17 percent), when they were asked if they would describe themselves as overweight, over a third of girls (36 percent) said they would, compared to 26 percent of boys. Of course body image concerns negatively affect both boys and girls, but these figures powerfully demonstrate the concentrated impact of beauty ideals and pressure on girls, regardless of the reality of their bodies.

Meanwhile, the excellent Representation Project reports that the number-one "magic wish" for young girls age eleven to seventeen is to be thinner. It takes awhile for that last fact to sink in. Just think of all the other things in the world that teenage girls could wish for . . .

In all my interviews, school visits, and interactions, I have not managed to find a single girl who doesn't agree that this is a huge area of focus and worry.

Girls worry about being fat, because people judge them a lot.

My friend's sister was getting bullied and being told she'd be better off if she had an eating disorder so she could get thinner. She was 13.

One girl, age fourteen, tells me girls worry about their weight "all the time":

Guys look at Tumblr girls and Tumblr girls are meant to be perfect—that's the whole idea. The girls on the internet are perfect—amazing boobs, amazing figures, legs, everything and the girls know the guys talk about it and I guess they want to please the guys. They need that idea of perfection . . . if you don't have a thigh gap you NEED to get a thigh gap.

For those not in the know, a "thigh gap" is achieved when a woman stands with her legs straight and together and a gap is present between her thighs. When I ask her how the girls try to achieve this quest for "perfection," she confidently explains:

Year 7 or 8, it's really common not eating, but when you get to fourteen to eighteen it's more diet pills and exercising all the time.

One American girl draws links between the culture requiring young women to be obsessive about boys and fashion and the need to be thin. Her account gives the impression of an exhausting daily onslaught:

▸ Sick at the pressure all the way through high school to conform to an ideal of "teenage girl" that was out of the dark ages. This appeared to mean silent, submissive, meek and conformist, but attractive. It made the idea of "girl" into something degrading.

Examples: My peers saying I should be happy when someone made disgusting comments about my body, because he is "popular." Getting sexual harassment during PE just for having breasts. Being mocked for having interests that aren't stereotypically feminine. Being insulted and called a "dyke" and "prude" for not being sexually active. Getting disapproval for speaking up in a class and showing my intelligence. That is just a small example of what many of us have gone through, and still are doing even in the 21st century.

There is so much pressure it seems designed to beat, batter, and shape a happy, tree-climbing, adventure-novel-reading little girl into something else entirely—imagine an insecure, diet-obsessed, self-doubting, silent, depressed young woman emerging from this factory,

and you have many of my peers. And they wonder why so many young women are unhappy these days.

Another girl, an eleventh grader, meets me in a quiet café. In a voice barely louder than a whisper, she tells me:

I don't think I know any girls who don't have some sort of self-esteem or body-image issues. I have about six friends with eating disorders and so many friends who don't have eating disorders but they're disordered eaters—they'll only eat fruit for a day or something. And so many people who just feel anxious about it—they won't wear short-sleeved shirts because they're embarrassed about their arms. It's so common.

I ask her how far back the problem goes, and her eyes glaze as she recalls a childhood of intense self-scrutiny:

I remember being embarrassed about my thighs aged six . . . I remember girls comparing their bodies in the toilet in Year 5. I would have been about nine.

She is utterly, unutterably beautiful, a seventeen-year-old girl who speaks with the eloquence and sadness of a much older woman as she tells me, "I feel like people are watching me all the time . . . judging me . . . I never show skin or anything. I feel way too self-conscious to do that."

I've sat in front of a screen full of threats and sexist jibes, I've watched stories of harassment pour in at a rate of one per minute, but I have never felt as angry or as frustrated as I did that afternoon, wishing there was anything in the world I could say to make this teenage girl realize how very much she had to be proud of, and knowing that nothing I could say would change the way the world had made her feel about herself.

My interviewee attributes her own slide into the grip of an eating disorder, at age fifteen, to the increasing levels of street harassment she was experiencing at the time:

There was a man who ran his hand up my leg on the tube—that was one of the first times I ever came to London to stay with my sister. I felt embarrassed and scared—mainly scared because I didn't know what he was doing and I was unsure. I didn't want to make a fuss . . . Losing weight seemed like the appropriate reaction to being looked at as a sexual being; it felt like the natural step . . . It's simultaneously fitting into this ideal of womanhood and running away from it; losing your period while getting complimented about how thin and sexy you look. It's kind of reclaiming your body, but in a really negative way . . . I remember feeling completely powerless.

This theme has come up again and again—with the girls I've spoken to in schools, the girls who've written in to the project, the girls I've met at events and speeches and interviewed for this book. Every one of them described sexual harassment and even assaults, such as unwanted touching and groping, as a regular part of life.

A recent national study by the U.S.-based organization Stop Street Harassment found that for 80 percent of women who had experienced street harassment, it had started between the ages of thirteen and twenty-five.

According to a nationally representative survey of students in grades seven to twelve commissioned by the American

Association of University Women (AAUW) in 2011, 56 percent of girls were sexually harassed at school. And in the UK, according to a 2010 survey by YouGov for the End Violence Against Women Coalition, nearly one in three sixteen- to eighteen-year-old girls said they had experienced unwanted sexual touching at school, and a huge 71 percent said they heard sexual name-calling (such as "slag" or "slut") toward girls several times a week or more.

And yet—whether because the extent of the problem is so little known, or because it is so normalized—it seems girls are being given neither the resources they desperately need to understand how to deal with it nor the information to understand that they shouldn't have to face it in the first place.

▸ Grabbed and verbally harassed every day when I was in grade nine. I was made to feel it was my fault because I was standoff-ish toward boys as a result of being bullied in elementary school. Also got plenty of comments about how I was so unattractive I should be grateful for any "attention" I was getting.

This despite the fact that a huge number of the incidents reported in school settings go far beyond sexual harassment.

▸ In middle school a boy followed me into the girl's locker room and demanded that I undress for him. I refused, told him to leave, so he forced himself on me.

When we were asked to create a video about the project for the Chime for Change initiative, we invited a group of young women to narrate their own firsthand experiences directly to the camera.

Sitting quietly, her hands folded on her lap and speaking hesitantly, one girl described how, at the age of thirteen, a man had followed her off one bus and onto the next, sitting down next to her each time. She had been taught to be polite, she said, so she answered his questions, even when he started asking her if she wanted to go with him to the park. And when he started running his hand up her legs, although there were other people on the bus, she said she didn't feel she ought to bother them.

When the director asked her how the incident had impacted her behavior, she whispered that she had learned you shouldn't wear shorts, even in the summer. Sitting in the corner, behind a screen, I wiped away tears and bit my thumb so I wouldn't ruin the recording. When the case went to court, she told us, it was dismissed for lack of evidence. If she had spoken up, or made anybody else on the bus aware of what was happening, she said, it might have ended differently.

By the age of thirteen, this intelligent, thoughtful girl had been taught by society to be polite, taught not to offend a stranger or to disturb other people on the bus. Because girls are socialized into submission and into acceptance of others' behavior—even when it invades their personal space. But nobody had ever taught her that she had the right not to be touched without her consent.

Similar stories repeatedly suggest that not wanting to cause a scene or upset anybody silences young women into feeling unable to protest.

▸ When I was a young, naive 15-year-old, I had to sit away from my mum and my younger sister on a flight. The business man next to me started chatting to me in French . . . I smiled and tried to look interested. I had always been taught to be polite.

After a while, he started to put his hand upon my leg. I felt really uncomfortable but didn't know what to say . . . I remember thinking that if I didn't make a fuss, he might stop . . . I hadn't been given the knowledge and the confidence to react and stand up for myself when I started to feel uncomfortable with his advances. Having been always taught to be polite and not make a fuss, I was totally unprepared.

Worst of all, countless stories suggest that teachers often respond poorly to incidents of school sexual harassment or assault—sometimes brushing them off altogether, blaming the victim, or even suggesting girls should be glad of the attention. The expression "boys will be boys" is repeated again and again.

▸ In elementary school, the boys would chase me on the playground, pin me down and try to pull off my clothes. This stopped after I headbutted one of them and broke his nose. I was nearly expelled for that. Not one of them ever got in trouble.

▸ I remember when I was about 13 in middle school when a few boys in my classes started groping me and several of my other female classmates. They would grope our asses and go for our breasts whenever the teachers weren't looking and other boys would just laugh it off. I don't recall ever telling the teachers because I didn't think they would believe us.

▸ When I was in elementary two of my fellow male classmates trapped me in one of the small tunnels on the playground. One held me down while the other pushed up my dress and pulled down my underwear. I screamed at the top of my lungs but it was a playground full of tons of other kids screaming. I finally managed to knee the kid pulling down my underwear and both boys left the tunnel. When I pulled myself together I found the nearest teacher and told her what had happened. The teacher didn't believe me and I never wore a dress again.

It is perhaps for this reason that many girls feel unable to report what happens at school, or fear they won't be believed. In the AAUW survey, even though such a high proportion of girls experienced sexual harassment, only 9 percent reported it to a teacher or other adult at school. And without recourse to adult support, girls find themselves modifying their own behavior instead.

▸ A fellow student in a few classes with me . . . always made inappropriate remarks about my legs and butt. He would look me up and down and express things he wanted to do to me. Instead of speaking up about it I tried to take it all as compliments but it never felt like it. I felt disgusted in myself and started to wear sweaters and long baggy pants, even in the summer time.

This idea that girls are somehow responsible for "provoking" harassment from boys is shamefully exacerbated by an epidemic of increasingly sexist school dress codes. Across the United States, stories have recently emerged about girls being hauled out of class, publicly humiliated, sent home, and even threatened with expulsion for such transgressions as wearing tops with "spaghetti straps," wearing leggings or (brace yourself) *revealing their shoulders*. The reasoning behind such dress codes, which almost always focus on the girls' clothing to a far greater extent than the boys', is often euphemistically described as the preservation of an effective "learning environment."

Often schools go all out and explain that girls wearing certain clothing might "distract" their male peers, or even their male teachers. (CBS reports that one teenage girl was kicked out of her prom because fathers chaperoning at the event in Richmond, Virginia, felt that her dress was "too provocative" and risked stirring "impure thoughts." Is there anybody else who thinks it wasn't the girls they should have been worried about?)

The knee-jerk response here is to protest that surely it's in everybody's interest for children to dress appropriately at school, but in reality these messages privilege boys' apparent "needs" over those of the girls (who often complain that they are prevented from wearing cool clothing in hot weather), sending the insidious message that girls' bodies are dangerous and provoke harassment, and boys can't be expected to control their behavior, so girls are responsible for covering up. When a girl is taken out of class on a hot day for wearing a strappy top, and she is accused of "distracting" her male classmates, his education is being prioritized over hers.

Consequently, a full-scale war is raging over the issue across the country. This may sound like an exaggeration. It isn't. Stuyvesant High School in Manhattan faced protests from students after implementing a new dress code that reportedly included a ban on showing shoulders. Girls at a junior high school in Petaluma, California, were reportedly taken aside and told they couldn't wear pants that were "too tight" for fear of distracting the boys. In Minnetonka, Minnesota, a high school principal sent parents an e-mail asking them not to allow their daughters to wear tight-fitting leggings or yoga pants because they could "be highly distracting for other students." At one high school in California, forty female students were sent home from a dance after reportedly being forced to twirl and flap their arms up and down as male staff inspected their attire. A New Jersey middle school mandated that no strapless dresses were allowed at an eighth-grade dance. When Haven Middle School in Evanston, Illinois, banned leggings and yoga pants, students complained after being told the dress code was designed to prevent boys from being "distracted."

Girls showed up in leggings to protest the sexist policy, bearing placards asking ARE MY PANTS LOWERING YOUR TEST SCORES? And one Georgia kindergartner was forced to change into another child's pants because her skirt (worn over leggings) was considered too short.

When such dress codes start so young, there begins to be a very valid argument that schools are not policing "sexy" attire worn by students attempting to be provocative but are in fact sexualizing students themselves by suggesting that their natural body parts are somehow titillating or scandalous.

And the codes aren't problematic only for sexist reasons. A student at one school I visited explained that the dress code didn't take different body shapes into account, making it much harder for her to conform to standards of what was considered "respectable" than some of her friends, who were naturally less curvaceous, even while wearing the same clothes. When two girls in Cincinnati, Ohio, were turned away from their high school prom for being "improperly dressed," the principal later clarified that they should have had "no curvature of the breasts showing"—an issue that wouldn't have applied to girls with a different body shape wearing the same attire. Multiple similar incidents have targeted or banned boys from school for wearing traditionally "feminine" fashion, from skinny jeans to skirts, makeup to wigs. A girl was threatened with having her photo barred from her school yearbook simply because she chose to wear a tuxedo to prom. A transgender student was threatened with having his photo omitted for the same reason. A twelve-year-old African American girl was threatened with expulsion for refusing to cut her natural curly hair. School administrators told her mother she violated school dress codes for being "a distraction."

At this point it starts to feel like such "codes" are less about protecting children and more about perpetuating strict social norms and hierarchies that refuse to tolerate difference or diversity. Why should it matter if a boy chooses to wear a skirt to school, or a girl feels most comfortable in leggings? Does it somehow damage their education? Whom is it hurting?

Boys are already harassing girls at school, regardless of their clothing. By putting the blame for such behavior at the door of female students, schools are actively initiating their charges into the hugely damaging narrative of victim blaming that sits at the heart of our society's problem with sexual assault.

These girls are voiceless. Their mistreatment, harassment,

and assault are so normalized that they feel unable to object. Then they grow up into young women and adults who don't feel able to speak up either.

Some are brilliant at fighting back:

Some random middle aged man was cat calling me (literally! "Pss pss pss") and I told him: I'm not a cat. I'm only 15.

Boys, if you want my attention, please don't refer to me as "Jugs" . . .

In seventh grade, on one of the days we played badminton, I approached an all-boys court. One of them said, "No girls allowed," but I walked onto the court anyway and demonstrated that I could play at their level. He left the court as soon as I aimed a successful smash shot at him.

But they shouldn't have to be! Not everyone is equipped to. And not every situation is "minor" enough to be dealt with by the victim alone.

At 15 in class, a boy felt my leg and went to touch my genital area. When I yelled in surprise and pushed him away he called me frigid. My female "friends" laughed at me and told me to lighten up. I felt even worse about it then.

I asked one teenage girl if she thought her friends understood that they don't have to put up with it, that somebody touching them in a sexual way without their consent is a form of sexual assault. She said, "They'd never report being touched—it wouldn't be seen as something you could report to the police. It's just so common. Normalized. None of the girls I know would describe any of this as sexual harassment. It's just "boys being boys."

And here's the worst part. As if all this wasn't enough, after they've been sexualized and hounded and harassed and bombarded from pretty much every angle with the notion that they are sexual objects, there to be sexualized and fantasized about and pursued, then they get ripped to shreds for being too sexy.

Enormous pressure is on very young girls to be sexually active, to give in to boys' "demands," and to acquiesce to various requests, from blow jobs to sending explicit photographs on mobile phones. But the moment they comply, they face a stringent backlash of almost puritanical proportions.

One fourteen-year-old girl tells me, "A lot of my friends have sexted and it's ruined their life; they've got so much hate for it." She breaks it down for me:

You'd feel like you don't want to let him down—you think he likes you for who you are and he promises not to show it to anyone . . . then you send the picture and then he'll never speak to you again. The guy shows his friends and then the friend puts it up on the internet and then for the girls it's horrible—her friends will all turn against her and call her a slut, and the guys at school will all come up and say they saw the picture and she'll lose all her friends.

As extreme as it sounds, this precise turn of events is relayed to me again and again, using near-identical language, by girls on their own, girls in groups, young girls, high school girls, girls from private schools, and girls from public schools. It seems to be, quite simply, the norm.

Sexting and sexual pressure is common. In my school when my friend was thirteen pictures of her were circulated. People teased her a lot . . . She was called a slut very often by boys in our class. If they were having an argument or banter, they'd just bring up the name of the guy she lost her virginity to. You could just see the color flooding from her face when they mentioned his name . . . That's something they did with me as well. They'd bring up my ex-boyfriend's name and just mention it—as a way of putting me down—sort of embarrassing me. A boyfriend is something to shame you with later, but for him it's like a victory.

Yet another story, from another school, corroborates the same routine:

When I was at secondary school, this girl took a personal picture of herself to send to her boyfriend. And when they broke up he showed it to all his friends, so it got around, a lot of names were called toward her—he wasn't spoken to at all about the fact he broke her trust, but she was called everything under the sun.

Stories of "slut shaming" mingle and clash with extraordinary tales of sexual pressure, leaving young girls in a helpless situation. "You just can't win," four of them separately tell me.

If the girl doesn't want to, he'll break up with her, go around and say she's frigid and the girl will get so much hate for being frigid; but if

she does it she'll be called a slut, so you can't win—there's so much pressure on girls.

Branded a slut today by 2 random boys on Snapchat because I wouldn't send them nudes #logic.

Freshman in High School and my boyfriend stuck his hands down my pants. When I said no he broke up with me.

And, importantly, this potent mix of sexual pressure and sexual shaming, public humiliation and regular harassment is not only reported over and over again by students but is also corroborated by a large number of reports made by teachers to the Everyday Sexism Project:

I was volunteering at an elementary school, a boy said to a girl "if you were taller I could slap my dick between your tits."

I am a secondary science teacher and a form tutor in Yorkshire. I witness on a daily basis the girls in my classes being called "whore" "bitch" "slag" "slut" as a matter of course, heckled if they dare to speak in class, their shirts being forcibly undone and their skirts being lifted and held by groups of boys, (I WANT TO EMPHASISE THAT THIS IS MORE OFTEN THAN NOT A DAILY EVENT, AND OFTEN BORDERS ON ASSAULT). On a daily basis I am forced to confiscate mobile phones as boys are watching hardcore pornography videos in lessons and I have noticed sadly that as time has gone on the girls in my classes have become more and more reserved and reluctant to draw attention to themselves.

I am currently dealing with a situation whereby a girl in my form class sent a topless photograph of herself to her then boyfriend, said boyfriend then used this to blackmail the girl in to giving him oral sex which he filmed on his phone and then distributed both the photo and video amongst the boys in the year. This girl is now having to consider leaving the school and interrupting her [exams] due to the abuse she is experiencing from her fellow pupils.

What I am seeing every day is incredibly worrying and distressing. It is getting worse and worse. I wanted to share this snapshot of my working life with others . . . The problem is that people are too willing to brush this issue under the carpet and dismiss it as just natural teenage deviance. However, being on the front line and dealing with this day after day I can tell you this is a completely different animal. There is an underlying violent and vicious attitude toward girls, a leaning toward seeing them as products to be used.

For many adults, even parents, the lives of children are a largely closed book, perceived through a grown-up lens that leans toward trivializing negative experiences as just "boys being boys" or "the way kids are." It is easy to turn a blind eye—to naïvely believe that nothing *too* serious could really be going on under that unturned stone. After all, we'd know, wouldn't we? The school would find out, or the children themselves would speak up. But girls are increasingly finding themselves trapped in a hostile environment, hobbled by the fear of being labeled "uptight" or a "tattletale" and unlikely ever to mention what's going on. And so much of this is happening in a different world altogether, which for many adults is uncharted territory: the largely unpoliced Wild West of the Internet. Here, for boys as much as girls, there are strong underlying messages about their place in the world and how their "masculinity" or "femininity" must manifest itself—aggressive and controlling or sexualized and submissive. The lines are stark and uncompromising. The instructions are clear.

What makes the cycle of pressure and judgment even more powerful is that, thanks to the advent of new technology and ubiquitous social media, there is no escape from it, even at home, away from school and peers. It's a new world that provides a complex multitude of interactions—many of them positive. Girls form strong and supportive communities online, and many teenagers talk about the groups they've found through Tumblr or Facebook, often promoting body confidence and positivity. But it's also an avenue through which the ever-mounting pressure continues to proliferate. Not just from Facebook and instant-messaging applications but on countless other sites, too, like Snapchat, where users send images back and forth, or on anonymous "question-and-answer" Web sites like Spring.me (formerly Formspring) and Qooh.me, Web sites with little risk of adult intervention or punishment. Young people create a profile, including a picture, but other users can send them questions without revealing who they are. It's a recipe for disaster or, more specifically, for extreme sexualized bullying. One mother of a thirteen-year-old girl asked her daughter's permission to let me view her profile page on Ask.fm.

The questions come thick and fast, aggressive and overtly sexual, from boys claiming to be from her school. "Have you ever sucked a dick?" they ask her. "Do you shave your pubes?" "Bra size?" "Have you done anal?" "Can I bang you?" "Is your c**t dry?"

They call her "whore" and "slut," make sexual demands ("Eat my penis"), arbitrarily threaten her ("I'd like to put a nail gun to your face"), and even ask her to upload a video of "you cutting yourself" (she refuses).

And, of course, hand in hand with the Internet comes instant, easy access to online pornography, much of it offering misogynistic representations of sex in which women are hurt or humiliated. One project entry explains the kind of impact wide exposure to such material can have, particularly in the absence of good sex education:

▸ At age twelve, while searching for answers, I came across porn on the internet and my idea of what my role was supposed to be in a relationship was forever changed. That was the age when I first thought that being submissive to a boy and sexually open was how I was supposed to be.

In a group interview, one teenage girl told me:

The view of women through porn creates assumptions—it means [boys] just expect women will take it, the man's in control, the women can just like it; and I don't think they can separate that the woman is acting and that isn't what relationships are really like.

Porn shouldn't be viewed as documentary—that's the problem: boys are looking at porn and they're told it's really real—it's "amateur," it's real people—and they blur the line between entertainment and actual reality and that's the problem. Porn isn't the main problem. It's the fact that you're saying, "This is what girls are like, this is real life, this is how they're going to react."

And also the age: most of the boys in your year will probably have

been watching it since about fourteen—that's before you've ever seen your first girl naked—so that's how they learn about sex.

A seventeen-year-old girl agreed:

I know that boys in my school were watching porn in Year 7 [age 11–12]—possibly earlier. They started circulating pictures. And they were also making rape jokes—like saying, "You're so hot I'd rape you." Or just not seeing it as a very big deal. They have no proper understanding of what rape is. Some see it as a compliment. Some see it as just something they're entitled to. Or something women would enjoy anyway. "It's not rape if you enjoy it"—that was something that was said a lot.

These misconceptions about rape abound in the reports we have received, both on the project Web site and in interviews. One parent even reported that at her child's school a part of the playground that is difficult to see by supervisors was known as "the rape corner." Other accounts included teenage boys saying that "rape is a compliment really" in a classroom discussion and young boys thinking that a girl crying and saying no was "part of foreplay."

My stomach turned as I flicked through my e-mails one morning to see that a girl had contacted me in distress that her school's eleventh-grade prom was "having a biggest rapist award." Other awards included "biggest slut."

A sixteen-year-old wrote to tell us:

▸ **My younger brother's 13. He had his friends round last weekend and I couldn't believe it when I heard them sitting in the front room** discussing girls in their class in 3 categories "frigid," "sluts" and "would like to rape."

Another girl tweeted:

At age 11, a classmate on a school trip stated that "no-one would rape me anyway because I'm too ugly." Others only laughed at that.

And in a heartbreaking Everyday Sexism Project entry, one schoolgirl wrote:

I am thirteen and I am so scared to have sex it makes me cry nearly every day. We had sex education in Year 6 and I felt fine about it, but now some of the boys at school keep sending us these videos of sex which are much worse than what we learnt about and it looks so horrible and like it hurts and it keeps coming into my mind and at night I get really scared that one day I will have to do it. I don't want to speak to my mum or dad about it obviously and I feel like if I say to my friends that the videos and stuff scare me and upset me they will laugh at me and everyone will find out and pick on me for it. I try to think don't worry you won't have to do it for ages but everyone at school keeps acting like it's normal and we're meant to do it really soon like some of the boys keep asking me have I done it and can I do it with them and showing me the horrible pictures and things.

I know it sounds stupid but I just wanted to tell someone because I feel like it's unfair that girls have to have horrible things done to them but boys can just laugh and watch the videos and they don't realize how scary it is. Why did they talk about sex at school like it was okay but then the real life sex that we see is so scary and painful and the woman is crying and getting hurt?

Nothing has emerged more clearly from the Everyday Sexism Project than the urgent need for far more comprehensive mandatory sex-and-relationships education in schools, to include issues such as consent and respect, domestic violence, and healthy relationships. It's not just girls who need it so desperately. For boys, porn provides some very scary, dictatorial lessons about what it means to be a man and how they are apparently expected to exert their male dominance over women. It is as unrealistic to expect them, unaided, to instinctively work out the difference between online porn and real, caring intimacy as it is to demand the same intuition of young women. One recent project entry described a young woman's first sexual experience, in her late teens. Mid-intercourse, her boyfriend suddenly put his hands around her throat and started trying to strangle her. When she reacted in shock and horror, he broke down with relief and explained that, having watched similar acts in multiple porn videos, he had thought she would expect it of him.

If we don't talk to young people about these issues, clearly and informatively, we are failing them—and leaving them open to abuse.

▸ **Age 14: After splitting up with my first "boyfriend," another boy hit on me when I'd been drinking whilst we were out. I said I didn't want to go but he pulled me into the woods and lay me down in a ditch. He started to put his hands down my knickers and I told him no.**

He pressed his finger to my lips and whispered me to "shh," like I was a child. I was a child. I think I let him do that because I didn't really know what was right and wrong. I didn't know how to act, I didn't know if I was making a big deal, or being frigid. I never told anyone.

▸ **Age 18: After going out with a close long term friend to a party, I stayed over at his [house]. I slept on the floor and crashed out with exhaustion. I woke up with his fingers inside of me. I had no idea how to react. So I waited it out.**

Both boys and girls are seeing mainstream porn that suggests a woman's role during sex is to be subjugated or humiliated, to please a man, and often even to be hurt or punished. And without receiving any counterinformation to offset these norms, or mitigate them with ideas about consent, relationships, respect, and boundaries, it is easy to see how, for some, these things could simply become accepted as the "reality" of sex.

It's futile to attempt to prevent young people from accessing porn on the Internet. But that doesn't mean that we can't offset its impact with clear, targeted education to provide them, at least, with an alternative narrative and to prevent what they have seen from crystallizing into unquestioned, accepted assumptions. Such standardized information is desperately needed in a world in which many young people are still receiving damaging messages from abstinence only education and "purity balls," suggesting that the onus should be on girls to say no, not boys to seek consent, that sexual behavior is damaging or immoral and that girls are somehow forever tarnished after having sex, while boys largely escape unscathed, or reap praise and rewards. We should be providing sensible, age-appropriate information that allows for the notion that sex can be pleasurable and enjoyable for both partners, regardless of gender, rather than the antiquated message that it is something bad and scary that happens *to* girls, with boys as the active and always eager protagonists.

We might not be able to protect young women from the barrage of Photoshopped images and objectifying advertisements regularly bombarding them, but we can at least arm them with the tools to analyze and rationalize the manipulation—and in so doing offset some part of the impact.

Most of the teenagers I speak to tell me they don't think people their age really understand what rape is. One seventeen-year-old tells me it is surrounded by "gray areas":

If she said yes and then said no, is it still rape? If she's asleep, is it still rape? If she's drunk, is it still rape? Sometimes girls don't realize they can say no—they think it's their duty to have sex with men.

Her words are echoed by twelfth-grade girls at another school:

The boys seem to expect because you're their girlfriend that they have the right to have sex with you . . . We need more education at a younger age.

One girl who was raped twice as a teenager, by boys she knew, ended her account this way:

▶ I always thought I was the problem. Since reading everyday sexism I've learnt it's not my fault. I felt guilty for all the events. And they should be taught things like that rape isn't only stalking a stranger down a dark alley, but taking advantage of a vulnerable girl, and how to recognise and understand when they are doing so.

In one school I visited, staff members described a recent rape involving a fourteen-year-old student perpetrator. When a teacher asked him, "Why didn't you stop when she was crying?" he responded, bewildered, "because it's normal for girls to cry during sex." That was what he had seen online.

Friendship groups, family, magazines, films, cartoon characters, porn, Facebook—the wrong ideas come from so many places it's easy to see how they become accepted without question. Often, the misogynistic double standards, the normalization of assault, the cyberbullying, and more collide in horrifying combinations, exemplified by the now infamous August 2012 rape in Steubenville, Ohio. A sixteen-year-old girl was subjected to repeated sexual assaults and raped while the incidents were captured on video by other young people using mobile phones and later posted on social media. In the aftermath of the attack, she was subjected to intense scrutiny, shame, and blame by the national media, individuals, and local townspeople. It was a story that people wanted to see as a horrendous anomaly. But it is not. It chimes horribly clearly with stories reported to the project . . .

▸ I was raped by a classmate in the back of his car, while his friend watched and took pictures. I was thrown out covered in seamen [sic] into someone's front yard when they were finished with me. I kept quiet, but pictures got around the high school . . . instead of people standing up for me I was called a "slut" and a "whore" . . . I remember closing my eyes as I began blaming myself and thinking "why bother defending myself when no one else will, I deserve this." A group of men from our church payed [sic] for my rapists lawyer . . . why was my story so hard to believe and his so easy?

In every area—from the idea that they will be judged on their looks to the vital importance of weight loss; from the knowledge that only certain paths are available for them to the normalization of being groped and even raped—accepting these things without question means that many girls aren't even aware of the possibility that things could be different.

Inescapably, the earliest lesson they learn is that they will be judged not just more harshly than their male peers but on a different scale altogether.

A girl sends me a tweet explaining that she has been told to go home from school and change because her skirt is too short. She adds an image, showing what a boy in her class is wearing that day. He hasn't been asked to change. It's a T-shirt emblazoned full-length with a picture of a naked woman.

Chapter 4

Young Women Learning

I don't know any girl at university who hasn't been touched or groped without her consent.

Answer on a student questionnaire

Vital Statistics

1 in 5 women experience attempted or completed sexual assault while in college.
-Christopher P. Krebs et al., "The Campus Sexual Assault (CSA) Study," 2007

Around 90 percent of victims of completed or attempted rapes while in college knew the perpetrator.
-Bonnie S. Fisher, Francis T. Cullen, and Michael G. Turner, "The Sexual Victimization of College Women," National Institute of Justice, Bureau of Justice Statistics, 2000

80 percent of rape and sexual assault victimizations of students age eighteen to twenty-four go unreported to the police.
-Bureau of Justice Statistics, National Crime Victimization Survey, 1995-2013

13 percent of college women are victims of at least one stalking incident.
-Fisher, "The Sexual Victimization of College Women"

4 out of 5 college women who were victims of stalking knew the perpetrator.
-Fisher, "The Sexual Victimization of College Women"

Registrar at college wouldn't have recognized any female students' faces. Our chests? No problem.

At college orientation and heard that the only major for "girls" is early childhood education; "men" should be STEM [science, technology, engineering, and mathematics] majors.

Three people told me in one class because of how a women dresses, they are asking for "it." I feel so unsafe at college.

Told that being groped/touched/having a crotch rubbed against you unwantedly is "a normal part of university nightlife."

Having a guy at college say in a sleazy voice "hey baby, you look fine today" does not boost my confidence at all.

My freshman year of college, my roommate came home drunk and passed out. While I was deep asleep, her date penetrated me. I was raped.

Already, by the time they hit their late teens and early twenties, young women are learning that the business of being groped and grabbed, having their bodies claimed and touched in public places without their consent, is just something they have to live with. Their project entries described instances of having "my ass groped" as "constant," "always," "common," "regular." The consensus was that "during nights out, it is pretty much guaranteed." Many of those leaving high school and going straight into the workplace related dispiriting tales of harassment and discrimination in their earliest experiences of employment.

Age 18 first job. Supervisor follows me into walk-in fridge and tries to kiss me EVERY DAY. Managers laugh.

The experiences of many young women, from the office to the sidewalk, are dealt with throughout the other chapters of this book, but there was one particular area that stood out so blatantly it demanded closer attention. For young women, college is a gauntlet.

There is no other way to put it. It isn't here and there, or every now and then. The project entries, bolstered by a plethora of headline news stories and regular visits I've made in person create a picture of a student culture literally suffused with misogyny and harassment.

To begin with, women's very presence at higher education institutions is constantly questioned and undermined:

I got accepted to an Ivy League University. When I tell people where I'm going to school in the fall the response (normally from women) is how wonderful it is that I can go find an "Ivy husband."

I studied computer science in college. I was told when I was a freshman that "Girls don't really do well in computer science because of how it is" by one of the guys who were in my class.

I am currently an undergraduate student at a relatively non-prestigious state university in the U.S. In the fall, I will be attending a very very good, top 20, law school on a scholarship. Why? 'Cause my LSAT kicked butt and I make amazing grades. A lot of people have been very supportive but there have also been a lot of people who have pretty much immediately asked me "Who did you sleep with for that?" or some variation thereof. Funnily enough, no one has asked my boyfriend, who got into the same law school, that same question.

Even when students have surpassed society's apparently depressingly low expectations and gained a college place, some find themselves facing the same undermining doubts from the very people who are supposed to inspire and educate them:

▸ Sophomore year of college, I took an Intro Physics course, and the professor for the section I was in was a misogynist. He repeatedly stated during lectures that women did not belong in the physics field, whether as students or as physicists.

▸ I went to a talk at my University by an esteemed male professor who was giving advice on how to be a scientist. He said that if we want to succeed in academia as a scientist we needed "male traits," those being competitiveness, confidence and impatience. Also mentioned that having children may be problematic career wise for women unless we had very understanding husbands. One female academic challenged him afterward at question time and got dismissed. Left feeling very sad indeed.

An engineering professor described in one project entry unfailingly greeted the class with "Good morning, gentlemen" while looking straight at the sole female student.

A student from Ukraine wrote that her professor described female physicists as being a bit like guinea pigs "(literal translation of guinea pig in Ukrainian = water pig): neither a pig, nor in the water (and hence, neither a woman, nor a physicist.)." And a woman in Mexico described being told by her lecturer, "*Calladita, te ves mas bonita*" (You look prettier when you shut up). "[He] also asks all the girls if they have boyfriends when they get a question wrong in class. He insinuates that we get our questions wrong because we are thinking about them, and not medicine."

Project entries on this theme poured in. After looking at her artwork, an examiner told one student, "I thought you were a man . . . but you should take that as a compliment."

Another was told by her lecturer that "all the best female academics write like men." One was repeatedly pestered for sex by a personal tutor with whom she had to meet weekly. Sometimes there was subtle, demoralizing gender bias; on other occasions the prejudice described was more overt.

▸ After approaching my tutor at university for help on an essay he had set (ironically) on "Misogyny in Paradise Lost," he told me that I should be happy with a [second-class honor] because women couldn't get firsts as they weren't able to "think outside of the box" like men. For every essay I wrote he gave me one mark off a first. He also told me "not to go running to the department to complain" as "girls" before me had. When I got a first for my degree I sent him a copy of my degree certificate.

There is hope in the fact that some (though by no means all) of these entries came from women who had already completed college; as enrollment numbers equalize, particularly in traditionally "male-dominated" subjects, such attitudes should fade. But in a wider social sense, far from finding themselves in a rarified academic environment, the extent of the harassment and abuse young women face seems if anything to intensify when they reach college.

▸ Now that I'm in college it's a lot worse. Guys here feel like they are entitled to me and it disgusts me. I've been walking to class or to get lunch and guys will say "Come sit on my face" or "damn the things I'd do to her." They refer to me as "yummy" "sexy" "you're mine" and so much more. Last semester two of my friends and I were surrounded by about 11–15 guys who made racist, sexual, and degrading comments since we're Hispanic and women. Most of them were directed to me, they said "I've always wanted to fuck a Mexican" "because you're Hispanic you're going to do sexy things with me"; one demanded that I get into bed with him, while another made it very clear that he was going to grab me and take me to his room.

▸ I am a male English professor at a state college in central Florida. One afternoon, as I was walking across the quad from the Admin building to the student center, I saw two young female students visibly upset walking in my direction. Behind them were two young men stating out loud their judgment of the women's bodies, in ugly, negative terms—about how ugly these young women were and how terrible they would be in bed.

What female students are facing is not just an on-campus manifestation of the same sexism and harassment women face elsewhere—there are also elements that are intertwined closely with college life and with educational institutions themselves.

One student forwarded me an e-mail she'd received from the physics society during her first week in college:

Freshers' Lunch . . . This will be mainly a chance for you to scope out who's in your department and stake your claim early on the 1 in 5 girls.

Before she even started her course, in an incredibly male-dominated sphere, before she had even met her male peers, she had already been marked out as sexual prey by the university itself. And seeing female students in this way wasn't an attitude that exactly needed encouragement from the university:

The boys who worked behind the Student Union bar used to play "fuck a fresher" at freshers week. There was a points scoring system . . . bonus points if you brought the girl's knickers in, took her virginity.

The othering of female students from official sources didn't end there. When several young women's entries mentioned their frustration at student nights expressly requiring them to dress as "sluts" and "slags," I started looking into the orientation events organized at universities. Here are just a few of the event titles I found:

Rappers and Slappers
Slag 'n' Drag
CEOs and Corporate Hoes
Golf Pros and Tennis Hoes
Tarts and Vicars
Pimps and Hoes
Geeks and Sluts

Over and over again, at events usually organized by university societies or student unions, often in their very first week at university, young men and women are being sent the message that men are powerful, talented, and successful while women are defined, every time, by their gender and sexual availability.

Freshman year of college I attended a party with the (common) theme "CEOs and office ho's." Didn't realize how sexist this was at the time.

This is not about a prudish distaste of girls dressing in a revealing way. It's about the apparent *pressure* for them to do so—their lack of choice in the matter—which was highlighted by a huge number of the accounts we received. For boys, it seems, dressing up offers a fun chance to wear something kooky or tongue-in-cheek. For girls, it is about something else entirely.

One female student I interviewed told me:

We had an event as part of Freshers' Week where some of our friends went on stage. Loads of girls were lined up and they had to take all their clothes off—they were told to race to strip. Then there were competitions where you had to do various sex positions. They make it all out as a great thing but you get pushed into it and it's not a matter of choice.

It's very different for people who feel shy or more uncomfortable, because you don't have a choice—there were strict initiations and you had to do what everyone else did or you were just missed out.

Such events are often dismissed as "harmless fun," and those who protest deemed prudish or moralistic, but within the compounding context of wider sexism on campus, they play right into the heart of the problem, as one project entry perfectly described:

▸ Three days after I was drugged and gang-raped by at least three fraternity men my very first night at college (and decided to defer the year), I was invited to a "Gangsters and Strippers" party at the same apartment complex. I go to a top 25 national university in Los Angeles. No one could understand why I was upset. When I explained "things like this objectify women, and when a woman is an object she is no longer seen as a human or sentient being; you cannot empathize with something you do not see as human, so that it is much easier to 'use,' sexually assault, or rape them," even people who knew I had been recently raped thought I was being dramatic and did not understand what I was talking about.

For some students, the impact of these "harmless" events and initiations on their academic career was devastating, as one UK project entry revealed:

▸ One of the Freshers' events organized by our halls of residence was a "girls and guys" pub crawl. We were split in to one group of "girls" and one of "guys" and each group went off on different pub crawl routes. All the girls were encouraged to wear pink and dress "slutty." We also had to come up with a "slut name" which the older students encouraged us to write across our breasts. Upon arriving at each bar, one of the older students would shout out a word which was code for us to flash either our "tits" or our "arse" or dance in a seductive way in front of men in the pub. I didn't take part in this (or adopt a "slut name") and was told that I was being too "uptight" and not "getting into the spirit of Freshers' Week." The whole thing culminated in the "girls and guys" meeting up in the student union, where we were informed that the older students had organized a competition with prizes. One prize was for the "slut" who collected the most ties from the guys and one for the "lad" who collected the most bras from the "sluts." I walked out on a scene of groups of drunk male students forcefully taking off the female students' bras.

On another occasion, I went out for the Freshers' night out of one of the women's sports clubs. Our group bumped in to the men's rugby club in a bar. They were putting their freshers through their "initiation ceremony." All the rugby freshers had their trousers around their ankles and were standing in their boxers. They were encouraged to pick one of us to "grind" with them (i.e. gyrate against them). One guy grabbed me and pulled me on to the dance floor and then told me I had to grind on him or else he'd have to do a forfeit. When I refused he told me I was frigid and grabbed a different fresher.

These two incidents made me feel extremely uncomfortable and alienated me from my fellow students . . . I couldn't believe I had come up against this kind of sexism in a university campus and it left me very disillusioned with higher education. These two "fun events" ruined my Freshers' Week and left me feeling isolated and humiliated. I dropped out after two months.

As well as verbal abuse and sexist events and initiations, physical assault is reported with breathtaking regularity:

At a bar for a college party and a drunk boy grabs my breasts as I'm coming out of the bathroom.

When I was in college, a man who was sitting beside me, put his hand up my skirt to grope me.

In college I'm wearing a sundress and climbing some stairs. Some guy passes me, yanks on my sundress and pulls it down enough to reveal my breasts.

In college a friend of mine was having a party. So I'm at the party just standing there and my friend's boyfriend grabs my crotch, smirks, and walks away.

I went to a party for the first time ever my freshman year at college. I was wearing jeans. I hadn't even been there 5 minutes when I felt someone pinch my butt hard.

I'm in college and it was the first warm day of the season so I wore shorts. I was standing at the post production center talking to my friend at work and a guy I knew from Freshman year (I'm a senior) walks past me. Instead of saying hi he slaps my butt super hard and then winks at me before going into the post production center.

I had just started college. I was in at a crowded house party dancing with some girlfriend when I felt someone slip his hand down my pants, under my panties and grope my vulva and vagina HARD . . . I saw his smiling smug face but I was too shocked and afraid to report him.

Just reading through the project entries relevant to this chapter took days and days. There are so many stories. One female student I interviewed told me:

It's not a common experience, it's an inevitable one. I don't know any girl at university who hasn't been touched or groped without their consent. I also don't know any girl at university who would consider it assault or report it.

At many of my visits to universities and colleges to talk about the project, I distributed anonymous surveys to students, hoping to get a sense of their experiences and gauge the status quo. I included questions about various forms of assault and asked whether survey participants had been on the receiving end of sexism from fellow students or professors.

In an empty train carriage rattling home in the dark after one of the first such visits, I spread the completed surveys out across the seats in front of me, read them, and cried.

Of the forty female students who responded to the survey that day, only two *hadn't* been groped or touched without their consent during their time at university. The bleak simplicity of the responses shook me. One student had circled "YES" for the question "During your time at university have you ever experienced sexism from university employees (e.g. Lecturers/Tutors etc.)?" and had then written: "Tutor groped me—" That dash felt like a kick in the stomach. It seemed to be a shrug of acceptance: What else was there to say?

Depressingly, though these cases were rarer, she wasn't alone in reporting incidents where the culprits were not fellow students but members of academic staff:

▸ I was in an English class during my sophomore year of college when my (older male) professor interrupted the class and made a random comment about how pretty I looked. I felt embarrassed as the entire class stared at me.

▸ Senior lecturer and tutor wrapping his arm around my waist every time I went to speak to him and slapping the inside of my thigh to make a point.

▸ When I was a PhD student my supervisor had a bad reputation for being lecherous. He asked one of the women who worked in the office what her chest size was so he could buy her a jumper as a present. When I finished my thesis and had submitted [it] he closed the door to his office and tried to kiss me when we were alone. I've also found out since he did this to a friend of mine as well. He shouldn't have a job in a reputable university.

▸ I am a male academic at a internationally respected state university. I supervise a number of female undergraduate and graduate students. It is typical for my male co-workers try to engage me in conversations about my students' physical attributes. The students are not aware of this but I do not want or need to think of my students in this way.

As a society, we are constantly questioning the issue with the "pipeline"—asking how it is possible that girls achieve such fantastic grades at school and yet fall so far behind their male peers before they reach boardroom level. So it is vital that we look unflinchingly at how utterly different young women's experiences of education are from those of male students, and how these differences are affecting them at this crucial period of academic and professional development.

▸ I have to wear high necklines or scarves to specific seminars in order to avoid a certain male lecturer staring down my top. As I feel uncomfortable being on my own with him, I do not ask him for help with work outside of lessons.

▸ At university my new lecturer asked me sexual questions and made a lot of sexual comments . . . it meant I didn't feel able to wait behind after class and ask him anything.

▸ Had an IT lecturer who would always sit very close on the bench to point out things you did wrong in your program (with "casual" touches, etc.). I declined his invitation to an advanced programming group simply because I knew it was him leading that group. My friend joined it and was constantly groped but she suffered in silence because she wanted to excel at programming.

For some students, the choice is very bleak indeed—succeed and learn at the cost of sexism, harassment or, at worst, *sexual assault*. Or choose to avoid it, within a system that condones and allows it to continue, and suffer the detriment to your educational opportunities.

While we're talking about young women's futures, there is an important point to be made here—while it is common to write off these issues as part of university life, college is the place where young people's attitudes and ideas about the world around them are cemented. If the scourge of misogyny currently infecting our higher education institutions continues, it is bound to carry over as students graduate and go out into the wider world. One interviewee told me:

The lads involved are intelligent, educated men who will go on to be leaders in industry, in politics, etc. If this behavior and these attitudes go unchecked, then they will pervade into all aspects of business and life in the future. Just as it seemed the "boys' clubs" in industries were disappearing, "lad culture" is forming new ones.

This sense of wider future impact is starkly revealed by the answers female students gave on their questionnaires. It was clear that the sexism they had already encountered had a major impact on their own aspirations and goals:

I want to go into academia. Very white male dominated. Have experienced frequent sexism. Feels like a boys' club.

As a science student, men are a lot more desirable to employers. I feel as a woman I would be taken less seriously than male applicants.

I feel that men are deemed to be the "professional" sex whereas stereotypes of "weak," "unintelligent" women definitely still remain.

One of the most glaring problems is that the sheer normalization and social acceptability of sexual harassment and abuse on campus is reiterated over and again, from female students feeling unjustified in reporting it to perpetrators expressing their surprise and anger when confronted.

▸ In college. I was at a school dance and was walking from the dance floor to find my then boyfriend when another student reached his hands between my legs and tried to touch me. I grabbed his hand

and threw it off of me and he just shrugged at me like "what? Why so hostile."

▸ When I was in college I went to a party and after it was too late to drive home. My friend said I could stay with him and considering we hung out all the time I thought that was fine. I woke up at 3 A.M. and he was fondling my breasts. I pretended to be asleep and waited for him to stop. I then left before he woke up. After I stopped talking to him he approached me and "didn't understand why I was suddenly being weird."

▸ My freshman year of college, I was out with a few friends, mostly new ones, when a group of guys some of the girls knew joined us. As we were walking up a hill, one of the men slapped and then grabbed my butt, while those below him laughed gleefully. When I turned around to yell at him, he called me a bitch and told me to calm down.

Within this environment, misogyny openly abounds, and rape jokes are plentiful:

▸ A guy at my college told me that I was "hot enough to rape." Am I supposed to be flattered?

▸ In college I was hanging with some guy "friends." I left the room and they proceeded to talk about how they wanted to have sex with me, going so far as to say they would tie me up and rape me.

In 2012, the Imperial College London student newspaper *Felix* published a "joke" article that furnished male students with a pretend recipe for the date-rape drug Rohypnol, which it described as a "fool-proof way" to make sure they'd have sex on Valentine's night "for cheaper than the price of a hooker."

Elsewhere one student reported being given a printed set of "rules" when he joined the university lacrosse team. It included the instruction: "Members don't date—that's what rape is for."

During Freshers' Week 2013, a video was posted online showing eighty student leaders at St. Mary's University in Canada chanting, "Y is for 'Your sister,' O is for 'Oh so tight,' U is for 'Underage,' N is for 'No consent,' G is for 'Grab that ass.' " The story came just weeks after a poster advertising a freshers' event at Cardiff Metropolitan University prominently featured a picture of a T-shirt bearing the words I WAS RAPING A WOMAN LAST NIGHT AND SHE CRIED.

Other high-profile examples showed students going out in T-shirts with "casual rape" slogans on them, playing drinking games called "it's not rape if . . . ," and being caught on camera chanting on a bus about miscarriage and sexual assault. Perhaps most famously of all, students in one Yale University fraternity marched across campus chanting, "No means yes! Yes means anal!" The slogan resurfaced on a sign in photographs allegedly taken at a Texas Tech University frat party.

Meanwhile, as with the experiences of younger girls, the Internet exacerbates and compounds the problem:

People at my college making a Twitter of pictures of girls' asses and rating them anonymously.

Boys in college made a "lad graph" where the amount of "lad points" you get depends on how fit the "wench" you sleep with is.

This is a culture in which "Spotted" and "Confessions" pages on social networks have proliferated faster than you can count. Students are encouraged to write in and "rate" their sexual partners; women you'd have sex with but not date are labeled "slam pieces"; there are graphic and explicit descriptions of young women, often with names tagged and often including photographs taken or used without their consent.

In this culture, Web sites like Uni Lad, BroBible, and the LAD Bible flourish. Here, across hundreds of articles almost exclusively about women, not a single female name appears. They are replaced with "wench," "slut," "slag," "hoe," "tramp," "slapper," "bint," "MILF," "bird," "gash," "clunge," "chick," "pussy," "bitch," "whore," "skank," "cunt." Here, "lads" are encouraged to describe sexual conquests in the most aggressive way possible, reducing women to scores ("I was banging a solid 5/10") and ridiculing the "wenches" afterward. Here, women who don't want to have sex with a man are described as "obstacle courses," as if the idea of finding a way around their lack of consent is an entertaining game. Here, users post comments about "smashing virgins and having the bloodstains to prove it," and articles say "85 percent of rape cases go unreported . . . that seems to be fairly good odds."

One post on a "lad" Facebook page boastfully and graphically describes a man knocking a woman "clean out with one smack" and leaving "her for dead on the side of the road."

A picture of Lady Gaga is captioned "Smash or Dash?" One of the top-rated comments reads, "Smash in the face with a brick."

Meanwhile, Total Frat Move, a U.S.-based Web site focusing on fraternity culture, perpetuates similar thinly veiled misogyny, describing sorority girls as "sorostitutes" and publishing totally hilarious frat boy statements on its "TFM wall" crowing about "Putting your girlfriend on hold to shotgun a beer" and "Shooting her with the finger pistol as she leaves unsatisfied," and boasting, "The only difference between a sorostitute and a can of dip is that I keep my cans when I'm done with them." Its article "38 Reasons Every Guy Should Date a Sorority Girl" included such perceptive gems as, "They might be freaks in the bedroom, but they're still the classiest on campus" and "She has over 100 girls to tell her if her dress makes her 'look fat,' so she'll never ask you." Then there's the "Instagram babe of the day" category (no explanation needed) and a separate digital library of images of women's breasts with fraternity names scrawled across them (known as "rush boobs") for frat bros' viewing pleasure. There are no heads on the pictures. Whaddaya mean that dehumanizes the female students? Boobs are all you need amirite? In the words of the TFM guys, "Let's keep the good times with titties rolling."

Attitudes toward rape range from ambiguous to misogynistic.

Forum threads started by TFM fans give a more explicit insight into the mind-set of those who frequent the site. One, titled "Slut Shaming," begins, "Any else getting tired of hearing this phrase? 'Stop slut shaming.' I love having sex with sluts as much as the next guy, but do sluts really expect us to respect them?" Another poster just gets it all off his chest, complaining how tiresome and annoying the fight back against rape has been for *him*: "College rape's been all over the news this week and it's pissing me off. The girl at University of Ohio who got her box munched in public is embarrassed and calling it rape, Huffpost 'writers' are calling on college men to drink less, etc. There's a group at my school trying to end victim blaming and these people are the fucking WORST."

Yeah, I'm still pretty sure rape is, in fact, the worst.

The idea of satirical sexist humor and the word "banter" has become central to a culture that encourages young men to revel in the objectification, sexual pursuit, and ridicule of their female peers. It is a cloak of irony that is used to excuse mainstream sexism and the normalization and belittling of rape and intimate-partner violence. And it is incredibly effective, because—as we know—pretending that something is "just a joke" is a powerful silencing tool, making those who stand up to it seem staid and isolated.

But as one young woman I interview explains:

I don't find it funny. These pages are not pages for jokes. There are no punch lines. They are not sexist jokes; they are just displays of sexism, displays of misogyny . . . I find it threatening, I find it terrifying . . . This is not banter.

Over on TFM's "sister" Web site TSM (Total Sorority Move, obv), an even more charming piece titled "Stop Crying Rape" laments all those stupid slutty girls having slutty sex and then regretting it and deciding to fix the whole thing with the joyfully simple stroke of pretending they were raped. "Yes, you were drunk. And yes, you flirted with him. And yes, you initiated the first makeout . . . and the second one. Yes, you whispered, 'Let's get out of here.' But you felt guilty this morning. And so you take it all back. No matter that he was drunk, too, and you were a willing participant—you take it back." It goes on: "We've created a culture where it is completely acceptable for girls to get drunk, make bad decisions, and then take it all back. And in the game of your word against his, you will always win."

Literally, what? Has this author ever glanced at a single statistic about the likelihood of getting a rape conviction?

There is evidence to suggest that this laddish "bro" culture is more than just offensive. Multiple studies have found that fraternity members are three times more likely to commit rape than those not involved in Greek life, while women in sororities are 74 percent more likely to experience rape than other college women. In 2013, one fraternity sent an e-mail to its members with the title "luring your rapebait," including this advice: "IF ANYTHING EVER FAILS, GO GET MORE ALCOHOL." It was the same fraternity where pledges were made to sing a song including the following lyrics:

Who can take a bottle
Shove it up her ass
Hit her with a bat and shatter all the glass
Who can take a tight slut
Fuck her 'till she cries
Then pull it out real fast and skeet into her eyes
Who can take a chainsaw

Saw the bitch in two
Take the top half and give the bottom half to you
Who can take a razor blade
give her a nasty cut
and then use the blood to lube up her butt

A leaked series of e-mails from another fraternity included such gems as "She's the kind of girl that you need to fuck hard and rape in the woods," "dumb bitches learning their place," and "She had a friend who got raped at our house? I would like to meet this lying cunt."

It is important (and pretty obvious) to say that these Web sites and e-mails are not representative of the entire male college population, and misogyny is by no means a universal characteristic among university-age men. In fact, many describe standing up to this "lad culture," saying it sickens them as much as it does their female peers. But they are usually isolated in their intervention and rarely report a successful outcome, suggesting that these often aggressive attitudes, though not universally shared, nonetheless dominate university discourse and experience.

▸ Couple weeks ago male friend says "9 out of 10 people enjoy gang-rape." I call him out on sexism, calling him disgusting, he shrugs saying it was a "joke."

▸ A couple days ago a girl in the year below walked past. After she was about 60 feet away a guy in my year came up to me and asked, "What do ya reckon is the ass on that?" I refused to comment saying it was wrong and that no woman wants their body judged in that way. His not-so-witty response is that, "If they didn't want their asses to be judged they wouldn't have them in the first place!"

It's pretty clear that in order for change to happen, the number of people (particularly young men) actively standing up needs to be far greater—and while we wait for that critical mass to be achieved, female students continue to suffer.

Worst of all, student after student reported experiencing rape while at college or university:

I was drugged and raped by a friend of a friend at age 19 on my college campus.

My first year of college I was followed home by a boy at a party and raped.

In my first week on my freshman year of college I was raped by a guy I had just met.

My first year of college, I was raped 3 times.

In the *majority* of such entries, victims reported being blamed by their peers for what had happened.

I was a freshman in college when I was sexually assaulted by two senior fraternity members. I was a virgin, on the other side of the country for college, away from all my friends and family. I had been drugged. All I remember is pain, trying to say stop (not sure if my voice worked or if he ignored me). The aftermath was just as painful, as my best friend of 7+ years accused me of "leading them on." She said it was a "bitch move" to accuse them of rape. I lost all friends at my new college, too, and spent a good portion of the year alone before transferring back home.

▸ I was raped in my second year of university. I had some great support from my family, and some great therapy. I thought this was the worst part, but when I felt safe enough to tell my friends, the questions started. "Was I drunk?" "Was I dressed sluttily?" "Did I know him?" "Had I led him on?" It broke my heart.

▸ Freshman year of college: a basketball player pushed me down on the floor of a private gym and pressed himself on top of me . . . I asked him to get off he said "why are you being such a tease? I'm not gonna hurt you" he began kissing my lips . . . everything inside of me was squirming as I held back the screams. I came back to my dorm crying and covered in seamen [sic] . . . my friends told me to "wash myself off, block his number and get a hold of myself, I shouldn't have put myself in that situation."

▸ Was raped by my roommate's friend my freshman year of college. She called me a liar when I told her, and told me that I was being a slut.

Eventually, this net of blame and sexism results in the inevitable curtailment of young women's freedom. Victim-blaming ideas blend in until they are regurgitated as fact.

▸ Told not to wear skirts + shorts + sleeveless in college because "you know what happens to girls these days."

And the blaming of victims doesn't just take a devastating emotional toll—in many cases, disbelief and misinformation are used to pressure and threaten the victim not to report.

▸ I was raped my freshman year of college. His friends got to me by claiming they saw my university's health records and said there were no signs of rape.

▸ I was 19 and went on a school trip out of town. We all had some drinks and I accidentally locked myself out of my hotel room, and knocked on the trip leader's room to get help. I trusted him. He asked me in and, after I had thrown up everywhere, invited me to sleep in his bed with him. I passed out and woke up to him licking my vagina. I was confused and afraid. In the morning I realized he had raped me while I was unconscious; I was covered in bruises and my vagina and anus hurt.

I told the university and several members of staff blamed me for drinking. The rapist told my friends I was a slut and wanted it. No one believed me, and people thought I was trying to get attention.

That was three years ago and I still haven't reported it to the police.

▸ The first couple times I was too afraid to report it, I live in Texas and have heard all sorts of stories about how if there's any alcohol in your system you don't have a chance, not to mention I couldn't bear the thought of facing any of those guys again. The last time I was raped I mentioned it to two friends of mine and they both asked me if "I was sure?" Then the rapist began sending hateful, harassing messages to me on Facebook, I reported it to Facebook but nothing ever happened. I deleted my Facebook after that and never reported the rape.

The victim blaming often becomes internalized, with some victims reiterating the abusive statements they have heard, attacking themselves:

▸ When I was a sophomore in college, I was raped at a party. I never reported it; I suppose I never really felt like I could. See, I had too much to drink and was passed out. I awoke to someone on top of me, raping me, and I did nothing. I let it happen, and when it was over I proceeded to do my best to forget about it and act like it never happened. I felt such shame and took on the majority of the responsibility. If I hadn't been drinking, this wouldn't have happened. If I had my good friends with me, this wouldn't have happened.

Even in the rare cases when victims do feel able to report what has happened, both in cases of harassment and sexual assault, the incidents are often dismissed by campus administration or police.

▸ Last year, I was sexually harassed by one of my lecturers. He would routinely invade my personal space, tell me to rub my breasts against him, grab me, stare openly at my legs and breasts, and talk about sexually explicit topics in class instead of what was on the syllabus. One day after class, he asked me intrusive questions about my sex life to the point where he became visibly aroused. Finally, I told him to back off and he lost his temper with me.

I wound up filing a formal complaint after he started throwing away my work instead of returning it. I was told by members of staff that sexual harassment is something that happens to women in academia and that I simply needed to learn to put up with it. I was shunned by staff and students alike for being a troublemaker.

A year on, I'm still dealing with the fallout from the sexual harassment case. I am getting absolutely no support from the university—quite the opposite, in fact. It may sound naive, but I was shocked that, in 2012, female students at a world-class research university are still treated as second-class citizens and unwanted interlopers in a world created by and for men.

▸ A (male) prosecutor for a sexual assault case that I was the victim of, made light of it by saying "it's just college and people are just trying out relationships and doing that kind of thing."

At one American university a student tried to report being raped and said the response from a university administrator was, "Well . . . Rape is like football, if you look back on the game, and you're the quarterback . . . is there anything you would have done differently?" At another college, a young woman who was raped by a fellow student at an off-campus party reported it to school administrators only to be asked about the length of her dress, her drinking habits, how often she partied, and whether or not she had climaxed.

Even for those who win the rare "victory" of being taken seriously by their school, the punishment—if there is any—is at best often pathetically disproportionate to the crime.

▸ Freshman year of college, I lived in the co-ed dorms. My neighbor across the hall would only hit on me when I had been drinking and would try to push the limits each time. I would fall asleep, and he would slip his hand down my pants or try to grope me. After a couple of months, he decided it would be okay to start coming into my room and into bed with me when I was asleep. I would wake up to him trying to make-out with me or touch me. After one particularly close call with him, I decided to report it. I was told to move dorms completely, move out, and make new friends in a new building. He received no punishment besides a "record" of the "incident."

Analysis released by the *Huffington Post* in September 2014 of more than thirty-two colleges and universities revealed that less than a third of college students *found guilty* of sexual assault were expelled and only 47 percent suspended. The *Huffington Post* also obtained a set of data from the U.S. Department of Justice on how 125 higher education institutions responded to reports of sexual assaults on campus. Once again the data revealed that less than one-third of students found responsible for sexual assault were expelled.

When a student at one university admitted raping a woman after she had said "no" and "stop," the school punished him with probation and a ban from university housing but decided that community service would be "too punitive." In another case, four students reported the same man to their university administrators for separate sexual assaults but heard nothing for months until they pushed for more information and learned, over a year later, that he had been "punished" with probation and mandatory counseling. When the leader of a student organization of which all the victims were members attempted to eject the male student from the group, university administrators allegedly said he should be allowed to remain, so that "he would have a community of friends to process it" and understand he had done wrong, if he assaulted somebody again in the future.

When a student at another university questioned why her

rapist had been punished only with probation, sexual assault education, and a $25 fine, the university told her it wanted "these types of situations" to be "learning situations for all parties involved." Quite what they thought she needed to "learn" from the experience wasn't clear.

In many cases, students found guilty of sexual assault have been barred from campus "after graduation" or allowed to finish the semester before beginning their suspension. Victim after victim has described her case being mishandled, belittled, or ignored by school administrators, who blamed, disbelieved, or tried to silence her, didn't make her aware of her rights, or privileged her rapist's needs over her own.

In July 2013, Yale University hit the headlines after issuing its semiannual report on "Complaints of Sexual Misconduct," which described rape as "nonconsensual sex" and revealed that the harshest penalty given to an undergraduate found by the university to have engaged in "nonconsensual sex" was two semesters' suspension. Many students accused of sexual assault were simply given "written reprimands."

At worst, it is the victim who is punished. At one university, a sophomore was told she had been charged with an "Honor Code violation" for speaking to the press about her rape and risked potential punishment for "intimidating" and "adversely affecting" her rapist—even though she hadn't publicly identified him.

In one UK case, an eighteen-year-old college student who reported that she had been gang-raped on campus was suspended for "demeaning sexual actions" before the case had been tried. In another, a group of female students who filmed the all-male hockey team chanting about sexual assault and miscarriage on a public bus and uploaded the footage to YouTube to raise awareness of misogynistic student culture later told how *they* were threatened with disciplinary action for "bringing the university into disrepute."

Any one of these incidents alone would be shocking, but together they represent a miscarriage of justice on an enormous scale. There are too many individual cases to list here, but at the time of writing, eighty-five U.S. colleges are under federal investigation over allegations of mishandling sexual assault cases.

I've used a lot of examples here, not by coincidence but to show that this situation is happening again and again and again. The problem is systemic. Thanks to the high-profile victim-blaming narratives like George Will's, articles like TSM's "Stop Crying Rape," and comments like those of Fox News host Bob "When was the last time you heard about a rape on campus?" Beckel, the reality of the situation needs to be stressed.

But there is reason to be cautiously hopeful that change is on the way. The spate of current investigations (fifty-five of which began in 2014) is testament to the enormous national interest and publicity surrounding the issue, thanks in large part to the incredible bravery of survivors and student activists who have spoken out to raise awareness of the problem.

The White House has taken unprecedented steps to counter college sexual assault, writing to all colleges to make them aware of their responsibilities with regard to handling campus sexual assault, and launching the "It's On Us" campaign, to which hundreds of schools have signed up. Sexual assault reports have risen by 61 percent at America's top twenty-five universities in the past two years alone, with students more likely to report assaults without delay, suggesting that the spotlight on the issue and the courageous actions of survivors have helped other victims to feel more able to come forward.

But there is more government and colleges can do, from appointing college Title IX coordinators, to improving reporting procedures; making clear and transparent information about their rights and options readily available to all students and putting victims' needs at the heart of the investigation process. In a historic move, at the end of September 2014, California's governor Jerry Brown signed a bill adopting the "yes means yes" model for sexual consent, under which colleges must take on an "affirmative consent" model in their sexual assault policies. This helps to shift responsibility for gaining active, affirmative consent onto both partners, instead of requiring an unwilling partner to say no. Indeed, it specifies "lack of protest or resistance does not mean consent, nor does silence mean consent," makes it clear that consent can be withdrawn at every stage of the process and cannot be given if an individual is asleep, unconscious, or incapacitated by drugs or alcohol. The bill also requires training for faculty reviewing complaints so that victims are not asked inappropriate questions when filing reports. Perhaps best of all, it is likely to lead to more active education of students about consent (mandatory "consent classes" have already been initiated at some universities) in order to make sure they are aware of their rights and responsibilities. This kind of concrete, perpetrator-focused education from colleges would be an important step forward, as would the wider adoption of the "yes means yes" model.

More work has to be done. Whether you look at the crippling impact of campus misogyny on female students' career aspirations or the devastating long-term damage of campus rape, if we fail young women at this stage, we are failing them forever.

While government and universities catch up, feminist student activists are leading the way. Inspirational women like Wagatwe Wanjuki, who was expelled when her grades began to slip after her university without explanation dropped the case against the fellow student she reported assaulted her, have worked tirelessly on campaigns like Students Active for Ending Rape (SAFER) and Know Your IX, which informs students about their rights in relation to campus sexual violence. Even in the most unbearable circumstances, survivors have shown the utmost strength in choosing to speak out, inspiring and supporting thousands of others to feel able to do the same. None more so than Emma Sulkowicz, a Columbia University student who found herself hitting international headlines after choosing to carry her heavy mattress to every class she attends on campus until the fellow student she reported assaulted her was expelled or leaves or until she graduates. Part senior thesis project, part awareness campaign, Sulkowicz's act eloquently speaks to the weight carried by survivors of sexual violence, despite the light or nonexistent punishments perpetrators so often face. She told the *Guardian,* "I could have taken my pillow, but I want people to see how it weighs down a person to be ignored by the school administration and harassed by police." What started out as a personal act of defiance sparked an international wave of solidarity, with ten thousand students later dragging their mattresses to class in a day of protest that epitomized the determination to tackle this issue around the world.

What we're seeing is a generation of young women who

refuse to be brushed off, belittled, or ignored—who have the determination, the strength, and the compassion to educate themselves about their rights and then pass on that information to their peers—who will endure the bruising court of public opinion if that is what it takes to raise awareness—who will take their cases to the federal government if their schools refuse them the justice that is their right. It is nothing short of a revolution.

Chapter 5

Women in Public Spaces

I committed the terrible crime of being female and out in public on my own.

Everyday Sexism Project entry

Vital Statistics

87 percent of American women age eighteen to sixty-four have been harassed by a male stranger.
-Penn Schoen Berland, 2000

41 percent of American women have experienced "physically aggressive" forms of harassment or assault in public spaces, including sexual touching, being followed, or being flashed.
-Stop Street Harassment, 2014

83 percent of Egyptian women report experiencing sexual harassment in the street.
-Egyptian Center for Women's Rights, 2008

95 percent of women in Delhi feel unsafe in public spaces.
-International Center for Research on Women and UN Women, 2013

More than 80 percent of Canadian women have experienced male stranger harassment in public.
-Ross Macmillan, Annette Nierobisz, and Sandy Welsh, "Experiencing the Streets: Harassment and Perceptions of Safety among Women," 2000

If you think whistling at me for my "nice ass" is going to make me swoon, then by golly, mister, you sure know women.

I've realized that it's sad I've had to take self defense, carry pepper spray, and run in areas with people and still not feel safe.

A guy actually growled and barked at me from his car, while I was walking on the sidewalk. I was 11 years old.

Being casually groped by stranger passing by on sidewalk—in broad daylight, not alone.

Guy simulated masturbating on my face on packed bus. Next month it happened for real, again no one said anything.

A man last night stopped me in the street and asked, "Do you ride a bike?" I shook my head and he said, "OK then, why don't you ride me." Obviously I had sex with him instantly and we're getting married.

It's nearly 8:30 A.M. and I'm going to be late because I've stopped to change my clothes again. I'd wanted to wear a pencil skirt, because I'm going straight to a friend's birthday after work and would have liked to have been a bit dressed up. But then I remembered the group of men who'd been lined up along the wall outside my office eating their sandwiches yesterday, and the excruciating embarrassment of their detailed comments on my breasts and bottom. So the pencil skirt is now lying across the back of a chair, discarded. I don't *think* there's any way my second choice—office trousers with a blouse—could be interpreted as an invitation for sexual appraisal, but I'm not fully comfortable until I add the chunky sweater on top. Extra armor. Just in case. I grab my bike helmet and head for the door.

I'm cycling faster than usual to make up time, but I still remember not to use the street where the traffic's particularly bad at this time in the morning. I'll avoid the worst of the beeping horns that way. I'm running through my notes for the morning meeting in my head, so I don't see the group of men in high-visibility jackets standing by the side of the road until a sudden shout makes me jump out of my skin, swerving dangerously into the path of the car coming up behind me. I force my bike back onto an even keel, my heart pounding and my hands shaking.

"Look at those tits!" "I would." "Nice view, love!" "All right, darling?"

It is not even 8:45. My face is only half visible, obscured by my helmet. This is the second day in a row that such harassment has ruined my journey to work. Everybody has a tipping point. With a sudden, impulsive rush of fury, I screech to a halt (almost causing another accident as the cyclist behind swerves to avoid me). Wrenching my bike up onto the pavement, I storm over to the now apprehensive-looking group of men and ask them, pleadingly, idealistically, to imagine how it would feel if *they* had been unable simply to reach their workplace that morning without enduring the sharp embarrassment of having their physique, their sexual merit, publicly commented on and appraised for all to hear. How might it impact their day to continue to work feeling dirty and ashamed and scared?

The men look at each other and laugh. "You want to calm down, love."

Adrenaline is coursing through my body. The act of the confrontation is absolutely, exquisitely terrifying. There are four or five of them and only one of me. With shaking hands, I pull out my mobile phone and dial the company number displayed on the side of the van parked next to them. The men start to look concerned. One of them says, "Now hang on . . ."

I hold the phone to my ear. My trembling fingers have misdialed the number. A tinny arpeggio sounds, then, repeatedly: "We're sorry. The number you have dialed has not been recognized. Please check and try again." The men are watching me closely.

"Yes, hello," I say brusquely, drowning out the tone. "I'd like to report a group of your workers sexually harassing me on the corner of——Road and——Street. They very nearly caused a road-traffic accident. Yes. Yes. Thank you." The men have retreated into the cab of the van. They look utterly bewildered.

When I reach the office, I Google the company name as the adrenaline slowly subsides, leaving a sick, weak feeling. The manager who answers my call says he is extremely grateful that I got in touch. "I know exactly which team you are talking about," he tells me. "We know it happens, but unless people report it there's very little we can do. They'll be seriously reprimanded when they get back tonight."

Until that day, in summer 2008, it had never occurred to me that the convoluted routes and extra precautions, the changed clothes and hastily swept-up hair were anything other than ordinary. Planning strategies to get through the day with the least possible exposure to unwanted attention and harassment was simply a part of being a woman that I accepted, as much of a necessary routine as carrying a spare tampon in my purse.

Of the tens of thousands of women's experiences collected by the Everyday Sexism Project, more than ten thousand of them have described street harassment—sexism, sexual harassment, and even assault in public spaces. In 2016, when we'd like to believe women are as free as men to go where they like, when they like, the reality is that thousands of women are running a daily gauntlet of harassment that leaves some "terrified to go out or walk home at night."

When I started the #ShoutingBack hashtag on Twitter to invite people to share their experiences, thousands of stories flooded in within a matter of days, revealing the true extent of street harassment and the frequency with which it impinges on women's lives: "Every day since I was 14," "I've lost count of the number of times," "Too many times to mention," "At least once a week and often much more, regardless of what I wear, where I am, how I behave." One woman said, "There isn't a day . . . where I don't get shouted at, followed or stared down. It's like a disease." Another wrote:

The only story I will share is that it started for me in sixth grade. Every day.

In fact, street harassment is happening so frequently that many women report it simply becoming a part of their daily experience—and when something becomes part of your daily experience, the danger is that you'll unconsciously come to accept it as normal.

The sad fact is that now I just expect to be harassed or followed on my way home from a night out.

The women in my life tell me to ignore sexual harassment because "they went through it too."

My 14[-year-old] gets cat called and whistled at so often walking to school she thinks it's just part of life.

There is a common misconception, particularly among those who do not personally experience it, that street harassment is restricted to gentle praise, or a cheeky comment here and there. "Just learn to take a compliment," we often hear; "a wolf whistle or two is just 'harmless fun.'" One woman described how after being "followed home walking from school, I was told, 'It's not as bad as getting raped so get over it.'"

An instance of verbal harassment isn't a simple, single experience. It isn't even just about the person insulting or propositioning you. It's the shock of the initial approach, which often gets your attention with an unpleasant jolt. It's the prickle of embarrassment when that makes your harassers laugh. It's the unease of suddenly reevaluating your safety. It's the discomfort when they mention your breasts or your legs, and you start panicking, mentally checking your clothing—despite the fact that you're in absolutely no way responsible for what's happening. It's the horrible burning shame of imagining that, since your legs or your breasts or your backside are being so loudly commented on, everybody within earshot is probably now staring at them. It's the guilt (as counterintuitive as that sounds) of wondering whether those people are now also judging you for being sexually evaluated in public. It's the fear when the harassers you ignore start shouting that you're a bitch, a slut, a whore. It's the sense of dirty, overwhelming shame when nobody stops to help you and the message their silence sends is, "You deserve this. This is not unjust enough to warrant my intervention. This is normal. This is what happens to women. Get used to it." And it's the impact afterward, as you begin to associate your own body parts with the unsolicited judgments that strangers have passed on them, as you reassess yourself and consider a change of style or clothing or—in the case of some women—even *body shape* to avoid going through the same thing again. (One project entry described a fifteen-year-old girl who was "so depressed about constant harassment" that she "begged" her mother for a breast reduction.) Street harassment is *not* friendly flattery.

It begins with the shouting. The yelling, calling, summoning, whistling, evaluating, and insulting. The boundaries between "compliment" and curse are fluid and unpredictable; countless women have described cries of "Hey, sexy!" and "Come here" switching suddenly to "stupid slut" or even "YOU WHORE, I'LL BEAT YOU SO HARD" when they refused to respond.

And from verbal harassment the sliding scale progresses. The sheer number of women who have described not just verbal but also physical and sexual assault in public spaces is shocking. You can trace this escalation through the project entries: men "touching me, rubbing against me" becomes "took a photo up my skirt and ran off"; from "Yeah, I'd fuck that" and "Look at the tits on that" to "sticks his hand between my legs and gropes me"; from "being rubbed, dry humped or groped on a crowded train" to "grabbed from behind by a man demanding my underwear." The stories go on, and on, and on.

What the project entries make obvious is that every aspect of street harassment is interconnected. There is no "harmless." There is no invisible line beneath which it's okay to sexually appraise and force unwanted verbal or physical attention on a woman but above which it crosses into abuse. Since I started the project, countless Twitter users, cyberspace trolls, and even journalists have asked, again and again, "Why make a fuss about something as minor as a wolf whistle or a catcall?" One journalist even spent nearly forty-five minutes circling back to the question, wheedling, trying to get me to admit that it was all just a bit of fun.

Why make such a fuss?

Because street harassment is perhaps the clearest manifestation of the spectrum of sexism, sexual harassment, and sexual assault that exists within our society. Yes, it starts out small, but allowing those "minor" transgressions gives license to the more serious ones and eventually to all-out abuse. We've heard the same words and phrases crossing over and echoing and repeating from women who are shouted at in the street to women who are assaulted and women who are victims of domestic violence in their own homes. The language is the same. And if we say it's acceptable for men to assume power and ownership over women they don't know verbally in public, then, like it or not, we're also saying something much wider about gender relations—something that carries over into our personal relationships and our sexual exchanges. Because this is a line that doesn't need to be blurred. It should be clear and simple. Take it from the women whose experiences started out with just a little "harmless" street harassment—a sexual "compliment" or a wolf whistle or a "Hey, baby"—but then turned nasty, became full-blown attacks. Ask them what the problem is with a harmless bit of fun.

Harassment started on the street, asking if I was married, ended with sexual assault on my doorstep at 3 P.M.

And, crucially, screaming a judgment about someone's vagina as you speed past in a fast car is *never* really a "compliment." People who shout at women in the street don't do it because they think there's a chance the woman will drop her shopping and leap into their arms! It *isn't* a compliment, and to call it that disparages the vast majority of lovely men who are perfectly able to pay a *real* compliment. It is an exertion of power, dominance, and control.

And it's utterly horrifying that we've become so used to it that it's considered the norm.

I was flashed twice on my route home, I was groped between my legs in a club, and had a man masturbate whilst telling me he wanted to suck on my tits in the street in broad daylight. I was walking home from a grief counselling session. Countless shouted comments about how un/attractive I am over the years . . . I consider myself lucky, relatively.

When we discussed street harassment on Twitter using the #ShoutingBack hashtag, some women said the saddest thing about the conversation was that they identified with almost every experience being shared. One woman wrote simply:

I don't even know where to start with stories. I have so many. So many and I have not forgotten any of them.

For thousands of women, street harassment starts at a terrifyingly young age.

When I was 9 a man asked "the girl with the dick sucking lips" to come here.

One girl told us that she was just thirteen when a group of men in a van pulled over and asked her if she had a "tight pussy." She didn't even understand what they were talking about.

I started experiencing crude, cruel street harassment as soon as I started growing breasts at 12.

Stood on pavement with friend & van driver honks, it's been the usual since age 12 walking in school uniform.

So from an incredibly young age girls are being sent the message that it is normal—simply part of being female—to be sexually addressed, judged, and commented on by strangers in the street. The impact on girls' developing sense of self and of their place in the world should not be underestimated.

When I was about 11 or 12 I was walking to the high school that I lived near to watch my little brother in his elementary school's Race for Education and about half way there three guys, probably in their late twenties drove up to me, slowed down and cat called me. They whistled and told me I was really sexy . . . This was the first time I had experienced something like this and I was absolutely terrified. I was in a deserted part of town and completely alone. The first thing that ran through my mind was "what if they rape me." They sped off right after that but the saddest thing is that I didn't go home after that and lock the door or call anyone, I just kept walking and watched my brother run and got on with my day as usual like nothing happened. I didn't say anything for about three weeks because I thought I did something wrong. I thought that I provoked it, that I was to blame for it. And once I did say something to my parents all I got was "get used to it."

Not only is this girl, in her very early teens, already forming a causal link between women's choice of clothing and the harassment they receive, but she's also clearly connecting the entitlement strangers feel to her young body with a fear of sexual violence and assault. From there, she identifies feelings of shame, self-blame, and normalization. These are the formative experiences of young girls. These are the messages street harassment sends them. Men have the right to sexually appraise you in public. You are valued on the basis of what you look like and whether you provide men with sexual pleasure. If you dress in a particular way, you are bringing it on yourself and are at fault—but even if you don't, it is still something normal that will happen to you. You will experience shame. It is the precursor to the possibility of even more aggressive physical possession of your body in the future.

Just a harmless compliment.

And, of course, while the regularity and normalization of

women's harassment in public spaces sends these formative messages to young girls, boys are learning from them too. Many of the accounts we have received detailed street harassment performed in front of young children, both accompanying the victim and the perpetrator.

▶ Age 15—walking through downtown during the summer with two of my friends. As we walk, three elementary school-aged boys and their (presumably) fathers start to walk behind us. They (little boys included) catcall us, saying things like, "Hey ladies, lookin' sexy," "Hey stop walkin' and gimme some, sweetie" and proceed to follow us down the street.

One woman told us that in the supermarket, one man commented to another:

"She obviously likes black c**k" . . . in front of my 8-year-old mixed-race son.

Another woman described a man who sexually harassed her from a van before he "turned and laughed," "winking" at the boy of five or six sitting next to him.

These inherently potent messages about gender-biased power and control surely help to shape the way our children see the world around them. We understand how it works: The everyday becomes the accepted norm, accommodated in the way we live. By making this allowance we reinforce the idea of acceptability and compound the sense of entitlement; that assumed prerogative is then exercised to an ever-increasing degree, and naturally we then find ourselves with even more of an everyday problem . . . To tackle street harassment, we have to break through that pernicious circle. We have to abandon the mistaken idea that street harassment is nothing more than a minor inconvenience, or a compliment taken the wrong way.

The problem isn't confined to only a small number of women, and certainly not only to "hot" women, or women who dress or act in a certain way, or go to certain places at certain times of day. These myths are part of the victim-blaming culture that protects aggressors while placing guilt on their victims. A survey by Penn Schoen Berland revealed that a staggering 87 percent of American women (age eighteen to twenty-four) had experienced sexual harassment in public spaces. And most women experience it over and over again. The Washington, DC–based organization Stop Street Harassment's 2014 study found that 86 percent of women who reported being harassed said it had happened more than once. Our reports concern a huge age range, from children as young as seven to women in their seventies and eighties. Many women have written to us in disbelief, finding it hard to cope with the fact that their daughters and granddaughters are now putting up with the same ordeals they faced themselves. They ask me, "Is it really still going on?"

And often this weary normalization goes a step farther, as women begin to internalize the perceived public attitudes toward them and their bodies.

The reason I hate my breasts is due to the unwanted attention they attract. I try to cover them up.

There are times I wish I wasn't female because I'm fed up of being scared of walking down the street on my own.

This sense of self-blame and the lengths to which women go to try to avoid street harassment was a recurring theme.

Walk down the street with eyes on the ground, hood pulled up, and never leave the house dressed provocatively because I cannot stand the attention of cat-calls, honking horns.

I want to take up jogging but [not] without a buddy too intimidated due to previous experience of heckling.

I do things like put my hair up in a certain way that means it's hard to be grabbed at or if I'm really scared holding my keys between my fingers . . . I wear my headphones with the music turned up in town so I don't have to hear catcalls. I walk at a certain distance from groups of men in front of me. If they are behind me I take a different route. This is all just normal to me now. It's normal for a lot of women I know. It's every day.

Women describe the emotional and psychological ways street harassment affects them to an extent that those who do not experience it might struggle to imagine.

Sexual remarks made to me when obviously pregnant made me feel like my unborn daughter was being molested.

Men "just having fun" yelling abuse (often sexual) at me in the street has been known to trigger panic attacks.

The annoying part about street harassment is the feeling that I should then change myself. I victim blame me.

One woman's description of a single week's harassment in public spaces started like this:

In the last week, I have had comments about my appearance at least every day. I have had three different men try to get me to go home with them, including one man who stated: "I will fuck you and then you can fuck off home." I was spanked by two different individuals, had my hair pulled and [was] pinned against a wall by another in a night club.

Yet despite experiencing such aggressive abuse, her account ended with her taking the blame upon herself:

It makes me feel so used up . . . I'm tired of it. I'm 26 now and sometimes I hate myself so much.

The ingrained public acceptability of street harassment is clear from the hundreds of stories we received of perpetrators becoming aggressive and violent when women tried to stand up to them or even simply ignored them. The phenomenon suggests that they are so accustomed to feeling entitled to harass women that they get angry when such behavior is denied.

A man in the street groped me then got angry and threw a brick at me when I protested. It missed me and hit my Mum.

Held against a wall because I refused to kiss a man much older than me when I was 16.

Propositioned by 3 older men . . . when I ignored them, one hit so hard across my upper thigh it bruised badly.

And another, and another, and another. These were not isolated incidents. There were countless reports—from women who'd rejected unwanted catcalls and had men hitting them, throwing objects, or trying to back their cars into them; from women whose harassers physically pursued them, threatening violence and rape.

Man leant from car window to ask directions, I said I was running for train (true) so he drove on pavement and pinned me against shop window, I had to clamber over bonnet to escape, him swearing at me.

Many women reported perpetrators expressing their sense of entitlement outright, reacting with apparent shock (and not a hint of self-awareness or irony) when their victims tried to deny them the "right" to harass and touch them.

At a club, last year. Repeatedly groped. Told him to back off. He grabbed me roughly and said women can't talk to men like that.

Man put his hand up my skirt when walking down the road. Shouted at him that he had no right to touch me. He seemed shocked.

Walking home, guy stopped me, grabbed my breasts and tried to kiss me. I yelled at him, he looked shocked and annoyed.

Several high-profile cases throw into sharp relief the devastating and very real threat of street harassment developing into even worse abuse. A young woman who told a man to stop groping her at Notting Hill Carnival in London in August 2014 found herself in the emergency room with blood pouring from her nose after he punched her in the face. A female runner in California who declined a man's offer of a ride was left in critical condition after he deliberately hit her with his car. And in the space of a single week in autumn 2014, two women were brutally attacked for turning down the advances of men in the street. The first, in Queens, New York, had her throat slashed after she rejected a man outside the lobby of her building. Just three days later, Mary "Unique" Spears was shot dead in Detroit after refusing a man's advances as she left a relative's memorial service. That Spears was a woman of color is not a coincidence. Women of color, trans women, and members of the wider LGBT (lesbian, gay, bisexual, transgender) community experience disproportionate levels of street harassment (the Stop Street Harassment study found that 41 percent of people of color of any gender experienced street harassment regularly, compared to 24 percent of white people; 45 percent of all LGBT people surveyed experienced physically aggressive harassment or assault compared to 28 percent of all heterosexual people).

Not only that, but for many women of color and trans women, like Islan Nettles, beaten to death opposite a police station in Harlem after a group of young men realized she was transgender, the escalation of street harassment can be deadly.

Just a bit of fun?

I am encouraged to see that there are definite indicators that speaking out about the problem—naming it and describing it, thrusting it, in all its forms, into the limelight—does have a positive impact.

For example, during our #ShoutingBack discussion, while women expressed their resignation and lack of surprise at the stories being shared, men were speaking up, voicing shock and outrage and, crucially, pledging to take action to tackle the problem.

▸ I had no idea that these things happened to women walking the streets day or night. I am shocked after reading some tweets.

▸ Makes me realize as a man who hates this crap, how much more there is to do. WE are the ones who can influence.

▸ Definitely think the awareness is useful from a male point of view. Has definitely led to me thinking more about what I say and do.

To catalyze such realization, women around the world have found unique and innovative ways of starting conversations about street harassment. One woman in Kolkata started photographing her street harassers, turning the discomfort of an unwanted gaze back on them. In New York, the artist Tatyana Fazlalizadeh started pasting beautiful and defiant posters of women with slogans like MY NAME IS NOT BABY in public spaces. And after a man ejaculated on her legs on a crowded subway, Londoner Ellie Cosgrave returned to the crime scene on International Women's Day and performed a dance she'd created to express her frustration, anger, and resilience. Beside her was a placard that read ON THE 4TH AUG 2011 A MAN EJACULATED ON ME IN THIS CARRIAGE. TODAY I'M STANDING UP AGAINST SEXUAL HARASSMENT EVERYWHERE.

Opening our eyes is the first step. Once we understand the scale and severity of the problem, we then have to act—and to see success we need to act together. The project entries we've received overwhelmingly suggest that, as with other forms of abuse and bullying, perpetrators of street harassment are often able to get away with it because others simply turn a blind eye.

2 P.M. on a main road a man groped me. When I screamed no one bothered to help, they all looked away as he casually walked on.

Standing on crowded bus in summer, seated man puts his hand up my skirt. I shout for help. Not one person responds.

Sat on train, man sits puts hand up my skirt [and] tries to convince me to go with him. Loudly protest, no one helps.

Crowded bus stop, loudly invited by man to "sit on his face" . . . No one reacted. I was 14.

To ignore what is happening is to be complicit, which perpetuates and exacerbates the problem by effectively telling harassers that they are free to act with impunity.

A guy leaned out of his car and shouted that the guy behind me was going to rape me. The guy behind me laughed.

The impact of such inaction lasts long after the incident itself. Not just by offering sanction to harassers but also by suggesting to victims that the abuse they have received is somehow deserved and their problem to deal with. When I walk down the street and a man shouts sexually explicit comments about my breasts or what he'd like to do to me—often referring to me as an object ("Look at the tits on *that*!")—it's not the comments that sting the longest but the memory of the people on the other side of the road who kept walking, diligently scrutinizing their shoes.

As one woman described:

[I was] cornered on a train in a two-person seat by a man who came on very strong and touched me, which I repeatedly, loudly objected to. When he refused to let me out for several minutes I tried to escape past him feeling incredibly scared—and he grabbed my behind with both hands. I screamed at him in shock and disgust and went to sit with a family further down the carriage, tears in my eyes. Everyone in the carriage had seen and heard what he'd done and how I protested. He continued to sit in the same seat and no-one reacted in any way. I went home feeling terrified, violated and dirty.

It's not always easy for passers-by to intervene, just as it's not always easy for women being harassed to stand up for themselves. The same complicating factors may apply: the location and nature of the attack, the possibility that the perpetrator might be armed or become violent, and the danger of being outnumbered. But frequently another pedestrian or commuter *could* safely step in. And all too often they *don't*—perhaps simply because it's a bit embarrassing or they think it's none of their business.

The simple act of sharing stories and raising awareness gives both women and men the strength and the impetus to make changes. Holly Kearl, the founder of Stop Street Harassment, says:

Street harassment is often an invisible problem or one that is portrayed as a joke, a compliment or the fault of the harassed person. In reality, it's a human-rights violation that restricts harassed persons' access to public spaces and the resources there. The best way to raise public awareness about the reality of street harassment is by sharing personal stories, and so initiatives like #ShoutingBack are extremely valuable because they give people an opportunity to share their story as an individual, but also as a group, to show how pervasive this problem is.

There are a lot of myths that exist about street harassment, including that it's a compliment and that women secretly love it. The thousands of stories shared on #ShoutingBack disprove those myths. I doubt that anyone who reads story after story about men groping, grabbing, flashing, stalking, or making sexually explicit comments at women can see it as anything other than gender violence and the human-rights violation that it is.

The sense of solidarity that also comes with sharing stories can make a huge difference, because women no longer feel they're standing up to street harassment alone. One woman wrote to tell us she was introduced to the project Web site by a friend and read reams of women's stories . . .

▸ Then on the 4th of November while out running on a reasonably busy street in broad daylight, I was stopped and asked for directions . . . I obliged and as I showed him on the map on my phone he looked down my top, made a sleazy remark then grabbed my breast. On protesting he muttered [that] I'd "a nice pair, what did [I] expect?"

The usual anger-but-not-quite-sure-what-to-do-about-it was replaced with something else . . . I'd read enough versions of same story just a few days previously.

I calmly took his registration and went straight to the police. I was surprised by how seriously they took it. They thanked me for coming in! They agreed with me—this guy was out of order and his behavior was not ok! He's been charged and I'm realistic, it may or may not make it to court. DNA tests are still pending. There were no other witnesses.

Regardless, thanks to this website and a couple of well-trained police officers, there is one guy who got the message, it is not ok to see women as there solely for your sexual gratification.

The woman who sent in this entry was unusual in having reported the incident. Yet according to the United States Department of Justice,

Sexual assault is any type of sexual contact or behavior that occurs without the explicit consent of the recipient.

Included in the examples listed as part of the definition is the euphemistic "fondling." Under the Department of Justice's definition then, every one of the thousands of women who have reported being touched, stroked, grabbed, or groped in public spaces was the victim of sexual assault.

Yet we are living in a society that not only downplays and accepts this crime but also deliberately normalizes it—telling women not to overreact, not to make a fuss out of nothing, or even to be glad of the attention. It is only when you really spell out the definition that the realization begins to dawn, even for many of the victims. Many women contacted the project after I wrote about the similar UK legal definition of sexual assault in the *Huffington Post*. Their comments testified to the great anomaly of our passivity to the crime.

Never thought about it before, but have now worked out that I've been sexually assaulted at least five times.

One of the blokes put his hand up my skirt and grabbed my crotch! Groping is too common on a night out! Never gets reported because it happens so often!

It seemed minor, scared the hell out of me though. I was crying by the time I got home.

We have created a social disconnect between the offense and its perception that is so strong even its own victims deny it. Which, of course, creates the ideal environment for such crimes to flourish.

But things are changing. The very fact of us sharing our experiences of street harassment and protesting against it has begun to spark a movement to shout back. The British Transport Police has used thousands of the accounts collected by the Everyday Sexism Project to help them retrain two thousand officers for Project Guardian, an initiative specifically designed to fight back against these crimes and their normalization. Within a mere two months of the launch of the campaign, it had already increased reporting of sexual offenses on public transport by 20 percent and detection of offenders by 32 percent. In just a single week of action, fifteen people were arrested.

For every woman who manages to stand up and say no, there's another harasser who will think twice the next time. For every bystander who intervenes, there's another crack in the culture of complicity. For every report made, either to an individual company or to the police, there's another perpetrator who will face consequences for his actions.

It's not always easy to stand up. The moment I confronted my aggressors is stamped on my memory so clearly because of the sheer shaking terror I felt. It's not always safe to shout back, for a victim or a passer-by. But across a variety of situations, there is a range of actions both victims and observers can take.

On Kearl's Stop Street Harassment Web site, it is suggested that indirect interventions can be the safest and most effective. Bystanders don't have to confront the harasser directly—they can also check in with the victim, simply stepping toward her and asking if she is okay. Sometimes, distracting the harasser with a simple request for directions, or the time, can signal in a calm and neutral way that somebody else is aware of and active in the situation, making the perpetrator feel less of a sense of impunity and sometimes giving the victim time to move away.

Many victims' accounts to the Everyday Sexism Project explained that their own silence often arose from a sense of shame or embarrassment. If you can find the strength to speak up, one way to win support from dithering bystanders is to clearly name what has happened and identify your aggressor—another clever tactic suggested by Stop Street Harassment. "Man in the red T-shirt, please don't touch my legs" is a strong statement that draws attention and focus onto the perpetrator instead of the victim and clearly indicates what the situation is to those around you, who may then feel more empowered to step in.

It may be helpful to draw inspiration from the strength of other brave and brilliant women who have stood up to their harassers in witty and wonderful ways—and there is no shortage of them reporting to the Everyday Sexism Project! Sometimes it's just the way they describe the incident:

Drive-by "SLAAAAAG!" from white van man this morning. Speed of vehicle precluded discussion on gender politics.

I'm currently traveling round Europe & am amazed by the amount of men that are compelled to tell me I have large breasts. It's as if they think I need a reminder or something.

Was just told to "cheer up" by two men. When I didn't, they yelled "slag" and "dirty little cunt." This didn't cheer me up.

Every time I get cat-called and respond with a finger wave, the aggressors explode in anger. Feeling insulted? You don't say!

Then there are the brilliant comebacks . . .

Guy at bus stop "I've a spare room, you can live with me." "Dude. Women are not Pokemon, roaming in the wild. I got a place."

Getting rated a "7.5" whilst in a queue because I have a "great arse." I rated him back as a −2 as he's a chauvinistic pig.

Once had a guy ask "Would you mind telling me your bra-size?" I replied "No, but tell me first how big your cock is." Amazingly he was shocked and found MY comment highly inappropriate.

Guy on train after I asked him to move his bag off seat: "Why don't you grab my cock?" Me: "I didn't bring any tweezers."

Last time a man called me a bitch for ignoring his unwelcome advances, I barked at him loudly and repeatedly until he ran away.

And my all-time favorite . . .

A man once pointed out loudly that I have big boobs. I looked down and screamed like I'd never seen them before.

In situations where it doesn't feel safe to act in the moment, it is often possible to report the harassment later, especially if it happens in a particular location or the perpetrator is clearly working for a specific company. The reports we've had of women reacting in this way have been overwhelmingly positive, with almost all experiencing not just an attentive response but also, like I did, a sense of gratitude and willingness to take action from the companies involved. I interviewed one woman who had reported a group of builders to their construction company after they shouted sexual abuse at her while she walked with an eight-year-old child. Two days later she was surprised by a knock on the door. It was the co-owner of the company, holding an enormous bouquet of flowers and a card.

[The owner had] had a heated discussion with the men involved . . . and told them it had to stop. She wanted me to go back with her so they could apologize in person. I declined, but I appreciated the sentiment, and how seriously my complaint had been taken. She told me that she had pleaded with them to think of their own wives and daughters before making "comments" to, or about, women on the street. She was horrified.

Sometimes the simplest arguments are the strongest. As obvious as it might sound, just forcing people to stop and think about the reality of what they are doing and what it means can go a long way toward challenging received ideas about entitlement and anonymity in public spaces. One story we received illustrated this to perfection and demonstrated the value of a simple, strong reaction to street harassment when it is possible.

▸ **Walked past a group of men—one of them started shouting at me: "Whoah! Come on darling!" and whistling, egged on by his friends. Crossed the street, went right up to him and said: "Yes?" He looked** really puzzled and the laughter stopped. I said: "Well, you obviously wanted my attention. Here I am—what did you want to say to me?" He looked embarrassed then and sort of turned and shuffled away. I felt like the strongest person in the world.

Chapter 6

Women in the Media

She made a mean beef Stroganoff, followed her husband from job to job and took eight years off from work to raise three children.

Opening of the New York Times *obituary for rocket scientist Yvonne Brill, 2013*

Vital Statistics

Only 28 percent of speaking parts in the 100 most successful films of 2012 were female (fewer than in 2007).

–Stacy L. Smith et al., "Gender Inequality in 500 Popular Films," Annenberg School for Communications & Journalism, University of Southern California, 2013

Just 4 percent of directors and 12 percent of writers of the 100 most successful films of 2012 were female.

–Smith, "Gender Inequality"

Nearly a third (31 percent) of female characters in the 100 most successful films of 2012 were shown partially naked (compared to just 9 percent of male characters).

–Smith, "Gender Inequality"

80 percent of the reviewers and authors of books reviewed in the *New York Review of Books* in 2013 were men.

–VIDA: Women in Literary Arts, 2014

Only 21 percent of the "notable deaths" reported in the *New York Times* in 2012 were women.

–*Mother Jones*, 2013

37 percent of staffers in U.S. newsrooms are women.

–American Society of News Editors Newsroom Census, 2014

Just 9 percent of sports editors and 16 percent of sports columnists in the US are women.
–Institute for Diversity and Ethics in Sport, 2013

Life according to music videos, men wear suits & women gyrate topless & decorate them. I am no man's or woman's decoration.

There I was thinking it was fat, sugar and lack of exercise! Cosmo reveals "your co-workers are making you fat."

No wonder I never watch commercial TV, 1 ad break & I'm told to worry if my feet are scabby, my legs hairy, my skin spotty.

Working on a TV program called "Hollywood's Best Film Directors." Twenty-nine episodes. Twenty-nine men.

A council candidate told by radio show panel is full (all men) but asked would she appear on a women's issues panel?

Thank god, an all-male panel show. Finally, after all our waiting, TV totally owes us this.

Throughout history, everything that we do—everything we believe about ourselves and other people, everything we plan for and work toward—has been shaped by stories. The stories we hear as children help us to imagine and dream what the future might hold. The stories we learn as we grow up help us to work out our place in the world. And the stories we tell when we are adults determine the legacy we leave behind.

So it is impossible to underestimate the impact of the fact that still, in 2016, women's stories are not being told. That women, in the stories we hear, are still portrayed as so incredibly limited, pigeonholed, and stereotyped. And that so very few of those stories are told in a woman's voice.

As an alien coming to Earth for the first time and taking the media as your reference point for how the human race works, you could be forgiven for coming away with an incredibly distorted picture. The 28 percent of speaking roles given to women in 2012's biggest films might give you the erroneous impression that the females of the species are significantly outnumbered by their male counterparts, though the sexualization of almost one in three of those roles would leave you in little doubt of their function.

The enormous age gap between the stars (disproportionately male, leading you perhaps to conclude that men are either higher functioning or simply more important) and their leading ladies would suggest a marital gulf of at least ten to twenty years. Meanwhile, your understanding of the optimal age of females for reproduction would be deeply skewed by the idea that a woman like Angelina Jolie could have given birth at the age of one (to Colin Farrell, who plays her son in *Alexander*) while a woman like Francis Conroy (Peter Krause's mother in *Six Feet Under*) must have done so at just twelve.

If nothing else, you'd come away with the certain understanding that there are *very* few circumstances in which it is acceptable to see an older woman on the silver screen. You'd realize that women's looks are the crucial factor in defining their value, that black women are to be sexualized and exoticized and disabled women pitied and portrayed as "strivers," that lesbian and bisexual women's entire lives revolve obsessively around their sexuality, and that fat women are generally reserved to provide the butt of a joke. You'd discover that women can be virgins or whores but rarely stray into the territory in between, that we despise one another's victories and find it impossible to resist bitching behind each other's backs, and that in order to achieve success we are either strident, masculine, and mean or sexual and manipulative. You'd see that sexual violence is our greatest danger but also a strangely erotic and titillating fate, and that the main function and purpose of our lives revolves entirely around finding an appropriate mate.

Though we consider it a single entity, the role played by the media in men's and women's lives is immeasurably different. For men, it largely reflects their reality, albeit a polished and aspirational version, and with the caveat that some groups are still underrepresented. We see men of all ages and sizes and shapes, in all different kinds of roles, usually at the center of their own story. But for women, the available roles are far narrower and less realistic. The media is both harshest critic and adoring fan—it reflects not our reality but rather a constant and suffocating stream of unattainable ideals and derided failures, dehumanizing sexualization and crushing reminders of our own marginalization and inadequacy.

A staggering number of films still fail to meet the incredibly low standard of the Bechdel Test, which merely requires them to include two named female characters who talk to each other about any subject other than a man. According to the Bechdel Web site, of the 5,506 movies in its database in 2013, an extraordinary 48 percent fail to meet these ludicrously simple criteria. Failures include mainstream Hollywood blockbusters like *The Internship, A Million Ways to Die in the West, The Avengers, Jack Reacher, Killer Joe, Men in Black 3,* and *Star Trek: Into Darkness* (which should get a bonus point for an underwear scene so blatantly gratuitous even the writer subsequently saw fit to make a public apology for it).

Small wonder, then (according to a study by the University of Southern California), that only four of the top one hundred U.S. films of 2012 were directed by women. The same report showed that women made up just 17 percent of all directors, producers, and writers on such films, translating to five men for every woman working behind the camera.

And the impact of the misrepresentation starts young—when the Geena Davis Institute on Gender in Media looked at gender in family films released in the United States (that is, those specifically aimed at children), it found that male characters outnumbered females three to one, a ratio that has remained the same since 1946. Gender stereotypes are also rife in these early thought-shaping films—from 2006 to 2009, the research found that "not one female character was depicted in G-rated family films in the field of medical science, as a business leader, in law, or politics."

Remember the young girl who wrote about early aspirations?

We were asked what we wanted to be. I wanted to say a doctor but didn't because I thought girls couldn't be doctors. I was 4 years old.

Later, of course, these girls—and boys—grow up to become consumers of the music industry, to learn that women are, almost without exception, required to bare as much skin as possible when singing, despite the lack of correlation to their vocal performance, while male artists, remaining fully clothed themselves, strew writhing, bikini-clad women around the sets of their videos like Christmas decorations.

They'll grow up with lyrics like those of The Wanted's "Walks Like Rihanna," reminding them that their accomplishments are meaningless without an ability to shake their booty. They'll hear songs about sluts and songs about players and see the bodies of women of color in particular being used as disposable, dehumanized objects. They'll learn that low self-esteem is the sexiest thing about a girl, that dangerous and volatile relationships are the most desirable, and that girls should blame themselves if they're badly treated. And they will also learn, with pointed clarity, what is expected of them.

Some musicians, like Flo Rida, are at least subtle enough to slightly mask their sexual demands with metaphors about blowing whistles. Others, like Tyga, with "Rack City," are more explicit, using the word 'bitch' 45 times and describing sexual domination over strippers and grandmothers alike.

And in everything from Justin Timberlake's "Tunnel Vision" to Robin Thicke's "Blurred Lines" they will see completely naked women surrounding the fully clothed men as they sing about how certain they are that their sexual partners want it (it sounds like they're trying to convince themselves if you ask me). Some singers don't even bother *pretending* to consider the woman's consent—in the song "U.O.E.N.O." by American hip-hop artist Rocko, featuring Future and Rick Ross, Ross raps about putting "molly" (a colloquial term for the drug MDMA/Ecstasy) in a woman's champagne before taking her home and 'enjoying' her without her knowledge.

The titillating depiction of women in positions of vulnerability is also a worryingly frequent trope, from videos like "Hold On, We're Going Home" by Drake (which sees a helpless, doll-like woman wearing only white underwear being violently kidnapped) to "The Show Must Go On" by Famous Last Words (which shows an unconscious woman tied to a chair, the tension ramped up with close-up shots of her terrified face before she's strangled to death).

Both videos strikingly perpetuate the sort of gender stereotypes the project has found to be rife among young people. The former makes explicit that the woman has been kidnapped because she is considered to be property; she is being taken to wreak revenge on her male partner. Meanwhile, the men storming to her rescue are hypermasculinized, armed to the teeth, and blowing things up during a violent gunfight.

In sexy cutaway scenes she is a terrified, vulnerable victim; we see her trying to escape, her bottom wobbling above her garters, before being thrown to the floor by her captor—who then aggressively lies on top of her, suggesting a potential rape scenario. A clear link is drawn for boys between loving a woman, owning her, and acting with extreme aggression to protect that right of ownership, while the woman's worth is clearly tied to her sexuality.

The "Famous Last Words" video portrays the male singer with a split personality; we see him battling against an inner demon who goads him into attacking a woman. The video does at least imply that the violence is wrong but still plays into damaging myths about masculine violence as aroused by women (suggesting this is inherent and difficult to control). And that violence is still presented in a melodramatic, sensational manner.

Such undertones are not niche- or genre-specific. Robin Thicke's "Blurred Lines"—which refers repeatedly to something resembling a rape scenario—hit Number 1 and got untold airplay, although it explicitly mentions tearing a female sexual partner in half.

We hear that the singer *thinks* he knows she wants it but never that she has consented; he goes on to decide that he *is* going to have sex with her anyway, and later must ominously check whether she can breathe . . .

In One Direction's 2014 hit "Steal My Girl," we're reminded again about male ownership of female partners. The lyrics refer to "my girl" whom others want to "steal", while the singer insists they will have to find a different girl because she is his property. Talk about influence—the band has millions of tween fans worldwide.

Again and again, violence and intimacy are linked. "Hit the Floor" by Bullet for My Valentine describes the singer approaching a woman from behind as she walks home; he shocks her by touching her unexpectedly, asks her not to scream, and comes down on her with heavy force when she does. In "Breezeblocks," meanwhile, Alt J cheerfully remind their listeners that any woman wishing to run away can be pinned down with breezeblocks. Problem solved!

I know I've said it before, but I could go on, and on, and on.

The significance of misogyny in music culture is twofold. First, it's extremely explicit—both lyrically and in the accompanying visual imagery, which is highly effective and easily absorbed; these videos, with their close-ups on the writhing, naked, available, sexualized female form, send a very clear message. Second, this particular form of culture is immediately accessible, from televisions to Web sites to mobile phones, making it a direct line of communication with teenage boys in particular.

Collectively, songs like those above—and the videos produced to sell them—with their casual stereotypes and sexualization and derogatory put-downs of women, form the background noise that seeps into our consciousness without us necessarily even realizing we're absorbing it. Just like *FHM* and *Maxim* and all those publications that exist purely to send the message, loud and clear, that women are there as sexual objects to titillate and amuse and entertain and satisfy men. We rarely stop to think about how it must feel, as little girls, to grow up surrounded by this kind of wallpaper.

▸ I was in the supermarket with my 7-year-old daughter. She was looking for a comic and spotted the lads' mags—a woman in the front wearing a thong and sticking her bum into the camera. My daughter looked embarrassed and made a comment about why that lady isn't dressed. So we went along the shelf and turned all offending magazines over. It gave her the giggles.

There is a feverish desperation to portray any young woman as a sexual object among a large swathe of the media that is so powerful as to transcend both relevance and respect. (A fact epitomized by the incredible University of Southern California finding that of female characters age thirteen to twenty in the one hundred most successful films of 2012, 56 percent were shown fully or partially naked.)

In the recent past, this rabid tunnel vision led to the portrayal of Amanda Thatcher (in mourning and speaking at her grandmother's funeral), Amanda Knox (on trial for murder), and Reeva Steenkamp (shot dead by her partner) as sexual objects for mass consumption. All—regardless of their very different reasons for being in the spotlight—were paraded in countless photographs for the delectation of the tabloid readers. Within minutes of her taking the lectern to speak in her grandmother's memory, nearly twenty high-definition images of the "elegant Miss Thatcher" littered the *Daily Mail* Web site. As soon as news of Meredith Kercher's death broke, slavering tabloids coined the moniker "Foxy Knoxy" for Amanda Knox; and when Steenkamp was murdered, the *Sun* ran a full-front-page photograph of her in a bikini alongside a lurid, titillating headline and a "Blade Runner" subhead that didn't even mention her name. (Betting company Paddy Power would later offer odds on the trial's outcome in the "novelty bets" section of its Web site, using the tagline, "Money back if he walks.")

We're repeatedly given the same animalistic, one-dimensional view of women afforded by the same obsessive lens. It's this worn-out single setting that saw our finest athletes covering themselves in glory at the Olympic Games only to be depicted across the media as "beauties," "angels," "radiant blondes," and "babes," and being grilled about their prerace beauty regimens with the same intensity that male athletes were asked about their technique. The same obsessive template that mysteriously sees only white, thin, long-haired blond girls (who happen to show off their toned midriffs as they leap in the air with delight) gaining top exam results year after year.

The same frame that focuses with morbid glee on the bright blue eyes of three-year-old Madeleine McCann year after year while scores of less photogenic and nonwhite children quietly go missing and are quietly found or mourned.

In the relatively new world of online media, where outlets find themselves scrambling for fresh headlines every few hours instead of every day, there's been an explosion in the practice of creating "news articles" out of the dress, behavior, and appearance of female celebrities. Here Web sites trample over one another to "report" the appearance of an actress in a low-cut top or a reality show star's barely noticeable weight gain, all in the name of easy "filler" pieces to provide new links and headlines. Women's individual body parts are expounded with such detachment that they become almost entirely dehumanized—and occasionally even strut their newfound autonomy on the red carpet, if you believe this surreal *Mirror* headline from 2013: "Rihanna's boobs go to fashion week in a lovely long red dress." All the while, repeated and reinforced, is the message that a woman is valued and judged solely on her looks.

What's worse is the way that women of color are portrayed and judged in the media through an entirely different lens, which often characterizes them as "angry" or "scary," "exotic" or strange, sexualized, or dirty. While certain hairstyles worn by black women for generations are described as "ghetto" or "ratchet," white women who appropriate them are suddenly praised for fresh, high-fashion breakthroughs. When white women draw attention to their bottoms they are praised for being sexy or subversive, but when women of color do the same it becomes offensive, or unacceptably raunchy. When actress Zendaya wore her hair in [dreads] to the Oscars, one of the hosts of E!'s *Fashion Police* program commented: "I feel like she smells like patchouli oil." (Another added: "or weed.") Yet the same host praised a similar hairstyle sported by white TV personality Kylie Jenner, describing it as "edgy." Sometimes the comparisons are even more blatant, as in a 2015 *Cosmopolitan* feature on beauty trends that were either "gorgeous" or needed to "die." Almost every "gorgeous" trend was illustrated with a photo of a white celebrity, but a significant number of the looks labeled "R.I.P." were illustrated with images of women of color. (*Cosmopolitan* apologized, claiming some of the images had been taken out of context.) When *Seventeen* magazine ran a fashion spread labeled "Navajo," it featured a white model wearing a printed sweater and feathered necklace instead of featuring a Navajo woman or introducing its readers to any real sense of Native American culture. A piece in *The New York Times*, which chose to focus on the "body image" of top female tennis players, mused over Serena Williams's "large biceps" and "mold-breaking muscular frame" even as she neared the Wimbledon finals, comparing her to other (mostly white) players and proclaiming: "Her rivals could try to emulate her physique, but most of them choose not to." The piece went on: "For many, perceived ideal feminine body type can seem at odds with the best physique for tennis success," and comments about Williams's "muscular frame" were contrasted with a quote from Agnieszka Radwanska's coach, declaring it a conscious decision to: "keep her as the smallest player in the top 10. Because, first of all she's a woman, and she wants to be a woman." Meanwhile in the UK, the *Daily Mail* ran an article pitting Williams against Russian player Maria Sharapova, describing it as: "The most bitter catfight in tennis," and claiming: "One's a human volcano, the other's an ice queen." The toxic combination of media sexism and racism was perfectly encapsulated by the piece, which declared: "Williams, 33, is the more physically powerful, with a ferocious temper. . . . However, she cannot compete with Sharapova's media-friendly combination of blonde Siberian beauty and sponsor-friendly image control."

And it's not just the messages *about* women that are so damaging, but the messages the media sends *to* us as well. Never has a more apt photograph been sent to the Everyday Sexism Project than the one someone tweeted showing a clear disposal container full of discarded magazines with a sign saying SHED YOUR WEIGHT PROBLEM HERE.

In the world of women's magazines, the "flaws" of women's natural bodies are headline stories week in, week out. Hence such dazzling anatomical facts as "She's got a belly," placed above a picture of Kelly Brook bending over momentarily on a beach, becomes front-page news.

"OMG! What has Madge done to her face?" shrieks a caption below a zoomed-in, unflattering picture of Madonna. Never mind that when it was taken she was speaking passionately to a concert audience about women's rights to education worldwide and the life-and-death struggle of girls in Pakistan to go to school. Who cares? She's *clearly* had work done, right?

There's a sort of shorthand you pick up as you wade through women's magazines, a bit like the one you eventually realize is there to help you fathom cryptic-crossword clues ("confused" might indicate an anagram, for example, while "goes back" signals a word spelled backward, etc.). Gradually you come to understand that words like "curvy" and "confident" and "full-figured" are code for "fatty" and "fatty" and "fatty"; that "brave" means "HA! Dumped!" and "flaunted" means "happened to wear while ten miles away from and completely oblivious of our long-lens paparazzo."

So a headline like "Brave Khloe steps out looking curvy as

she puts split behind her" translates to: "Try to restrain your glee—Khloe piles on the pounds as she's dumped by her boyfriend!" Of course what we're really looking at is more likely "Khloe happens to turn sideways slightly as she walks past camera after popping out in varied company for the past few days; her relationship's perfectly fine, thanks for asking."

Weight is a major fixation. The tiniest fluctuations are picked apart, scrutinized, and swamped with intense and lascivious commentary—whatever it takes to find enough text to run alongside several close-up photographs. And there's a vindictive joy in being able to draw criticism.

"Supermodel Kate eats pizza shocker" is a genuine headline from one mag, while another cattily declares, beneath a photograph of Cara Delevingne wearing no makeup, "There is a God!"

An article purportedly praising Sharon Stone's looks is betrayed by the breathtakingly snarky headline: "How to look amaze at 105."

The sentiment extends to a whole world of *vital* breaking analysis of female celebs, from those "circle of shame" pictures damning their shoddy unplucked eyebrows and sweat stains (the horror!) to entire features lamenting their ill-considered outfits and physical "flaws." "What a beautiful embroidered kaftan, Ashley" starts one such piece, before cackling, "Shame you're not anywhere near a beach—and next time wear a bra!"

There's also a nasty classist undertone sneering beneath these features, like the one in the *Daily Mail* that smirks: "Tulisa really is a 'chav in a tracksuit' as she heads to Tesco in sportswear."

And then there's the dual Holy Grail of weight loss and

boyfriend, the importance of which is emphasized by the sheer desperate urgency of these headlines:

NEW BODY PANICS!

Gemma's SOS to Josie: "HELP ME GET THIN"

COLEEN'S BODY PANIC: Extreme yoga and juice diet to be size 8 in three weeks "I'm terrified of getting fat again!"

KELLY'S SECOND THOUGHTS: I worry I shouldn't have let Thom go!

Frustrated Lauren: Why hasn't Jake proposed?

And the inevitable sensationalist conflations of the two:

KELLY COMFORT EATS AS DANNY FAILS TO COMMIT

"I've got my perfect body—now I can't wait to marry Jake!"

"Kieran won't fancy me if I keep bloating!"

Having absorbed the message that romantic success is directly proportional to weight loss, women are ready to be assaulted by a baffling barrage of commandments, directives, and mandates: what to eat and what not to eat, what to wear and what to avoid wearing at all cost and—most crucial of all—how, EXACTLY, to give the perfect boyfriend-pleasing, man-snaring blow job.

The most frustrating thing about all this is the unadulterated, blatant hypocrisy.

Women's magazines are experts at creating precisely those hysterical "problems" they claim to teach their readers to "fix" and thus profit from in the meantime. And, as time goes on, the list of fabricated defects of the female body becomes increasingly ludicrous as new problems are desperately conjured up in order that reams of copy can be spun teaching us how to diet, what to buy, and how many sit-ups constitute sufficiently self-despising penance for the crime of being normal. (If you didn't think things could get any worse than the ridiculous invention of "cankles"—fat ankles—you clearly weren't prepared for the advent of the even more stupid "kninkles"—knee wrinkles. I'm not joking—Google it.)

The hypocrisy only deepens. Some women's magazines and media outlets, particularly in the last decade, have begun to leap, posturing and preening, onto a bandwagon of faux concern about eating disorders and body-image problems while simultaneously continuing to peddle the quick-fix extreme diets, airbrushed underweight fashion shoots, and obsessive calorie-counting features that perpetuate them. "Curvy girls really do have more fun!!" they squeal, in an issue that criticizes a celebrity for daring to have white bread in her cupboard and extols the virtues of the all-kelp detox to "fight the flab." "Curvy beauties hit the beach!" they proclaim, featuring Jessica Alba, or Katy Perry, or another celeb who happens to have worn a top in which her boobs are visible but who otherwise remains slimmer than the slimmest of the magazine's readers.

Perhaps the most flagrant example of this came in June 2012, when two editions of *Now* magazine hit newsstands at the same time. One was a regular issue, featuring a front-page image of model Abbey Clancy beside the melodramatic headline, "Oh no! Scary Skinnies," and a caption that warned, "Girls starving to be like her." Inside, an article claimed that Clancy had become so dangerously thin she was a role model for damaging pro-anorexia Web sites. The second issue, which appeared directly alongside it on the shelf, was the *Now Celebrity Diet Special.* This too featured Clancy on the cover, this time beside the headline, "Bikini body secrets . . . The stars' diet and fitness tricks REVEALED." Yes. In the *same week* they claimed that emulating her look could make young women dangerously ill, they used the promise of helping readers look like her to sell copies.

To be such a huge part of the problem is one thing; to pretend to be part of the solution while still pushing the same unattainable, unrealistic "standards" is immeasurably worse.

And it's not just in matters of body image that magazine and fashion industry irresponsibility hits women where it hurts. In a disturbing recent trend, designers and magazines use violence against women as a titillating theme for fashion spreads and photo shoots, because what says glamour like a beaten woman?

Less than a year after the horrific Delhi gang rape and murder case, the fashion photographer Raj Shetye published photographs depicting women fending off male attackers on buses in scenes clearly mimicking that of the infamous incident—but all attired in glamorous ball gowns, of course. *Vogue Italia* tried a similar technique in its April 2014 issue, depicting fashion-clad models as terrified and bloodied victims of domestic abuse. One lies dead and spread-eagled in a pool of her own blood while her male killer sits in the background. But hey, she's wearing Prada! Another "beauty" spread in Bulgarian fashion magazine *12* showed models sporting horrific injuries, from slit throats to acid mutilation.

Indeed, the depiction of fashion and beauty models as abused and beaten women is an inconceivably well-trodden tradition, from Guy Bourdin's images of dead and bloody models to a 2006 Jimmy Choo ad featuring a model's lifeless body being transported in the trunk of a car to be buried in the desert.

Many such spreads have been defended by their creators with the protestation that they were intended to raise awareness, but there is very little in the glamorization of violence, the artful, carefully lit bruises and perfectly slim spread-eagled limbs to substantiate the assertion. Whether intentionally or not, these advertisements can cause far more problems than they solve, as the deeply problematic title of the *12* magazine spread "Victims of Beauty" perfectly demonstrates. (Suggesting that an abused woman is a "victim" of her own beauty plays right into deeply harmful stereotypes about women's attractiveness driving men to distraction and provoking their passion and violence—the very myths that can help cause partner abuse in the first place.) What comes across instead is an ugly and greedy sense of exploitation, excused once again beneath a hypocritical and wafer-thin veneer of care.

Whether it is used as fodder for "controversial" discussions on panel shows, as clickbait for deliberately victim-blaming tabloid opinion pieces, or as gross titillation across fashion, news, and entertainment, the media uses sexual violence for its own ends again and again and can rarely be said to have victims' best interests at heart.

It doesn't help that the narrative voice running through all this inequality—the newspaper inches reporting and reflecting it, the opinion pieces analyzing it, and the talk shows discussing it—is also (you guessed it) heavily dominated by men. Only 37 percent of staffers in U.S. newsrooms are women, and a 2013 *Gawker* study found that, of the regular opinion columnists at the *New York Times,* the *Washington Post,* the *Wall Street Journal,* and four of the largest press syndicates (providing opinion columns for many of the nation's smaller newspapers), just 27 percent were women. A separate two-month study of *New York Times* front-page articles in 2013 found that only 19 percent of sources quoted were women.

In some specific areas, like sports journalism, the problem is even worse—just 2 women (1.09 percent) appeared among the 183 sports talk radio hosts on *Talkers* magazine's 2014 "Heavy Hundred" list.

The findings were echoed in the UK by a 2012 Women in Journalism study, which revealed that an enormous four out of five front-page stories were written by men, and 84 percent of those stories were dominated by a male subject or expert.

When women did appear, it was most likely to be in the capacity of window dressing: Kate and Pippa Middleton were by far the most frequently pictured women.

Naturally there follows a male-dominated influence on how stories are reported and opinions are shaped. This became gradually clearer and clearer in my own experiences with the media as the Everyday Sexism Project gained prominence. I've been told by newspaper photographers that their editors have sent them to take extra pictures because I'm young and blond, and they'll put in more pictures than words to keep the male readers happy. (I said I'd really rather the words.)

When the picture editor of one of the country's biggest

newspapers confidently tells you (presumably *after* reading the article about your quest for gender equality, which this picture is to illustrate) that the key thing is to make you look "as sexy as possible," you start to wonder about giving up altogether.

This media gender imbalance has particular relevance when the issues being reported directly affect women and their safety. It is this male-dominated sphere that has seen commentators deliberate over rape victims' guilt, male contributors argue vociferously against women's right to control their own bodies and reproductive systems, and all-male panels discuss issues like the impact of breast cancer on women. It is from this male prism that articles emerge like the 2014 piece in the *Bombay Times* listing "Bollywood's Favourite Rapists," arguing that rape scenes were used in the past to "stimulate and excite" and are perhaps now seen less in films because, since the advent of porn, "today's youth just doesn't watch cinema for titillation." The male gaze becomes the mainstream voice.

Consider the Canadian radio station that ran a recent poll asking listeners to vote on the question: "It's very controversial but do you think victims of sexual assaults share any blame for what happens?" Or the *Glenn Beck Program* ridiculing campus rape statistics with cross-dressing men acting out pick-up style scenarios before someone jumps out with a red "RAPE" arrow to claim victims were encouraged to overstate the problem.

The heavy male bias in newsroom staff and the sexist attitudes that often make their way onto our television screens and front pages also tend to shunt aside initiatives and news that would be considered progress toward equality. So, for example, instead of celebrating the achievement of Major Mariam al-Mansouri, the first female fighter pilot in the United

Arab Emirates, when it emerged that she had flown a successful mission in the campaign against the Islamic State, Fox News commentators instead used the opportunity to make sexist jokes. "The problem is, after she bombed it, she couldn't park it," said one, while another quipped, "Would that be considered boobs on the ground?" When the Russian cosmonaut Yelena Serova hit the headlines in the same month as she prepared to travel into space after years of expert training, journalists bombarded her with questions about how her parenting would suffer and how she would wash and style her hair in space. When Rona Fairhead CBE, Cambridge and Harvard graduate, British business ambassador, former chair and chief executive of the Financial Times Group, and nonexecutive director at HSBC and PepsiCo, was announced as the preferred candidate to lead the BBC Trust in 2014, the *Telegraph* headline read, "Mother of three poised to lead the BBC." And when Nicola Sturgeon was about to make history by becoming the first female first minister of Scotland, two major national newspapers ran front pages about the appointment: One chose a headline about her "baby hopes," and the other featured analysis of her fashion transformation from "death row hair and awful trouser suits" to being "sleek as an otter."

The effect of this kind of sexist reporting on high-achieving women and their strides toward equality isn't only undermining, insulting, and demeaning to the subjects themselves. It also has a major impact on the aspirations and perceptions of young women, learning from the media that they will be judged on their looks regardless of their achievements, and that even their most groundbreaking successes will be acceptable fodder for sexist jokes. Multiple young women at university talks and events have told me they've reconsidered a career that might take them into the public eye for exactly this reason. We lose them before they even begin.

Part of the problem is that it is difficult to have a conversation about the impact of media on a culture awash with violence against women without being accused of leaping to hysterical conclusions, or violating the important right to free speech. On June 19, 2013, UK MP Caroline Lucas stood up in the House of Commons during Prime Ministers Questions to raise her concerns over media sexism. She pointed out that the government's own research showed a link between the media's portrayal of women as sex objects and greater acceptance of sexual harassment and violence against women. She also asked Prime Minister David Cameron whether he would support a ban on the *Sun* newspaper being sold on the parliamentary estate until Page 3 was scrapped.

In response, Cameron and the men on his front bench laughed at her. Chancellor George Osborne openly laughed as Cameron stood to address the question, and even Cameron—our prime minister—was unable to suppress a snigger as he finished his sentence. He refused to back Lucas's call for a ban and ignored her question about sexual harassment and violence against women.

Those front-bench men might say that a headline is harmless. They might scoff at the idea that what is printed in the newspaper, or played on the radio, or seen on the television or movie screen can have any real, measurable impact on women's lives and safety and self-image. Perhaps they think that way because it's difficult to realize, when the media reflects you and protects you and demonstrates your power and importance, how oppressive it can be when you're invisible. For a white, middle-aged, middle-class man who sees his own face staring back out of every page, every news bulletin, every panel show, it must be difficult to imagine being one of many women looking through paper after paper, magazine after magazine, watching film after film and rarely catching a glimpse of yourself.

So to help them understand, I'd like them to hear about some of those women and their stories. I'd like them to know about the fifteen-year-old girl who wrote that the media portrayal of women has made her feel that she will always be worthless unless boys find her "sexy," no matter what she achieves. I'd like them to hear from the gay women and trans women and older women and fat women and black women and women with particular accents who all told me they looked at the media and never saw or heard themselves. This made them feel invisible—and convinced them that to be treated as invisible was inevitable, and natural, and excusable.

▶ We so rarely see a woman play the lead in good films or TV shows, we're always in a supporting role, as women are throughout life really. As we age we don't even get that it seems.

▶ I'm 43 and have two teenage daughters . . . I was thinking back to the women who I watched on TV when I was young. Lucille Ball & Vivian Vance, both women in their 40s. Ms Cunningham on happy days. Jean Stapleton. *The Golden Girls.* Just a few examples. A person could write for a long time about the stereotypical roles they did or didn't play in their shows, but there is something physically striking about these women. They looked like normal everyday middle-aged women. So different from today's hyper-sexualized TV moms; Sofia

Vergara, any of the Desperate Housewives, Mary Louise Parker. I'm at the point where I don't want to turn on the TV or go to the movies anymore. I end up feeling terrible, insecure, inadequate, angry. It's not worth it.

I'd like them to know about a girl of just fourteen, who went to the same school as I did, who killed herself, it was suggested in part because of worries about the size and shape of her beautiful teenage body. They should hear that in his verdict, the coroner declared the fashion industry "directly responsible for what happened" and begged "particularly the magazines in the fashion industry, to stop publishing photographs of wafer-thin girls . . . because at the end of the day for their benefit, families like this must suffer . . . and until they control themselves it will continue."

And I'd really like them to hear this woman's story, most powerful because she told it in her own, brave words.

▸ I went to a nightclub in London last year for a friend's birthday celebrations. When we walked in I was really shocked to see the walls decorated with pornographic pictures pulled from lad's magazines and page 3. It was everywhere plastered all over the walls like wallpaper. It made me feel so uncomfortable but as it was a birthday party and nobody else was voicing any opinion on it I didn't say anything.

About an hour in I went to the toilet and didn't realize someone had followed me. He forced me into a cubicle, hit my head against the wall, which was also still covered in pornography, and sexually assaulted me. I was shouting but the music was too loud. I was struggling but he was too strong. All I could do was stare at the pictures of naked women on the wall he was pressing my face into.

I reported it but after a year of toing and froing nothing has been done really. One of the officers I spoke to even commented about the nightclub I was in in front of me to his colleague saying something along the lines of "oh isn't that the place with all the tits on the wall? Oh yeah, ha ha ha."

It makes me feel sick now when I think of it. And when I see pornographic pictures on newsagent shelves and mainstream media, just accepted like it's normal and okay. I wondered and still think to this day whether the man who did this to me would have done it if he wasn't raised in a country where women are advertised as products to be used. That's what I felt like that night, like an object, like I was just one of the women on the wall and that's what he wanted so he took it . . .

I just think how can we fight the other forms of sexism if every day the work is undone and undermined by the big booming message that screams from all of these "WOMEN YOU ARE NOTHING, YOU ARE WORTHLESS, YOU ARE HERE FOR OUR ENTERTAINMENT AND WE WILL USE AND TREAT YOU HOW WE WANT."

It's taking a lot of time and soul searching to try and make myself feel like a valid human being again, the law and legal systems have not helped me in doing that, I feel dismissed and ignored, yet again like a naked woman on the wall that's okay to use and abuse because I'm not a person. I really hope that one day I am really convinced that I am worth more than that, and that these voices from everywhere telling me I am not worthy of human status stop.

We live in a society where, like it or not, the media is controlled by men, for men. There's really no arguing about that. And this media—which perpetrates and perpetuates all manner of ill-advised ideals and norms—*does* affect women, and their lives, every day in every way. There's really no arguing about that either. And for the media to offer women more than a place as a commodity or a seat in the audience, something big is going to have to shift.

We need to have a conversation about the impact of the media on social attitudes and ideas about women—and it is a conversation that is loudly and angrily resisted, even when song lyrics refer explicitly to abusing women—even when a study in December 2011 showed it was virtually impossible to differentiate between the copy printed in men's mags and the words of convicted sex offenders, even when the hottest new games let players experience the vicarious virtual thrill of beating women senseless as part of the fun. And no: Of course this isn't to say that men's mags and song lyrics and video games turn innocent men into rapists, or that a single image of a scantily clad woman in a newspaper directly causes immediate harm to the viewer; of course it's not that simple. But these are not a few unique examples. This is a culture steeped in misogyny and the objectification and subjugation of woman—and yes, it does have a real impact, both on the way society sees and values women and on the way women feel about themselves.

How do I know? I know because there's a lot of documented evidence to this effect—particularly in relation to printed media. According to the Miss Representation campaign, for example, three out of four teenage girls feel depressed, guilty, and shameful after spending three minutes leafing through a fashion magazine.

Meanwhile the UK government's recent review into the sexualization of young people found "a clear link between consumption of sexualized images, a tendency to view women as objects and the acceptance of aggressive attitudes and behaviour as the norm." That report concluded: "Both the images we consume and the way we consume them are lending credence to the idea that women are there to be used and that men are there to use them." Then there's the recent UK government report showing that "between one third and half of young girls fear becoming fat and engage in dieting or binge eating" and "over 60 percent of girls avoid certain activities because they feel bad about their looks." It specifically cited media criticism of body weight combined with a lack of body diversity as a contributing factor.

Most of all, though, I know the impact is real because every week I receive project entries like this one:

▸ I look at images of women everywhere I go—in shop windows, on the sides of buses, in the tube, on the backs of newspapers, in magazines open in women's laps, on billboards, on videos, on TV, on the internet, popping up on my screen. They are all the same. They are taller than me, so much thinner than me, beautiful, flawless, perfectly made up. Many, many of them are revealing their long, toned legs right the way up to the tops, their flat, flawless stomachs in all their tiny, tiny glory, their ample cleavages looking perfect—not fat but perky. They are all that way—there aren't any that I can look at and think, she's a bit like me, that's OK. And they are everywhere. There is no escape. When I look in the mirror, I see myself and over the top I superimpose that image and all I see is the difference between us. When I meet new people I feel like they are looking through me to those differences too. She is everywhere and I can't escape her and I'm terrified my boyfriend compares her to me

constantly and finds me constantly wanting. Know the funniest part? I'm a very normal size. I'm not obese or fat, I have a pretty good figure. But it's nothing compared to hers. And she's everywhere.

From *Blurred Lines* to the Circle of Shame, men's mags to sexist advertisements, from the erasure of older women to the devaluation of women's voices in debate, the media, and those in power who turn a blind eye to it, have a lot to answer for. No, not in terms of direct cause and effect, but in terms of the creation and maintenance of a culture that fuels a continuum, from force-fed unattainable body image and mixed messages about "real" solutions for imaginary "problems" all the way through to teenage suicide and commonplace sexual assault. And, strangely enough, those who claim the media has no real impact on society or attitudes are the very same newspaper editors running proud campaigns against racism in football, or awareness-raising drives about breast cancer. They proudly trumpet the success of their campaigns on their front pages, so it seems their concept of their own impact on society must be very strangely selective indeed.

And when I say we need to talk about it, I'm not advocating censorship, or trying to stifle freedom of speech. I'm just asking that the speech of those affected by the media is heard as well as those who benefit and profit from it. I'm asking that we seriously consider taking steps to offset those negative effects, whether that means teaching young people about airbrushing and its impact, or considering age ratings for music videos like those already normal in the film industry, or appealing directly to filmmakers to think about how they represent women onscreen.

In 2014, U.S. media consumption was approximately fifteen hours per person per day. If that media continues to present women as aesthetically unrealistic, two-dimensional objects, more often than not sexualized, and to present violence against them as titillation and entertainment, it's not unreasonable to argue that we need to take a moment to look at the bigger picture. And maybe, just maybe, change the record.

Chapter 7

Women in the Workplace

I'm 21 and being asked at job interviews if I'm getting married, or pregnant.

Tweet sent to @EverydaySexism

Vital Statistics

Women working full-time in the United States in 2013 earned 78 percent of what men earned.
-American Association of University Women (AAUW), 2014

Over the past decade, the pay gap has remained stagnant, from 77 percent in 2002.
-National Women's Law Center, 2012

Among financial managers, the pay gap rises to 30 percent.
-AAUW, 2014

Just one year after college graduation, women are paid 82 percent of what their male counterparts earn.
-AAUW, 2012

Women hold just 5 percent of CEO positions at Fortune 500 companies.
-Catalyst, 2014

1 in 4 U.S. women reports experiencing workplace sexual harassment.
-Langer Research Associates for ABC News/*Washington Post*, 2011

When starting my first job as a welder 4 of the men went to the boss and told him he couldn't employ me because I was a girl.

Patient at work: "I don't want to see some uneducated woman, I want to see a real doctor."

A male boss said he'd "love to bend me over" and more, I reported it to female supervisor who said I was being "sensitive."

Saw my hours cut every time I complained to a manager about the co-worker who sexually harassed me.

Male customer demanded to see manager even though I was manager on duty. I said: you mean you want to see a man? He shut up.

Chatting to a man on the bus home, was fine until I said I was a scientist. Apparently that's not a job for women. He really didn't like it when I said my qualifications disagreed with him.

Perhaps to a greater extent than with any other form of sexism recorded by the project, reports on workplace sexism are often immediately and utterly denied. There are many understandable reasons for this. For a start, legislation on workplace discrimination is good, and, that being the case, many who would not dream of perpetrating find it very difficult to imagine others getting away with it. It often follows particularly covert and elusive patterns, too, frequently occurring in complete seclusion, in an empty corridor or a private office.

On the misguided assumption that perpetrators must be overt, lecherous monsters, people often believe that nothing could possibly be going on in their own workplace. Frequently there are significant power dynamics at play: Victims may feel unable to report the behavior of a senior colleague, manager, or boss; they may be afraid to risk losing their job or being branded "troublemakers" for speaking up. The inherent difficulty of proving a pattern of what can be very subtle behavior, often with little evidence, gets weighed against the cost of a legal claim and the potential resulting career suicide. Consequently, only a tiny number of cases ever go to court or even come to light.

In short, the vast majority of victims simply suffer in silence.

Besides the obvious, the trouble with this is that when the issue of workplace harassment does arise, it's often met with skepticism or a stubborn refusal to acknowledge that the problem exists at all. In addition to the usual dismissal, silencing, and disbelief, other gems that come up in such situations include:

If she's a strong enough woman to work in that industry, why didn't she just deal with it/knee him in the balls/give him a swift slap [delete as appropriate].

It's very easy for those signals to be misread in a friendly workplace environment—one person's encouraging hand on the shoulder is another's sexual harassment.

If you ban all flirty interaction between men and women in the workplace you'd be preventing a huge swathe of couples from ever getting together.

Such respondents would have it that workplace sexual harassers are poor bumbling buffoons who misread ambiguous situations and accidentally come on too strong—what's all the fuss about? They suggest that the issue is caused by little more than clumsy, misplaced attempts at flirting between peers. The strong implication is that the poor perpetrator has every reason to expect his advances may be welcomed and thus—whoops!—*misguidedly* oversteps the line.

This misleading idea of a man making a move in good faith (as if he really doesn't know it will be unwelcome) feeds into the narrative that women somehow "inadvertently" send out confusing "signals." And who can blame a poor hapless businessman for grabbing your crotch if you have the audacity to attend a meeting in a pencil skirt with your hair in a sleek chignon, you brazen hussy? Never mind that you're expected to look smart and presentable, or that so many other women have reported being sacked or sidelined for *not* wearing enough makeup. Never mind the countless magazines telling you that a businesswoman who doesn't dress in catwalk-chic, day-to-night, power-lipstick glory is an unsuccessful one. Never mind how mind-blowingly offensive it is to the average male to suggest he's too stupid to tell the difference between a well-pitched business plan and a come-hither seduction play. It's the same school of thought that starts squawking about "political correctness gone mad" every time there's an allegation of sexual harassment or inappropriate workplace behavior. How will anyone ever create a fun, cooperative workplace atmosphere, they ask frantically, if nobody can take a joke anymore? For God's sake, women, when will you give up this ridiculous insistence on bodily autonomy and START LEARNING TO

TAKE A COMPLIMENT? Unless you're living in a 1940s movie or a *Mad Men* fantasy, it's difficult to understand such reluctance to concede that in fact *most* people would quite like to work in an environment in which they aren't subjected to harassment.

It's laughable, really, to think that people have such a difficult time understanding the definition of *unwanted* sexual advances. Or the difference between consensual two-way banter and uninvited, sleazy sexual comments, or wandering hands. And for me—having worked in a brilliant office that happened to be all straight and all female yet somehow still mysteriously managed to remain full of laughter and camaraderie—it's really difficult to understand the argument that a lack of, ya know, "illegal" sexual harassment will somehow put the kibosh on All. Levity. And. Repartee. EVER.

Worse still, this "misunderstanding" narrative utterly fails to recognize two vital factors: the severity of the majority of the incidents and the inequality of power frequently reported between victim and perpetrator.

Believe me, across all the thousands of women who've told us their experiences of sexism in the workplace, not a single one of them could possibly have been a simple case of "misunderstanding." We aren't talking about a gentle "You look nice today" being met with outrage and a full-on banshee attack by an outraged, uncompromising female. We're talking about professional women being told to strip at office Christmas parties, told to sit on their bosses' laps if they want their annual bonus, seriously sexually assaulted by senior male colleagues, groped, grabbed, touched, licked, fondled against their will and subjected to regular vitriolic and offensive misogyny. We're talking about sixteen- and seventeen-year-old girls, in their first jobs, being accosted, groped, intimidated, and harassed on a regular basis by much older bosses, managers, and overseers. We're talking about regular and serious harassment, prejudice, and assault.

▸ Male colleague after putting the phone down to a client, "I wish I could stick my c**k in her ear and f**k some sense into her." I am not over exaggerating, this kind of thing is an everyday occurrence in my office, along with comments about the size of my breasts.

▸ My manager bullied and sexually harassed me over a period of a year. In December last year he grabbed my face with both his hands and licked around my lips as if he was kissing me. I pulled my lips tightly together to stop his tongue in my mouth. When he released my face I put my face in my hands and said go away. He then said "mop the wet patch up from under your chair woman."

▸ My first male boss repeatedly made passes at me on a work night out. Literally grabbing me and pushing his drunk, sweaty face at mine, trying to kiss me, hands all over me. I told him he was married, too old for me and I worked for him. He told me he didn't care, didn't care, and didn't care.

Many of the workplace experiences women relayed to the project were serious enough to constitute sexual assault. And yet, again and again, women also reported feeling unable to speak up, for a variety of complex reasons. For a start, there is often a power dynamic to consider. Innumerable entries recount stories of harassment perpetrated by senior male colleagues whose authority amplified the victims' feelings of fear and hopelessness and ultimately constituted a firm obstacle to formal complaint.

A guy at my work told me he'd get me fired if I didn't have sex with him. His brother was the boss.

It frequently being the case that there's no physical evidence of the crime, a victim may have to rely on her word being taken at face value. At best, an employer will take an allegation of harassment seriously, investigate fully, and ensure that the victim's job and career are not negatively impacted by the experience.

At worst, victims have reported losing their jobs and even being blacklisted within their industry. And in between is a murky gamut of risks, from being labeled a "troublemaker" to losing clients or opportunities and being marginalized and unable to properly advance in an existing career. Little wonder, then, that so many of the women who told us their stories felt unable to register complaint through official channels.

When I was 23 my ass was regularly pinched at work. I was too afraid of losing my job to report it.

I work in a male-dominated business environment, every off-site meeting one of the male team members try to get off with me, last time the Director tried to sleep with me, dragging me to his hotel room and leaving finger shaped bruises on my upper arm for over a week.

I didn't and won't report it to HR as I want to get on in my career and don't want to be sacked.

▶ Two senior male colleagues made jokes about my knickers . . . I had no idea why they were speculating about my knickers. I felt utterly humiliated and belittled. Handling the ensuing meeting was difficult. I felt ashamed, but they should have felt ashamed.

▶ I worked in a shoe store when I was 16. The manager walked past me one day and slapped my ass. It completely freaked me out, but I felt I would be ridiculed if I complained, so I didn't say anything.

And, so often unreported, the problem runs rampant. The project entries on workplace harassment testify to its complexity and the many different ways it can be manifest.

It starts at recruitment stages: from interview questions about pregnancy and family plans to inappropriate sexual demands. Before they even land the great pleasure of working in a job where they might face extreme sexism and harassment, women often must navigate a downright biased selection process.

▶ I worked at a top law firm in recruitment and have heard partners assessing female candidates according to their attractiveness.

▶ Male professor at a uni I used to work at doesn't hire "attractive women" to work in the laboratory as it would "distract the men from their work."

One of the most commonly reported problems in the recruitment process is phrased in various ways across the entries but remains essentially identical:

I'm 21 and being asked at job interviews if I'm getting married, or pregnant.

Sometimes there is no subtlety at all: One woman was simply asked outright for oral sex during an interview.

Once employed, many women notice quietly pervasive sexist norms within the working culture around them that serve to indirectly belittle and dismiss their value.

International visitors from company's head office came for a meeting at which I, the only female in management, had to report. I walked in with my report and they asked for coffee, white with two sugars.

Others describe their ideas being disregarded without consideration only to have male colleagues repeat them verbatim moments later to praise and reward.

A female friend of mine in an office meeting proposed a logical, simple solution to a recurring issue. Blank stares from the group and a "We've never done it that way" from the senior (female) manager. A male colleague then makes the exact same suggestion and the room nods enthusiastically and congratulates him on the idea.

Many reports to the project suggested that the simple fact of *being* a woman is frequently sufficient to warrant derision. We've heard some charming stories on this theme. One woman described a male colleague whose answer to any disagreement from his female peers was a loud announcement that they must be "on their period" because they were "all hormonal." (Cue one of the wittiest of all comebacks reported to the project: "If I had to bleed to find you annoying, I'd be anemic.") Another referred to a boss who'd told her, "I don't know what you are saying, I don't do woman speak."

Reports also suggest that this commonplace nonsensical assumption of *female* inferiority often translates into a similarly casual assumption of women's *professional* inferiority, whereby women are naturally perceived to be junior to their male colleagues. In fact, I received the following entry on the very first day I launched the Everyday Sexism Project:

▸ Me, "I'm an architect"
▸ Man, "An architectural assistant?"
▸ Me, "No . . . an architect"
▸ Man, "Oh . . . gosh . . . well done."

And since then similar stories have just kept coming.

▸ Told a guy where I work and he replied "Oh are you a receptionist?" "No actually, I'm a DNA scientist." *awkward silence*

An attorney described a conversation with a law student on work experience:

▸ . . . the student turns to me and asks: "So, are you Steve's secretary?" Seeing the look on my face he realizes his mistake and splutters: "Oh sorry, I mean his PA?"

Leading on from this gently insidious atmosphere of inequality is the steady drip, drip, drip of verbal harassment—and by that

I mean everything from inappropriate sexual questions to misogynistic comments to rape jokes.

▸ I am a computer scientist and work at one half of Oxbridge. I'm in my 30s, have a doctorate, a good number of independent publications and several years' experience. My male head of department refers to me as a "clever girl."

▸ In an office that I used to work in, I have been told I am a prude by a male colleague for not wanting to discuss my sex life or for being unhappy with listening to his sexual comments. Another colleague suggested that I should get a boob job as a joke and reacted badly when I told him I did not want to overhear his commentary on the appearance of all of the women in our office. One further male colleague told me that I obviously just didn't have a good body and this was the reason why I disagree with strip clubs.

When only a single instance of this kind of socially accepted dialogue is noted, it's perhaps difficult to appreciate the potential cumulative impact on a woman's work experience. But in fact the scope for injury is huge, not only because it can create a downright unpleasant and off-putting work environment but also because such discourse, given license, will generally increase over the course of time.

▸ Every day I am subjected to verbal humiliation from my male colleagues. They think that it is one big joke but it is extremely upsetting to be the victim of their jokes. If I am to wear a piece of new clothing, I get shouted at . . . This doesn't happen to any of the men in the office. Once they have finished shouting and silence falls, there is always one

man that will shout "show us where you piss from." They proceed to break out in hysterical laughter. This is incredibly embarrassing.

In fact, when researchers at the University of Melbourne reviewed 88 studies involving 74,000 women, they found that continual and repetitive low-level sexism in the workplace was just as harmful as overt incidents and could have serious psychological consequences. Writing in the journal *Psychology of Women Quarterly*, they referenced sexist jokes, repeated questions about women's competencies to perform their roles, lower pay, and fewer opportunities to progress. The researchers said: "The pervasiveness of these experiences makes them very harmful over time and with repeated exposure across situations. Our results suggest that organizations should have zero tolerance for low-intensity sexism the same way they do for overt harassment."

And of course there's also physical contact, groping, and assault. Many such incidents fall into the category of the unseen and vigorously doubted—almost (like the actions of Roald Dahl's atrocious Miss Trunchbull) too outrageous to believe. But much of this physical touching is also minimized or disguised as harmless, friendly fun. A bit of opportunistic fumbling around the office watercooler of a morning is, apparently, both flattering and hilarious. The odd office-party-breast-grope-tongue-down-the-throat-bottom-squeeze is a jolly good hoot! But let's face it: "Friendly molestation," in the workplace or otherwise, is something of an oxymoron.

I used to get my bottom slapped by the male managers at work, once with a fly [swatter] by the deputy manager—all a joke, you know.

▸ A colleague in my previous job used to grab me inappropriately. For example, grabbing me by the waist to pull me toward him, touching my bum. He was very explicit about how he fancied me and even though he knew I was in a relationship he continued to make inappropriate comments and behavior. I complained to my line manager who instead of supporting me, gave me excuses.

▸ On a night out, stood in a crowd of male colleagues who were considerably older than me (I was 19) when one of them interrupted me by leaning through the circle and touching my boob while the rest laughed. Not one of them said anything or even seemed to think it was wrong.

Like the normalization of street harassment and the multilayered media culture that so desensitizes us to the use of women's bodies as currency, the frequency of many of these occurrences in a single workplace can lead to a wider acceptance of such sentiments—whether in company policy or around the boardroom table. The more such incidents crop up—from a "little" sexist joke here to a "cheeky" pat on the bottom there, a "tongue-in-cheek" comment about the hassle of maternity leave to a "joke" about a colleague's sex life—the more they lubricate the wheels of a system that comfortably maintains the male-dominated status quo. And, just like any hierarchical status quo, the more it repeats itself, the more comfortable it becomes for its beneficiaries to maintain it, whether as perpetrators or passive bystanders or ostriches with their heads in the sand. And the harder it becomes for its victims to speak out, as they stand on ever shakier ground.

So, far from being the rare or nonexistent problem so many

people would have it, workplace harassment not only manifests itself in nasty, diverse variations but also often exists in horrifying combinations that pile up to create an unbearable atmosphere for victims. Each different incident adds greater cumulative weight to the next, while every indication of employers' and colleagues' acceptance of the prejudice presses down even harder on top.

▸ When I was 16 and in my first job, a sales rep visited the company and grabbed my breasts when I was in an office on my own. A few years later I overheard a couple of senior managers talking about me with some of my peers in the corridor—they described me as the small, skinny bird with big tits. One replied that he would like to bend me over the desk and give me one—several others jeered their appreciation of this comment.

The obvious key factor in harassment and abuse that happens in the workplace is the potential for career damage it carries. No other scenario yields quite the same implications. One can't help but wonder, judging by the number of women who report workplace prejudice, whether the ramifications of such a persistent bias might be far greater than the sum of their parts.

▸ A senior adviser to me, while working late during our busiest period of the year: "What are you still doing here? Isn't your boyfriend getting hungry? He must be lonely."

Same guy a couple of days later as I'm preparing to take some work home with me: "You know, a married woman should never take work home with her. I mean, it's natural for a married man, but a married woman shouldn't be distracted at home."

This guy affects the projects I get to work on, so I mentioned the comments to my boss. He said they were inappropriate but "what can I do, it's just how he is." Didn't push it further because I didn't want to be labeled as "difficult."

▸ As the owner and Director of a company, I would sometimes attend bank meetings alone. Nine times out of ten, the manager would greet me and then ask "when will your husband/the owner be here?"

It was fundamentally satisfying when I bought them up short on it, but ultimately, I'm pretty sure it affected the business. The perception was I couldn't quite be the boss, there had to be some murky male owner lurking in the background, or back in London, whereas the truth was I owned the entire company.

It seems possible that gender bias affects women's overall representation in the workforce. A recent study by scientists at Yale University, reported in the *Proceedings of the National Academy of Sciences,* seemed to indicate that such inherent assumptions about gender, made without employers even realizing it, could be having an enormous impact on women's professional prospects. In the randomized double-blind study, applications for science-based jobs were sent to research-intensive universities. The CVs were identical, but some carried male names and some female. The study revealed that recruiters (both male and female) rated the "male" applicants as "significantly more competent and hireable" than the identical "female" applicants. What's more, they also offered the "male" applicants a higher starting salary *and* were more likely to offer them career mentoring. Mediation analyses concluded that "the female student was less likely to be hired because she was viewed as less competent."

Food for thought indeed.

Many of the project entries support this unconscious bias and illustrate where the intricacies of the problem make it very difficult to challenge the status quo.

▸ When I was in my early 20s I was kept on clerical grades whilst male colleagues advanced to management level. When one of the male managers left and I was given the job, it was down-graded to a clerical grade. I was told the previous incumbent had been overpaid. When I left, the job was upgraded to management again!

You might think (this being the twenty-first century and procreation generally being considered in the best interests of society as a whole) that women's rights in terms of pregnancy and motherhood would be pretty watertight. But project entries from working women on this subject have regularly indicated that some time-honored sexist attitudes prevail here too.

Women who chose to have children described how their competency and dedication were brought into question. One woman was told by her boss not to return to work with "leaky boobs," and a common swipe seems to be the idea of "baby brain"; many women were automatically thought to be no longer "up to the job" even when they returned to work with full dedication.

One PR executive was banned from pitching to new clients while she was pregnant, because bosses said her "future commitment to the account" would "clearly be in doubt." A waitress described her boss's straightforward instruction to "have an abortion or resign as my colleague was pregnant first & 2 pregnant workers was unfair."

It very often seems to be the case that when a woman's career suffers subsequent to having children it's because external forces have conspired to cap her potential. Her own intentions or decisions apparently have little to do with it.

▸ A female colleague recently announced she is pregnant. Everyone in the office assumes she will quit work and are already talking about replacing her even though she is discussing maternity leave, not resignation from the company.

▸ After College one of my jobs was as a Park Ranger in Alaska. The place I worked employed all men with stay-at-home wives. No other women at a professional level . . . As soon as I announced my pregnancy, they started ignoring my work, assuming I'd never come back from maternity leave.

▸ I am in my early 40s, a professional, with a PhD and 15 years of experience. I recently came back from maternity leave to my overseas posting, to meet the new boss for the first time. In our first meeting, he explained that I would no longer be in charge of the unit I had been setting up for a year due to my "special circumstances," and because he wanted to make sure that he respected the rights of my baby to have his mother around. He also stated that while I was nursing it will be difficult for me to focus on my job, so he was being generous by giving me less responsibility, and downgrading my position.

That this is appallingly discriminatory is even more starkly evident when you realize that U.S. law provides for the protection of women at work during pregnancy and motherhood. The Pregnancy Discrimination Act (PDA) forbids discrimination based on pregnancy in every aspect of employment, including hiring, firing, pay, job assignments, promotions, layoff, training, and fringe benefits. The law states that if a woman's ability to carry out her job is temporarily compromised as a result of pregnancy, her employer must treat her in the same way it would treat any other "temporarily disabled" employee.

It is categorically illegal to select a woman for redundancy because of pregnancy, yet the UK Equal Opportunities Commission estimates that around thirty thousand women *every year* lose their jobs as a result of pregnancy discrimination. This represents about 8 percent of all pregnant workers. In the United States, nearly six thousand charges were brought alleging pregnancy discrimination in 2011, but if the silencing of victims is anything like as bad as in the UK, where the EOC estimated that just 3 percent of those affected took legal action, the actual number is likely to be far higher.

Perhaps the greatest injustice of all is that the same handicap is by default served even to those women who have no intention of having children. Countless women have reported that their careers have been disadvantaged for no reason other than that their age and gender put them in the "baby risk" category.

Myself and my female business partner were turned down for a contract last week as we're too much of a "pregnancy risk."

For one woman who was biologically unable to have children, missing out on a job because she was considered a "baby risk" was a bitter blow.

So if women are facing sexism, harassment, discrimination, and even sexual assault in the workplace, why aren't more people aware of the problem and why isn't more action being taken? Under Title VII of the Civil Rights Act, individuals are protected from discrimination based on sex. This means it is illegal for an employer to discriminate in matters of hiring, firing, promotion, or pay because of an individual's sex. Sexual harassment in the workplace is also illegal if submitting to or rejecting such conduct is used as the basis of employment decisions, or if it constitutes a course of conduct sufficiently severe or pervasive that it creates an intimidating, hostile, or offensive work environment.

It is difficult to see how a single one of the experiences quoted in this chapter—or, indeed, of the thousands of workplace-related entries submitted to the project—does not fall firmly under at least one of these categories. And yet the problem persists. The complex and interwoven difficulties making it nearly impossible for victims to speak out are exacerbated by flagrant flouting and circumnavigation of the law.

Many women who do find the courage to speak out—via their company's HR department, perhaps, or a manager—are met with rebuttal. Reports to the project suggest that there's an alarming propensity for denial and disregard, even from those whose job it is to combat such problems and ensure fair treatment of all employees.

Went to HR about sexist and flirty CEO. Told to put up with it as I'm "young and pretty and they're men, what do you expect?"

▸ I have taken my case to HR but they simply ignore me due to the sensitivity this case could bring to the press.

▸ My boss, who was in his 40s, tried to kiss me after the Christmas Party. I was 22. I went to the woman who coordinated the graduates and told her what had happened. I was told that this was to be expected in an office and if I ask to move it would affect my future career. So I continued in my position but felt so uncomfortable I would . . . throw up before I met with him.

▸ HR manager told me on our first day "If you are going to report sexual harassment, first think about what you were wearing that day."

Sometimes the options are laid starkly bare:

▸ I'm 18 years old and work as a receptionist in a car showroom. As the only female member of staff I'm forced to endure sexually charged comments on a daily basis from men old enough to be my father. I've complained to my boss about this (also male) who dismissed it as what passed as banter in all-male workplace. The message I got from the meeting was if I couldn't handle the situations other workers put me in, then leave.

Unfortunately, this pattern of dismissive response is evident even in those women's stories concerning allegations of serious harassment and sexual assault.

One woman was sexually assaulted by a male colleague at a conference and reported the incident to the event organizer. Her complaint was met with a conspiratorial wink and an indulgent, "I hear he recently got divorced."

A young female engineer who was physically assaulted at

work reported the crime to her boss, only to be told to "sweep it under the carpet."

One woman was raped by a colleague on a work night out. "Guess who lost their job?" she wrote grimly. "Not him."

The impact of such reactions on the victims, both emotionally and in terms of their career, cannot be underestimated. The young engineer told us:

▸ Because there were no witnesses or evidence of assault nothing could be done. I left the company shortly after that and now have a good career, although for a long time after I blamed myself, lost a lot of confidence, and went through a period of deep depression. Nine years later I still experience the odd sexual comment which makes me question as to why I remain in the industry. At the end of the day however, I've put a lot of hard work into getting to where I am and am passionate about what I do so why should I give it all up? Sadly though, I feel that if I were to give advice to a young female looking to follow a similar career path I would be very [wary] indeed.

When we talk about workplace harassment, people tend automatically to think of women putting up with the odd sexist joke. The common and simplified response is the question, "Why didn't she just complain about it?" But of course in many cases women do not have direct recourse for such action. For thousands of people working freelance, or in jobs like bartending, there is no access to an HR department at all. Sometimes the option to report through official channels simply isn't there.

According to the National Women's Law Center (NWLC), women make up around two-thirds of minimum-wage workers across the United States, and two-thirds of tipped workers, such as restaurant servers. This means that they are disproportionately likely to find themselves without recourse to HR grievance procedures if they experience discrimination or harassment in the workplace, and also disproportionately likely to feel pushed into suffering in silence for fear of losing their job in a precarious economic climate. As of June 2015, the NWLC reports, the federal minimum wage was only $7.25 per hour, and full-time earnings of $14,500 a year leave a family of three more than $4,000 below the federal poverty line. For tipped workers, where employers can legally count a portion of tips toward wages, the federal minimum cash wage has been frozen for twenty-four years at just $2.13 per hour. With women disproportionately making up minimum-wage and tipped workers, this presents a clear intersection of gender and class inequality.

And if the Everyday Sexism Project entries have demonstrated anything, it's that harassment and sexism occur across the whole gamut of job types and descriptions.

A female vicar was repeatedly asked if there was a man available to perform weddings and funeral services ("Nothing personal!"). A young DJ described how constant harassment and groping had brought her to dread the job she'd once loved. A midwife and a marketing consultant suffered nearly indistinguishable experiences of sexual assault by senior male colleagues. A teacher was heckled with sexual comments and jibes from young male pupils. A woman working in the office of a world leader was filing documents when she was told, "That's where I like to see a woman: on her knees." An office worker was told to sit on her boss's lap if she wanted to get her Christmas bonus. A junior hospital registrar received the same demand from a senior consultant when she asked him to help her interpret an X-ray. The captain of a wind-farm support boat found that many male recruits rejected jobs because they didn't want to work for a female skipper. A racehorse owner wouldn't trust a female vet to touch his prized animal. A female pilot was scorned by passengers and colleagues. Again and again, women have to make an uncomfortable choice: Deal with the harassment or discrimination and get on in your career, or report it and risk losing everything.

Be open about your plans for motherhood and risk being sidelined; keep quiet and you'll be affected anyway by ingrained stereotyping and assumptions about your life choices and biological urges. It isn't the way it should be. It isn't even legal. But right now it certainly seems to be the way it is.

One woman's story completely summed up this status quo:

▸ An arm round my shoulders with the hand resting on my breast . . . I had a senior manager who frequently used to try and do this to all the female staff necessitating a side-step movement to get away. A complaint was made but nothing changed.

The onus is currently on women in the workplace to develop coping mechanisms and contingency plans rather than on perpetrators to stop offending or on companies to deal with the problem. "Advised against pursuing an investigation in my sexual harassment case," one woman told us, "because it would 'harm my career' as a woman in science." That's a conclusion as ironic and misguided as the one drawn by some media outlets that the women who spoke up about being groped by a senior immeasurably larger than any individual. And, yes, even though a single individual may well be able to take certain measures to advance her career within the existing framework, it is the framework itself—and the wider cultural attitudes surrounding it and influenced by it—that have the greatest impact. *These* must be tackled in order to see meaningful, widespread change.

You need only glance at the relevant statistics to realize how much greater the problem is than any individual woman's attitude. A stubborn pay gap of 22 percent persists, despite equality legislation and apparently equal opportunities.

The gap in pay is mirrored by a gap in attainment at the highest professional levels. According to the National Women's Law Center, although women make up around half of law students, only a third of Supreme Court justices, 35 percent of judges in the federal courts of appeal, and 32 percent of district court judges are women. Only 4 of the 112 justices ever to serve on the highest court in the land have been women. In the UK, only 7 out of 38 lord justices of appeal and just 18 out of 108 High Court judges are female. Data from the U.S. National Science Foundation reveals that women make up just 20 percent of architects, 17 percent of economists, and 11 percent of engineers. Only 5 percent of CEOs at Fortune 500 companies are women. Around the world, there is a significant gap between the proportion of women obtaining university and postgraduate degrees and their representation at professorial levels. In Canada, women are 55 percent of master's graduates but just 22 percent of full professors. In Belgium, in 2008, women made up 55 percent of PhD holders but just 15 percent of top professorships. In Finland, 49 percent of PhD graduates in 2003 were women but they made up just 22 percent of professors in 2005. Figures for the Netherlands show that in 2008, women were 53 percent of graduates and 42 percent of PhD students but only 12 percent of full professors. And change doesn't seem to be coming fast. When the American Association of University Professors began measuring data on the salaries of female faculty members in 1975, it found that they earned 81 percent of what their male colleagues were paid. When it released its 2010 report, they earned . . . 81 percent.

The reasons for these inequalities are many and complex, but the glib argument that women make "different choices" and choose to "sacrifice career for family" falls short on two counts. First, even if this argument is accepted at face value, it fails to entirely explain the pay gap or women's enormous underrepresentation in the top tiers of so many professions. The 2013 report "Graduating to a Pay Gap," released by the American Association of University Women (AAUW), revealed that women one year out of college who were working full-time were paid, on average, 82 percent of what their male peers were paid. And in the UK, research released by the Higher Education Careers Services Unit in 2013 showed that, directly following university—long before many people even begin to consider families—female graduates are already earning thousands of pounds less than their male peers. The problem persisted across almost every career path and remained even between graduates who majored in the same field. The AAUW found, for example, that among business majors, male graduates were paid an average $7,000 more per year than their female counterparts.

The second problem with the rationale that women "make sacrifices" for family is the very notion that having children must necessarily impact a woman's career but not a man's. This reality, compounded by inflexible working hours and a lack of shared parental leave, is often cited as if it were an immutable fact that women must simply accept, rather than a long-existing prejudice that could and should be challenged.

Rarely does anybody stop to peek a layer farther and ask why women have those different "priorities." *Why* is it that deciding to have a family is something that we talk about as a reasonable cause for a setback in a woman's career but never consider in relation to a man's? *Why* is it women who have to make these choices at all, while men are seemingly able to waltz serenely into the sunset with a top-flight career, 2.4 children, and company car?

Why do we continue to insist, even in the twenty-first century, on asking the archaic question, "Can women really have it all?" instead of unpicking the deep societal bias that allows such rhetoric to persist in the first place? Why don't we stop to question the sexist paradigm in which women are the primary caregivers of children and the elderly, and the part-time work they frequently must take on in order to maintain these responsibilities is paid less per hour than full-time jobs and has few if any prospects for career advancement? Why do we keep asking why girls aren't as "interested" in business and engineering or as "driven" and "ambitious" as boys, instead of stopping to consider the impact of the repeated background nonsense that tells them science isn't feminine, strong women are "shrill" or "bossy," and that their natural role—as the thousands of dolls and playhouses and stoves in the girls' section at the toy store will affirm—is to care and clean and cook and keep house?

It is vital that we address these underlying inequalities, because overcoming the gender pay gap and the underrepresentation of women at the top of business, politics, and other fields cannot otherwise be achieved. Take, for example, the fact that the roles traditionally associated with men (such as firefighting) tend to be higher paid than those traditionally associated with women (such as social work or nursing), even when a similar level of skill is required. A simplistic analysis might conclude that the problem could be solved if more women were encouraged to enter those fields considered more "male," and vice versa. But what happens when that movement takes place? Those fields women move into begin to be considered less prestigious, while the fields men start to infiltrate rise in value and estimation. So it isn't enough to tackle the problem on the surface—the underlying societal stereotypes must be tackled as well.

Similarly, many of the victim-centered solutions commonly suggested may be more problematic than they initially appear. It is often said, for example, that women should simply get better at putting themselves forward and demanding pay rises, but that ignores the inconvenient truth that for many women in the workplace, the sort of traits this would require (assertiveness, self-promotion) are considered negative and unattractive, in a way that doesn't apply to men exhibiting the same behavior, meaning that such tactics could actually backfire. Consider, for example, the results of a study by the linguist and tech entrepreneur Kieran Snyder published by fortune.com in August 2014. Snyder compared 248 workplace performance reviews from 180 people at 28 different companies. Only 58.9 percent of the reviews received by men contained critical feedback, compared to 87.9 percent of those received by women. Snyder pulled out any reviews that contained what she described as "negative personality criticism," including words such as "bossy," "abrasive," "strident," "emotional," and "irrational." Out of the eighty-three critical reviews received by men, just two contained such personality criticism. But it showed up in seventy-one of the ninety-four critical reviews received by women. The only negative word that showed up in both men's and women's reviews was "aggressive." This word came up three times in men's reviews, but two of those three times, the man was being encouraged to be *more* aggressive.

The playing field obviously isn't the same for men and women, as is painfully exemplified by the firing of Jill Abramson (former executive editor of the *New York Times*, so often held up as a shining example of women's strides forward) under a cloud including reports of a gender pay dispute and seemingly gendered accusations that she was considered "difficult," "brusque," and "abrasive." And by the extraordinary case of Melissa Nelson, a dental assistant in Iowa who was fired for being "too sexy."

Though her boss openly admitted his only reason for terminating the dental nurse after ten years of exemplary service was that he had become attracted to her and feared that would threaten his marriage, both the Iowa district and supreme courts rejected Nelson's gender discrimination suit.

We have to tackle the wider cultural issues at their root if we expect to see meaningful change. But there are other steps that could be taken to improve things in the interim. It's important to make employees aware of their rights and responsibilities, because so few victims even realize what they are experiencing is illegal, and many perpetrators may not understand that their actions are unacceptable, due to massive normalization.

Companies should introduce clear and transparent reporting procedures, and ensure that there is an option to report to somebody other than a victim's immediate manager, since, in many cases, the superior is the perpetrator. They should take action, in line with the law, to ensure that women who report sexual harassment face no negative impact or retribution as a result, and make sure women are aware of such policies, to increase confidence in reporting. Audits should be introduced to compare men and women's pay and to hold companies accountable for addressing disparities. And, above all, we need to take on the cultural factors holding women back in the workplace, starting before they even reach it.

From childhood onward, both implicitly and explicitly, women are discouraged from certain careers or from having a career at all. They are subjected to subconscious and overt bias at every stage of employment, starting with applications and interviews; they suffer verbal harassment and physical assault in the workplace, then face being silenced or sacked when they complain about it; and they are written off and marginalized merely for approaching biological fertility. Isn't it time to set aside the questions about what *women* should bring to the equation and focus on some of these things instead?

When I told my marketing-director boss I was pregnant for the first time she said, "Well, this isn't a part-time job."

Everyday Sexism Project entry

Vital Statistics

Out of 185 countries and territories, the only country besides the United States that doesn't offer cash benefits to women during maternity leave is Papua New Guinea.

-International Labor Organization, 2013

The Pregnancy Discrimination Act applies only to employers with fifteen or more employees.

-U.S. Equal Employment Opportunity Commission, 2014

In just the first six months of 2013, U.S. lawmakers passed 43 separate restrictions to abortion access.

-Guttmacher Institute, 2013

More than 10 million women with children under eighteen were not in the labor force in 2011 (compared to 1.7 million men).

-Bureau of Labor Statistics, 2013

Mothers working in restaurants spend more than a third of their income on child care.

-Restaurant Opportunities Center United, 2013

Almost 1 in 3 U.S. women will have an abortion by age forty-five.

-Guttmacher Institute, 2014

324,000 women report experiencing intimate partner violence during pregnancy in the United States each year.

-U.S. Centers for Disease Control and Prevention, 2013

I'm so tired of people on the street calling me sexy. I'm 6 months pregnant, bro. You literally just need to leave me alone.

Friend of mine works in a law firm, recently got pregnant. They're hiring for her replacement. She won't have a job after.

I am constantly expected to justify my reasons for not wanting or having babies and put up with people telling me that I will change my mind.

Met a man who said he'd never employ a woman of childbearing age as they could "ruin" his company if they got pregnant.

"All single mothers are sluts who get pregnant to get benefits and housing."

I was 8 months pregnant, walking through the pub I worked at. A regular says: "I heard pregnant women need a good seeing to, want help?"

From contraception to abortion and baby weight to childlessness, the common misconception that women's bodies are public property is never stronger than when the subject is reproduction.

Once more, it starts minor. So minor, in fact, that you'd be chided for making a fuss. Newlyweds being repeatedly asked when they're going to start popping out tiny humans as if it's suddenly their urgent, public duty. Intelligent women, quite in command of their faculties, stating their intention to remain childless and being condescendingly assured, "You'll change your mind, just you wait and see." The inexplicable erosion of boundaries that turns a pregnant belly into an electromagnet for the outstretched, groping hands of passing strangers. To object to such "well-meant" intrusions would be considered churlish—an overreaction. But the idea that we should listen to anyone and everyone's advice and opinions about what we should do with our own uteruses stems, ultimately, from the notion that women's reproductive systems (and, by extension, women themselves) exist for one purpose, and one purpose alone. Somehow, this seems to translate into a merry free-for-all that mysteriously doesn't extend to penises despite their equal role in the initiation of the whole process.

This sense in which everybody has a say amounts to nothing less than a public invasion of pregnancy. Albeit that it's supposedly joyful and friendly, it's easy to understand why women might resent being swamped by unsolicited advice and comments or having strangers touch their bodies willy-nilly.

My pregnant wife's bump was apparently an invitation for strangers (men and women) to cop a stroke.

This is a common theme, stemming, I think, from the fact that when a woman conceives, that single fact takes over her whole identity in society's eyes, as if her individual features somehow melt away and she morphs into a cookie-cutter "pregnant lady."

But there are numerous reasons why a pregnant woman might dislike someone touching her body without permission. (For a woman who has previously experienced abuse, it could be terrifying.) It is ironic, given the alienating isolation women often face in the workplace when they become pregnant, that in the public sphere they battle the opposite problem—the idea that everybody in society at large seems to think they have a stake in the process. Likewise, women may feel very exposed and vulnerable when they're at the receiving end of a barrage of "well-meaning" advice. For some, this uninvited commentary can feel very disempowering and invasive, particularly if they are already experiencing anxiety about the pregnancy for myriad possible reasons. For others, it's simply annoying. At best it's downright rude. Male-pattern baldness affects around half of men by the age of fifty, but we don't see strangers approaching them in the street and commenting on the sparseness of their follicles, or copping a confident feel of their scalp, as if the biological process, by dint of its visibility, was somehow a public matter.

▸ I was out for dinner and a musical event at a local venue . . . As I was paying for our bill the (male) owner of the venue asked how my pregnancy was going and said, much to my shock, "It is so good that you've kept your weight down, that is so important."

These invasions say much about attitudes toward women generally. The indignity of public ownership crosses the boundaries of just about every aspect of sexism in our society. Clumsy overenthusiasm about our reproductive state might come from an inherently well-meaning place, but the fact is that it also denotes the idea of women as passive objects of utility.

If the reports we have received are anything to go by, many, many mothers find themselves subject to harassment not *aside* from their maternal status but *because* of it.

▸ I was walking my 5-month-old son in his buggy, down Oxford Street. Middle of the day, wearing a knee-length black dress. A man stopped me, told me I was a "fucking MILF" [mother I'd like to fuck] and then proceeded on his way with a grin. This isn't the only time this sort of thing has happened—in fact it's more vulgar when I'm with my son. I believe it's because women appear more vulnerable when they're with small children—usually I'd challenge that sort of behavior, but I wouldn't put my son at risk so keep quiet.

▸ As I was waiting for the bus, a man came up to me and started an awkward conversation. I tried to just be nice and then he started asking me personal questions about if I'm with my "man." I told him that I don't need to answer that question because I hardly knew him . . . especially when he kept licking his lips. The bus came and I choose to sit in the back and he followed. He said that I'm going to have a beautiful baby and then he reached over and touched my face and said it was because I was beautiful that my kid will inherit my looks. I took his hand as nice as possible and gave it back to him. Then he leaned over and brushed my left breast down to my stomach. This time I grabbed his hand and handed it back to him and said "please don't do that—DONT TOUCH ME!"

▸ Walking down the street today, wearing sports gear (I'd just been for a run). I'm twenty weeks pregnant and am showing . . . a group of men stopped their car and started yelling at me to "put it away" (presumably, hide my bump or my body in general). I ignored them but they kept yelling "you . . . pink top . . . put it away" so I knew it was me. So weird and very upsetting.

▸ While heavily pregnant, as the sun was starting to go down, I was walking with my husband when he realized he had forgotten something and ran back to our home. I waited for him on the pavement outside our local park, on a fairly quiet road. Not one, but two men slowed down their cars and hung out of the car calling at me (exactly what, I couldn't hear). I'm 40 years old and pretty streetwise, yet I felt really uncomfortable standing on my own on a summer night, obviously heavily pregnant and having to deal with this unwanted and intimidating attention.

As for the idea of reproduction as the primary purpose and function of women, well . . . What could be more limiting to our collective identity? Entirely preposterous it may be, but it nonetheless forms a background disquiet that helps mold the way women feel about themselves and their sense of validation.

For some women, the underlying message that childbearing is the single most exalted experience of every human female causes huge distress.

▸ Maternal, no children, mid-forties. Have been made to feel very much a lesser being and a complete failure for not having children. There are TV programs I can't bring myself to watch, adverts I can't bear to see. Images of the wonders of birth and motherhood bombard me. I don't/can't resent it and I'll still get excited and a surge of joy at the prospect of a friend/relative's pregnancy, but, I am grieving (and it is real, heart stopping grief) for the children I haven't produced. So, having not found the man to make the baby with, I guess I'm not ruling the world as I've failed myself and all womankind.

One woman told her own family that she didn't intend to have children and was asked, "What's the point of you, then?" Another told us:

▸ Telling people that I haven't the health or energy to parent a child never stopped the comments. Telling them I'm gay didn't stop them. Telling them my primary illness is genetic and likely to be inherited by any child didn't. Telling them pregnancy could leave me paraplegic didn't.

We received the following entry from a woman describing herself as "childfree by choice" but also citing a medical condition that leaves her unable to have children:

▸ I get insulted frequently for this. Told I'm unnatural, heartless, and most commonly selfish. I often get treated like a pariah among friends and family with children, or even strangers . . . I get treated like a child-hater, which I'm not . . . I get threatened, insulted, derided and told I'm not a real woman, or that I'll inevitably change my mind when I'm older/more mature. (I'm nearly 30, apparently old enough to do everything apart from decide I don't want a baby.)

A definition of womanhood based on a presumed ability and desperation to procreate is incredibly heteronormative, and gender essentialist too. Naturally there are many who don't subscribe to it for that very reason.

▸ My boss asks if I would want a family one day, so I say, "Possibly, but not for a long while yet. I'll probably adopt." He laughs and says, "No, I don't think you will. You just need to find the right man to change your mind. All women want a man to give them their own children, I don't think adopting would suit you." So, I reply, "Actually, it probably would. I'm infertile. Also, I'm a lesbian."

One woman wrote to the Everyday Sexism Project after seeing an article in the national press arguing that women of childbearing age (all women, not just those who are pregnant) should be denied antidepressants because they could be harmful to a hypothetical fetus. Her entry laid bare the very suggestion of reproduction above and beyond anything else as wholly counterintuitive.

▸ One of the things my body can do is carry a pregnancy and give birth to the baby. If I am going to use it for that, it is up to me. But I may (and do) also want to use it for a zillion other things, many of which require me to be in a fit state of mental health. I am a person living inside this body and I am more important than a theoretical future being that could exist or the abstract principle of what some other person thinks my body should be used for. It is MINE and it is going to be used by ME for whatever I want.

For many women, such an assertion of autonomy is simply not an option, though, so strongly are cultural beliefs entwined into legislation. Worldwide, one of the most basic forms of sustained gender prejudice is the denial of women's control over their own bodies and reproductive systems. In 2011 *alone,* the Guttmacher Institute for sexual and reproductive health and rights reported that legislators in American states introduced more than eleven hundred provisions relating to reproductive health and rights. Of those that were enacted, 68 percent restricted access to abortion services. And in just the first six months of 2013, U.S. lawmakers passed forty-three separate restrictions to abortion access. Meanwhile, forty-six states allow individual health-care providers to refuse to participate in abortions and seventeen states mandate that women be given counseling before an abortion that includes information on at least one of the following: the purported link between abortion and breast cancer (five states), the ability of a fetus to feel pain (twelve states), or long-term mental health consequences for the woman (eight states). In some states, women seeking abortions are forced to undergo medically unnecessary and invasive transvaginal ultrasounds. And according to "This is Personal," a National Women's Law Center campaign, in the first six months of 2013, state politicians introduced seventeen bills that would allow bosses to refuse to provide insurance coverage for birth control.

Moralistic panic over birth control and abortions can have devastating consequences. Providing for safe, legal abortions does not lead to a significant increase—women have abortions all over the world, regardless of legality. But women who are forced to seek unsafe illegal abortions may pay with their lives.

Worldwide, forty-seven thousand women every year die and millions are injured as a direct result of complications from unsafe abortions. And other basic health needs can also be compromised—58 percent of U.S. birth control users cite reasons for using it other than contraception. But in 2011, members of the U.S. House of Representatives voted to ban all federal funding for Planned Parenthood health centers, which, had it not been stopped by the Senate, would have prevented millions of women from getting not only birth control but critical health screenings, including mammograms, according to This is Personal.

In 2012. Savita Halappanavar, a thirty-one-year-old in Galway, Ireland, was denied the right to a lifesaving operation under legislation that prioritizes motherhood over autonomy. Following her death, her husband said that hospital staff citing Irish anti-abortion policy had refused to allow her the abortion she needed—despite her pregnancy being nonviable. A jury found that she died as a result of "medical misadventure." What a euphemism. (In 2013, Ireland revised its anti-abortion law to allow for abortions when the mother's life was at stake.)

Around the world, women are dying because of men's ideas about what they should and shouldn't be allowed to do with their own bodies. Childbearing carries enormous physiological implications and risks, even in healthy full-term pregnancies. The decision to carry and give birth to a child should not be made by anybody other than the woman whose body is involved. And yet here, once more, we see puritanical, archaic objections to female autonomy that aren't applied to other comparable situations. The fact that birth control and abortion weren't available many years ago doesn't mean that every child—even those conceived by rape or incest—is a "gift from God" that a mother has no choice but to bear. We *do* have a choice now; and, just as scientific advancement has given us far greater control over other "natural processes," such as disease, it has also allowed women far greater self-governance over their own bodies. Our judgments and decisions should be made within a modern framework, taking those advances into account.

While arguing about viability and the date at which a fetus becomes a "person," we often fail to take into account the absolutely definite, not at all hypothetical life of the mother. (See, for example, the untold psychological impact on a woman visiting an abortion clinic of being picketed and bombarded with abuse by protestors holding bloody signs or screaming curses.) It is most striking that in a debate that revolves almost entirely around the concept of "humanity," there is so very little humane thought given to women at all. Indeed, much anti-abortion advocacy rests on prejudiced and downright false assumptions about the "kind of women" likely to undergo the procedure, with the vague notion of promiscuous, selfish hussies (and irresponsible teens) having them left, right, and center with no maternal instinct or regard for human life. The reality couldn't be more different. Abortions are extremely common, with almost one in three American women having one before the age of forty-five, according to the Guttmacher Institute. The majority of women who have abortions are in their twenties, with teens accounting for less than a fifth of all abortions. And 60 percent of women who have abortions already have a child, often citing the need to care for existing children as a primary reason for their choice. Yet the shadowy idea that abortion is a shameful and immoral act allows those who, largely, have little experience of it or of the need for it, to frame the debate, while the voices likely to give us the most useful and relevant perspective are entirely silenced. And of course this skews the debate even farther.

▸ While in Year 10 my science teacher felt it appropriate to share his views on how he believed abortion was too flexible and should not be allowed up to 24 weeks. After telling him that I believed that it should be allowed up to 24 weeks he looked at me in disgust and told me that "those" women should not be allowed to have children at all.

▸ A male colleague told me men should decide about abortion law and time limits because women are too emotional and have a personal bias which is why we have 24 weeks which he says is "really late" and puts too much focus on "what the woman herself wants."

▸ I was watching one of those round table political discussion shows this morning and the topic of abortion came up. There was one woman on the show, and she was trying to speak up on several occasions. The three men next to her were in an intense discussion on pro-life (no exceptions) versus pro-life (exceptions like rape and health risk) and kept cutting her off and telling her to hold on. I could hear a woman off-set laughing because she obviously could not believe what was happening. The woman at the table had this smile plastered on her face as she tried several more times to get a word in edge wise. She even started sentences like "Well since this is a women's issue . . ." but the man next to her said "Hold on one second let me finish" and continued talking to the other men. It was painful and sickening to watch. On the topic of abortion the only woman at the table did not get to speak even once before they went to commercial and dropped the subject entirely.

▸ My husband just said that a woman should be able to decide to take her top off for men if she wants to that she should have control over her own body but that a woman should not be able to have an abortion because that is murder.

In among the censorious pseudoreligious, moralistic panic that forms the mainstay of most political debates about abortion, stories from real women are notably lacking. It must be so very simple to pronounce judgment and dust off your hands and walk away secure in the knowledge that you will never have to think about, feel, in your own body, the reality of what you have just said. It is real women's stories that are missing—stories that might reveal to these black-and-white thinkers the true depth and complexity of what they are discussing. But, of course, that would make things much more awkward to discuss in such handy, clear-cut terms. The comfortable myth of abortion users as selfish, irresponsible creatures rather than human beings like you and me would be quickly shattered. The reality is very different.

▸ I had an abortion, and I can't tell anyone besides my partner because I am so afraid. I chose not to ask for support from my family because they are very "traditional." I am a highly educated, bread-winning mother in a 15-year relationship . . . I am a successful human being, and I have a right to direct the course of my life and protect my own family. Although I am successful, we are not rich nor do we have infinite time. I want the best life possible for myself, my partner, and especially for my daughter. This was the best (not easiest) possible decision for all of us, and yet I still feel ashamed and silenced.

On top of the potentially traumatic experience of going through an abortion, women are often forced by societal prejudice to pay a heavy double penalty of guilt as well as self-blame.

▸ I was working for a firm when I found out I was pregnant. I decided to have an abortion and my boss gave me the time off for this. I was very upset at my decision and felt completely selfish, horrible and vulnerable. About two weeks later, we were on a works night out where I got horribly drunk and we all (about 5 of us) went back to my boss' house. I crashed out in the spare room my boss had offered me. I woke up at about 3 am to find my boss had crawled into bed with me and had put his fingers inside me. I was still bleeding from the abortion.

I never went back to work, and after a few days, I contacted him about this. I was told by a colleague (who obviously knew what he had done) that there was nothing I could do as I would lose all my benefits as I had walked out of the job.

I lost it. I felt that this was my punishment for the abortion. I had a breakdown and ended up back at my parents'. I was 26.

Our society has such a knee-jerk tendency to vilify and dehumanize women that in discussions of pregnancy and abortion the role of men is almost never mentioned. Still, the euphemistic and somehow judgmental description of a woman "falling" pregnant is used, as if reproduction is something she carelessly does all by herself, comparable to forgetting to buy milk, say, or getting an ill-advised tattoo. And in this relentless focus on women's responsibility, men lose out on crucial support and help, too. Precious little counseling or care is made available to those whose partners lose or abort a child, for example, because such things are portrayed so unremittingly as "women's issues."

For women experiencing some of the common mental-health symptoms frequently associated with pregnancy, sexist assumptions and stereotypes about women and motherhood can be deeply damaging. As one interviewee explained:

Honestly, until I became a mother I thought sexism had all but died out. I was largely unaware of it and had always achieved what I wanted regardless of my sex. Then I got pregnant and all of that changed.

After twenty years of happy infertility (I never wanted to be a mum) I accidentally got pregnant in 2007. I decided to go ahead with it (I kept being told it was a miracle conception) but the enormous shock of a baby I didn't want was devastating. From the moment I discovered I was pregnant the sexist pressure was on. I saw my doctor the day after I took the test to discuss my options but she instantly assigned me a midwife for the pregnancy. It didn't occur to her that I may not want a child. I recall clearly that it was at that moment that I felt I was "wrong" for not being overjoyed at my situation and all because, as a woman, I was supposed to be overjoyed.

I developed post-traumatic stress disorder and post-natal depression with suicidal tendencies after the pregnancy and this became a full breakdown in 2010 from which I am still recovering. My daughter—who I now adore—is five. The sexism came into it when seeking help. I was a woman with a new baby so it was assumed that I was delighted and fulfilled. My gender seemed to mean more to people than my individuality.

Everyone around me, apart from my very closest family and friends, thought that as an infertile woman all my dreams had been fulfilled. They were incapable of understanding why I had such a problem with this shock change in my circumstances. Even the mental-health professionals I've been in contact with have all struggled to understand why a woman would not want to be a mum. It was only the understanding of those closest to me—those who knew that I was never going to glow with maternal instinct—that saved my life.

There were so many times when I felt I was screaming but no one could hear me and during all of this time I became increasingly mentally unstable, isolated and desperate and I also attempted suicide. I wanted to be heard as an individual but all anyone heard was what they thought a woman "should" be. I feel as if I have spent the last five years fighting not just my illness but the inherent sexism that comes with being a mother.

This exalted status of "mother" as almost another category altogether, separate from personhood and individuality within our culture, can have lasting and deeply felt effects.

It's now been five years since the birth of my daughter and the sexism is as strong and pervasive as ever. Not a day passes without me having to battle the assumptions and expectations demanded of me because I am a woman and a mother. It's in adverts, on packaging, in magazines, on TV, in newspapers, in the comments of strangers, in the schoolyard and in children's books.

An average day will start with news reports about how the actions of mothers (not fathers) impact on their child's health. I take my child to school to be referred to by the teachers as "Mum" rather than my name. I go to the supermarket where the baby aisles are strewn with

pics of glowing women, rather than men, and where the clothes aisles are nothing but pink for little girls. When I use the internet, parenting websites are loaded toward women as the nurturers and carers (Mumsnet etc.). When I meet extended family on weekends I get asked when I am "having another one." (Never, by the way.) When I play with my daughter we are assaulted with images of princesses, puppies and pretend kitchens, which I fight with every atom of my body. It's endless and it's exhausting.

The whole area of maternity is fraught with a multiplicity of contradictions and hypocrisy—teen motherhood is sneeringly condemned, while "career women" who "leave it too late" are caught in a crossfire of pity and accusations of cold, hard selfishness. Women are constantly reminded that reproduction is their pressing raison d'être yet at the same time are bombarded with headlines like these ones suggesting that selfish women spewing out babies are ruining the very fabric of our society:

Now three in five doctors aged under 30 are women: fears for care standards as junior doctors fall pregnant.

What kind of woman gets pregnant just to take a year off work?

As one woman wryly retorted on Twitter:

How dare we go and have babies. The poor patriarchy.

Meanwhile, women are closely watched and pressured to stay fit and do everything right while pregnant, but too much exercise (or whatever other innocent activity the tabloids have deemed potentially harmful that day) may provoke a cascade of indignant outrage. "Pregnant women should avoid the sun" . . . "Pregnant women hit by rickets because they're not getting enough sun" . . . "Pregnant women who drink 'lightly' could have brighter babies" . . . "Pregnant women are told: Don't drink at all" . . . "How can pregnant women ensure their babies will be healthy? By eating fry-ups" . . . "Pregnant women who eat chips increase risk of having underweight babies" . . . "How healthy eating could STOP you getting pregnant" . . . "A fish-rich diet gives mothers silent nights" . . . "Pregnant women warned over tuna" . . . And my favorite: "Pregnant women are confused about their diets."

The list goes on and on—there's certainly plenty there to sustain a serious state of guilt-induced anxiety throughout your entire pregnancy ("Pregnant women should avoid anxiety at all costs").

It's enough to make the mind boggle at the miraculous survival of all those healthy pre–women's magazine babies.

And don't forget, when you have a moment's break from the brain-bending exhaustion of working out what you ABSOLUTELY MUST and DEFINITIVELY MUST NOT eat and drink, you're also obliged to take the time to pick a tribe—be a sexy MILF, a hockey mom, an earth mother, a full-time mum, a yummy mummy, a slummy mummy, a scummy mummy . . . Because here, as with every other aspect of "womanhood," there is a rigid categorization with little room for alternatives or gray areas.

The problem with pregnancy is that in a society hell-bent on judging you first and foremost as a woman (rather than as an individual person) in any given situation, your condition becomes the immediate focus of the lens through which your every move, outfit, and mouthful is analyzed.

Suddenly the decision to leave the house becomes, according to the media, an extrovert ploy to "put her bump on display"; the choice to carry a particular handbag, meanwhile, is a coy attempt to "keep her bump covered" (A *Daily Mail* headline: "Kate Winslet continues her pregnancy parade as she shows off baby bump at Toronto Film Festival." What the *Mail* has done there is to confuse "doing her job" with "parading" and "showing off.")

Then there's the media's inability to distinguish between the natural changing of a woman's figure during pregnancy and its usual hyperdriven disgust at an inch of female fat, leading to disturbing coverage that conflates the two. As scream a couple of recent magazine headlines:

Jessica Simpson's fat days are numbered . . . she just popped out baby number two

Pregnant Kim's Nightmare 65 lb Weight Gain!

The obsession with baby weight and the not-always-subtle suggestion that these lazy women have basically let themselves go and become disgusting fatties are reinforced by myriad articles interpreting everything a pregnant woman wears as a desperate attempt to "cover up" or "disguise" or "hide" her baby bump:

Keeping Mum: Drew Barrymore hides her baby bump under slimming horizontal stripes

Black to cover up the baby bump: Petra Ecclestone hides her heavily pregnant shape in dark outfit

Perfect and pregnant: Molly Sims hides her baby bump in a super chic dress and heels combination

All of this combines to promote the unhelpful dual fallacies that (first) gaining weight while pregnant is somehow "shameful" and akin to getting fat, and that (second) women are in control of the shapes of their bodies throughout pregnancy and immediately afterward. Both concepts are fueled by stories artificially pitting pregnant celebrities against one another and the relentless scrutiny of any woman's postpartum figure.

The parallel pregnancies of Kim Kardashian and Kate Middleton, Duchess of Cambridge, provided the perfect opportunity for the media to indulge in its obsession with competitive gestation, and revealed the arbitrariness with which it is possible to mold perfectly natural and uncontrollable bodily processes into cause for either enormous praise and admiration or denigrating disapproval.

As Kardashian's pregnancy advanced, the world went into a feeding frenzy over her weight and diet, with online memes springing up comparing her to a killer whale after she wore a black-and-white dress, and magazines fabricating stories about her apparent "despair" at her own burgeoning size. One newspaper plastered her photograph on the front page because she happened to eat a portion of french fries. Under the headline "Pregnant Kim Kardashian Succumbs to Cravings and Gorges on Burger and Chips," there followed a nonstory astutely inventing details about how eagerly she "tucked into the calorific meal."

Elsewhere, headlines focused unendingly on her swollen ankles and the size and shape of her bottom. In one particularly awful example from *Now* magazine's Web site ("Is it just me, or is Kim Kardashian giving birth out of her bum?"), the incredible inanity of the accompanying article was evidence of a desperate scramble for some text—any text—to justify the gratuitous cruel headline and a guffawing "look how big her bum is" moment: "Ever since her rapper boyfriend, Kanye West, got her up the duff, her bum is growing at a faster rate than her baby bump!" (It wasn't.) "So it totally begs the question: Is Kim Kardashian going to give birth out of her bum?" (It didn't and, needless to say, she wasn't.)

And just to lay to rest any remaining doubts we could possibly have about the intended spirit in which the piece was to be taken, it ended with the snide reminder: "Rest easy girls, no matter how many Easter eggs we eat this week, we will never have the biggest bum in the world. Great, isn't it?" (No, it isn't.)

Now compare this hyperbolic and gleeful mudslinging to the equally cringe-inducing sycophancy-fest that surrounded the Duchess of Cambridge during her pregnancy, with constant references to her "svelte" and "streamlined" figure implying some kind of virtuous, intentional suppression of her bump.

Multiple media outlets run "best-dressed bump" lists (evidence in itself of the idea that women are expected to use their nine months of pregnancy as some sort of fashion-plate opportunity, much like dressing for the races or a beach holiday). *Vanity Fair* voted [Kate] Middleton best-dressed pregnant celebrity, raving about her "bare minimum of a bump."

Meanwhile, the *Daily Mail* went a step farther, making it clear that they considered the difference in the women's appearance to be a matter of class, with a crass "bump off" article that compared a series of photographs of Kate in long, covering coats with images of Kim in tight dresses, describing the duchess as the "picture of maternal modesty" while Kim was branded "brash," "trashy," "mumsy and clumsy." The "mumsy" jibe (an ironic insult in an article *about* pregnancy) and the praise for Kate's "barely visible royal bump" once again reiterated the idea that while women are expected and demanded to fulfill their biological function, the ideal scenario is for them to magically not *look* as if they are doing so at all. Lest we forget that the media is driven by men, for men . . .

But it's the setting up of celebrities against one another that's the cruelest public spin on motherhood—the transformation of what is already a difficult, emotional, and physically demanding experience into some kind of endurance-challenge spectator sport, with all the added pressure and insecurity that will inevitably cause. Spare a thought for any pregnant mother reading the *TMZ* article headlined "Not All Famous Preggo Chicks Have to Be HUGE," which shamelessly clawed into Jessica Simpson and Kim Kardashian by lining them up next to the duchess and crudely concluding, "Well, one of these things is not like the other," while helpfully observing of Kate's physique that you could "BARELY tell she was with fetus."

Add to all this the slew of articles about losing baby weight, "showing off" svelte "postbaby" figures (always with a "celebrity steps out just x months after giving birth!" headline for comparison purposes), and a total dearth of media coverage of real women's postbaby bodies. The result is a toxic combination of shame, guilt, and self-flagellation for new mothers at one of the most vulnerable and draining points of their lives, complete with all the (let's face it) much more important things they could really be focusing on.

It's a strange quirk of our media that, while certain aspects of women's bodies (what they look like at eighteen, say, or after breast implants, or slathered in baby oil and airbrushed) are so overexposed that we come to automatically and inaccurately consider them the norm, some *actual* norms are so resolutely kept from our view that we're utterly unprepared for them. This is especially pertinent in the case of pregnancy—and never has it been more astoundingly exposed than on the Duchess of Cambridge's exit from the maternity wing of London's St Mary's Hospital just hours after giving birth, her postpartum baby bump clearly visible.

The media, both traditional and online, exploded. What was wrong with her? people *demanded* to know. Had she really had the baby? Was there another one in there? Had she got fat during her pregnancy? A quick-thinking Sky News reporter asked a midwife in an on-air interview why Kate still had a baby bump. Twitter exploded as stumped users searched for answers: "Why's Kate Middleton still fat with a bump? She's already had the baby," asked one flummoxed user. "Why does Kate's belly still look fat when they're outside holding the baby?" wondered another, concisely expressing the depth of their consternation with an added "wtf." Myriad commenters stuck to the plain facts: "Kate looks fat. Lol." Others flavored their observations of the new mother with extra objectification and misogyny: "I'd fuck Kate with or without her afterbirth bump."

The stunned reaction revealed the seeping of the media correlation between pregnancy and "fatness" into the public consciousness and gave an ugly glimpse of the extent to which, for some people, any woman, at any time, will always be seen as a sex object. But most important, it revealed a widespread lack of any kind of public awareness or education about the actual impact of pregnancy on women's bodies—the changes they go through and the reality of how they will look different at different times.

When the BBC capitalized on the inevitable ensuing slew of "Kate bump" Google searches with a story showing photographs of women's postbirth stomachs, there was an outpouring of emotion from women and a shocked realization that here, incredibly, was an angle on the female body that many of us had simply never seen before. As one woman commented on the BBC article, "After I gave birth I was shocked. And horrified. I had never seen an after-pregnancy belly with stretch marks and sags exposed. At all. I hadn't heard about it. I didn't even know that it existed."

And it's not only expectant mothers who are apparently fair game for public commentary, criticism, and condemnation, but any mother at any time, according to a range of recurring trite headlines about whether women can "have it all," what "moms" are feeding their children, how "moms" are letting their kids watch too much television, whether "moms" should be making different choices—with never a father in sight or mind. Fox News ran a whole segment in May 2013 to debate the question: "Are female breadwinners a problem?" And a recent episode of

TV talk show *The Wright Stuff* asked: "Should Mums Only Work for the Money? Is it selfish to leave your kids in nursery or with child-minders just because you fancy getting out of the house a few hours or days each week?" Because, after all, what other reason could women have for a career than getting out of the house? We all know it's only men who derive fulfillment from academic and professional endeavor! The study that led to this momcentric debacle referred to children left in the care of others, so it could have applied to moms *or* dads, but was (like so many "scientific" findings) interpreted as a potential slur against only women. (As in the *Metro* story of August 2013 that took a scientific study about both spouses' ability to tune out their partner's voices and turned it into the refreshingly original story: "NAGGING NOISES: Good news husbands: it's easy to ignore your wife.")

Such headlines expose and compound the inherent societal assumption that ultimately it is a woman's duty to produce children, a woman's responsibility to ensure their well-being at every stage, and a woman's fault if anything goes wrong. As the thousands of entries we have received from working women testify, workplace equality laws and initiatives have yet to truly make a dent in the stony conviction that it is a woman's career that should take the hit for the price of parenthood. And after all, people still ask, What "real" woman wouldn't care more, deep down, about her child than her career? It's natural for men, of course, who have worked so hard and put so much into their prized jobs, to want to maintain a balance and not allow new fatherhood to derail a promotion or an ascending career path. But for a woman to voice the same priorities? Cold. Hard. Selfish.

One woman who recorded her story on the project Web site was excited to return to work after the birth of her first baby, but:

▸ As I walked into the office . . . the first question asked by a more senior male colleague that I would be working for was: "Hi, so who is looking after your baby?"

That afternoon another senior colleague—friends with the first one—thought it was acceptable to ask straight whether I would be properly involved in the new project, as "women are not as committed to work after they have a baby." He has 3 children but apparently the commitment only affects women.

Other women had not even *had* their babies when impending motherhood began to negatively affect their careers. One was dismissed by her manager in front of colleagues with an airy, "Well she's just a ball of raging hormones." Another's boss insisted on waiting until after the birth before filling in the paperwork for her return from maternity leave, "in case I'm besotted with the baby." Another wrote:

▸ While pregnant, I was told by ex-boss I should resign. He said he couldn't plan around me having another baby in the future. And when I took it to HR, I was told he was "probably just thinking out loud."

Before they even begin to hit the issue of workplace discrimination, expectant parents in the United States must face the fact that it lags embarrassingly behind most other countries by failing to mandate paid maternity leave and offering only a paltry 12 weeks' unpaid leave. In Sweden, by comparison, parents receive 480 days' leave (including 390 at around 80 percent of their salary); in Germany, new parents are allowed 14 months on 65 percent of their salary; Australia offers partners 52 shared weeks of unpaid leave, and Japan allows each a year off. This means that for many American couples, what should be a joyful time is fraught with financial worry. Of course this only emphasizes outdated stereotypes about the world of work being a man's domain to which women are ill suited, a notion further exacerbated by the definition of pregnancy as a disability for the purposes of workplace legislation. Does it sound like an outdated principle for such a modern country? Just pop back on over to *Fox News,* where business host Lou Dobbs complained that the rise in female breadwinners was "concerning and troubling," while panelist Erick Erickson went even more prehistoric in his argument against career women: "When you look at biology, look at the natural world, the roles of a male and female in society, and the other animals, the male typically is the dominant role." Animals also live in small dirty holes and crap on the ground, Erick. Should we be returning to those good ole days too?

Sleepless nights and close attachment to their new baby are commonly cited reasons leveled at postpartum mothers to underpin the idea of their potential workplace incapacity. Myths about working mothers being less committed or reliable abound, despite a lack of evidence to support them. Ironically, of course, new fathers suffer many of the same sleepless nights and feel the same close attachment to their new baby, yet somehow this leads to far less "well-intentioned" concern about the potential impact of parenthood on *their* careers.

The strange habit of seeing mothers and fathers through

completely different lenses holds strong in other situations too. Witness, for example, the level of public vitriol reserved for teenage mothers, from reality-style shows to media debates such as BBC Kent's recent phone-in on the question: "Do teenage girls get pregnant just to get a council house?" Hearing such questions, you might honestly be forgiven for assuming that teenage girls are indulging in some sort of trendy new craze for self-insemination, so clear is the implication that this is something *they* do, a decision *they* make, a responsibility *they* must shoulder and, as is often suggested, a burden *they* are foisting on the poor overstretched state.

So acute is our hysteria about teenage motherhood that a 2013 poll conducted by Ipsos MORI showed that the average member of the UK public believes that 15 percent of girls under sixteen get pregnant every year (the actual figure is around 0.6 percent). And penises, once again, get a free pass. In fact, this obsession with the idea that pregnancy is somehow a selfish choice made by mothers alone comes across again and again—whether it's in stupendously ignorant arguments about maternity leave being a "burden" that women selfishly foist onto employers, or in public attitudes toward pregnant women more generally:

▸ I'm heavily pregnant at the moment and was travelling into the city, by bus. When I got on, I walked toward the seats which are reserved for elderly/disabled/pregnant individuals. A man was already sitting here and looked at me, knowing I wanted "his" seat. He asked me did I want special attention due to being in my condition. I replied that I would appreciate the seat. His response was that I "should have thought about that when doing the business."

▸ While I was pregnant with my oldest, I worked in a post-press mailroom . . . On my way to the bathroom, I crossed paths with a co-worker, a man in his mid-40s. He looked me up and down, glared at me, and said, "Oh, THAT'S exactly what I want to see on my lunch break. A pregnant woman going to the bathroom!"

It strikes me that the vast majority of these inequalities come back to the same bizarrely stubborn insistence on considering pregnancy and reproduction something that women do, by and for themselves. The idea that women are "selfish" for taking maternity leave, or that their jobs shouldn't be safeguarded if they "choose" to "go off and have children" is ridiculous when you consider the fact that society depends on reproduction in order to physically continue. These women aren't flouncing selfishly off to a spa for nine months with no regard for their professional duty. A lot of them are just as upset about the potential damage to their career as their employers are! But given that reproduction is something *people* do together—and, frankly, is something we can't carry on without—it doesn't seem outrageously demanding to ask that we all chip in to deal with the costs. And that means paying a lot more attention and respect to the role of fathers in this whole process too.

One new mother described her situation:

▸ I will be going back to work later this year while my husband stays at home to look after our baby . . . At a recent baby fair, various reps for part-time stay-at-home money-making schemes converged on me and ignored my husband completely. Because obviously, if anyone's going to stay at home it must be the woman.

All our local parent-and-child sessions are geared toward mothers and babies—except, of course, for the Saturday session, which is specifically for "dads and granddads."

Even among those who accept my going back to work as perfectly reasonable and normal, there is always surprise when I tell them my husband will be doing the majority of the childcare. As though it's inconceivable that a man might prefer to look after his own child rather than hand the baby over to a (presumably female) child minder.

Countless other situations have been reported to the project by men who have been variously ostracized, stigmatized, or praised for performing parental duties that are considered perfectly normal for mothers. Like the man who was standing right next to his child when a stranger loudly alerted everybody in the vicinity to the presence of an abandoned baby. "Yes," he said, "the baby one foot to my left is without its mother. She's my daughter."

This discrimination occurs not just in the phase of babyhood but throughout the child's upbringing as well—where the closer involvement of fathers and greater respect for the role they play would be beneficial for everybody, children and parents alike. Whether it's the media reporting on every study about parents as a revelation for "moms," the world of advertising showcasing weary mothers parenting away while dads prance mischievously in bars like overgrown schoolboys, or businesses refusing to provide adequate provision for paternity leave, dads come up against barriers and disapproval at every stage of the child-rearing process. This leads to a vicious cycle of social assumptions about their inability to parent properly, which are passed on loud and clear to young boys and feed straight back into narratives about female domestic responsibility and expected gender roles.

Many men even reported being "congratulated" for "babysitting" their own children as if it were some special achievement, or a sign of overcoming a natural incapacity. One woman told us:

▸ My husband and I had our first child last year; I go to work and he stays at home with the baby. I often get asked, "How is he doing with all that babysitting? Has it been hard to teach him how to take care of a baby?" He's her father. He doesn't babysit, he PARENTS. And since he's with her for forty hours a week that I'm not, he's frankly quite a bit better at taking care of her than I am.

Some women understandably express their frustration when dads are praised like dancing monkeys for managing to complete a few hours of child care, but this attitude is equally unfortunate for fathers themselves. One man reported shocked disapproval from the doctor when he, instead of his wife, arrived with their baby daughter for one of her early checkups.

Many men struggle to care for their children in public places where baby-changing facilities—if there are any—are restricted to the women's toilets. One man reported a baffled and stony-faced staff member asking, "Can't you just do it on the floor?"

Inevitably, tackling such prejudice—whether it relates to workplace inequality or stereotypical public assumptions about parenthood—is essential and will be beneficial to everybody, both men and women. But it has to be done in the right way. As with so many other forms of sexism, we need not only legislative change (in this case to ensure things like flexible working hours and shared parental leave) but also a cultural shift in our very ideas about motherhood and what it means for women. Schemes like Apple's and Facebook's new egg-freezing "perk" are the perfect example of how hard people will try to address the problem without grasping it at its root. Offering to help women pay for egg freezing might be a useful Band-Aid for women in the current unfair professional system where childbirth and parenthood impact negatively on their careers and negligibly on most men's, but it overwhelmingly fails to address that culture, reinforcing the idea that it is problematic or impossible for women to combine career and family. Compare this policy, dreamed up by two companies whose staff are mainly men, with the simple solution reached by Sabrina Parsons, CEO of Palo Alto Software. Inspired by her own postbirth experience, Parsons simply allowed employees to bring their new babies into work with them, thereby taking a huge stride toward eliminating the exclusion of women from the workplace rather than perpetuating the divide.

There are other concrete measures that would clearly make a big impact—implementing paid maternity leave or better child care support, for example, would help to offset the fact that it is mostly the youngest and poorest mothers who are unable to return to work after having a baby. And from a legislative standpoint, implementing the Pregnant Workers Fairness Act would be a positive strike against maternity discrimination.

But fundamentally, we need to let go of the stubborn belief that providing a vessel for a fetus is the pinnacle of female purpose and achievement. And no, this isn't an exaggeration: Women actually are faced with this archaic idea on a regular basis—the ridiculousness of which is laid bare by these women's dry comments in a recent conversation on the Everyday Sexism Twitter feed:

I've been told: "single childless women over the age of 28 have no right to live."

Damn it, I have less than three months to live. I didn't realize these things mattered!

Bugger. I'd like lots of astronomy at my funeral, please . . .

I should have been dead 12 years ago.

I'm over 28, married & childless. Does that mean I just need to lose a limb or summat?

Apparently I've been dead for two years. I actually quite recommend it.

Chapter 9

Double Discrimination

I've had men say that I'm "attractive for an Indian" & "one of the good ones."

Tweet sent to the Everyday Sexism Project

Vital Statistics

Women with disabilities have a 40 percent greater risk than women without disabilities of experiencing partner violence.

-Douglas A. Brownridge, "Partner Violence Against Women With Disabilities: Prevalence, Risk, and Explanations," 2006

Half of LGBT people in the European Union avoid public places because of harassment.

-European Union Agency for Fundamental Rights, 2013

As of September 2014, U.S. unemployment rates among black women stood at 9.6 percent, compared to 4.8 percent among white women.

-U.S. Department of Labor, Bureau of Labor Statistics, 2014

Native American women are 2.5 times more likely to experience sexual assault crimes compared to the national average, and 1 in 3 Native American women reports having been raped during her lifetime.

-U.S. Department of Justice, 2000

More than half of women sex workers have been raped or sexually assaulted, and 75 percent have been physically assaulted.

-UK Home Office, 2004

One of the problems that makes sexism so difficult to tackle, or even to talk about, is that we all view each instance of it from a very individual perspective based on our own experience.

Take, say, a man who, every six months, witnesses just one instance of catcalling, after which he goes about his business without giving the matter a second thought. And then take a woman who every day experiences several such instances of harassment and has also on more than one occasion ignored the catcalls only to have the situation escalate into something more aggressive. Those two people would, understandably, react very differently to a hypothetical description of an isolated instance of harassment. The man would probably consider it minor, insignificant, and even harmless, while the woman would likely view it as more serious and potentially damaging. This is partly why it's so hard to discuss the problem of sexism—and why, when we do, the narrative (often led by those in the first category) turns so frequently to whether the problem in fact exists at all, or whether it's simply exaggerated. Our limited ability to view things through the lens of another's experience is even more pertinent when considering the intersection of sexism and other forms of prejudice. Unless we've experienced something similar ourselves, it's virtually impossible to imagine how it feels to experience multiple forms of oppression at the same time.

The concept of "double discrimination" isn't conjecture—these are real, concrete problems reflected in alarming statistics. Many LGBT people experience harassment and violence on a regular basis. Trans people are at a greater risk of depression, harassment, violence, self-harm, and suicide than the general population. A recent study revealed that 42 percent of trans women surveyed had attempted suicide, compared to 4.6 percent of people within the general population. A Royal College of Obstetricians and Gynaecologists (RCOG) inquiry in 2004 found that in the UK, "Women from ethnic groups other than white were, on average, three times more likely to die" in childbirth than white women. Unemployment figures for nonwhite women are consistently far higher than for white women, and they experience a wider pay gap—for example, the American Association of University Women reveals that on average, Hispanic and Latina women were paid just 54 percent of what white men were paid in 2013 (compared to 78 percent for white women). According to Women's Aid, disabled women are twice as likely as nondisabled women to be victims of domestic violence.

Since the Everyday Sexism Project started, many of the stories we have cataloged have described not only sexism but sexism intermingled with other forms of prejudice—racism, homophobia, transphobia, classism, ageism, disablism, stigma around mental-health problems, and more. Again and again, we've heard from women in same-sex relationships being fetishized and asked for threesomes when they're just trying to walk down the street, trans women mocked and belittled and hounded from public spaces, Asian women being labeled as "easy" or "obedient," sex workers accused of being complicit in their own assaults, disabled women being infantilized and patronized, and countless similar stories.

I chose to include this chapter in order to put a spotlight on these issues of "double discrimination" (or, indeed, triple or quadruple) because it has proved to be a major recurring theme within the project and is a crucial focus for modern feminism.

The severity and frequency of the problem merit closer examination. However, it should be noted that, though this section is designed to give these intersections between different forms of prejudice the attention they deserve, they also run throughout the other sections of this book, just as they should be present in all feminist discourse and activism. This chapter does not conveniently distance and compartmentalize its subject matter as one clean-cut area of sexism, nor is it intended to "other" those subjected to such double discrimination.

Intersectionality means being aware of and acting on the fact that different forms of prejudice are connected, because they all stem from the same root of being "other," "different," or somehow "secondary" to the "normal," "ideal" status quo. So just as women suffer from sexism because our society is set up to favor and automatically take men as the "norm" from which women deviate, the same is true for people who are "different" from other dominant norms—generally heterosexual, white, cisgender, and nondisabled. (A person who is cisgender identifies with the sex they were assigned at birth—in other words, they are not transgender.) People also often face prejudice as a result of other characteristics, such as age, class, and religious belief.

When I go into schools and talk to young children, one of my favorite exercises is to ask the whole class to close their eyes and imagine themselves at the dentist's office. I ask them to picture the white walls and the bright light, to see themselves in the big chair, and imagine that weird dentist smell. Then I tell them the door has opened and the dentist walks in. Without opening their eyes, I ask them to raise their hand if the dentist they are imagining is a man. Almost every hand in the room is always raised.

Acknowledging double discrimination forces us to recognize that when we think of a "human," he isn't simply a man. He's a white man. A white, heterosexual man. A white, heterosexual, nondisabled man. A white, heterosexual, nondisabled, middle-aged man. A white, heterosexual, nondisabled, middle-aged, cisgender man. And so on.

The principle of intersectionality is simple: If all these different kinds of prejudice stem from the same root, then it is arbitrary and ineffective to attempt to eradicate one of them without acknowledging its intersection with others and trying to tackle all forms of inequality. Or, from a feminist perspective, if we are to tackle the fact that women have historically been oppressed because of characteristics that are seen to be "different" from the male norm, how can we protest such treatment while simultaneously excluding from our own movement the needs and agendas of those with other stigmatized characteristics? (This is particularly true in the case of our trans sisters, who some feminists believe should be excluded from some areas of the movement by virtue of not fulfilling required "characteristics" of womanhood—a deep irony for a group fighting for equality regardless of sex.)

And on a concrete, practical level, the importance of intersectionality when fighting sexism is reinforced by the huge numbers of project entries we have received that clearly demonstrate the multiple discrimination of two or more kinds of prejudice combined.

Many women of color, for example, describe suffering not

only from both racism and sexism but also from a particular brand of racist sexism that conflates and exacerbates the two.

▸ I am Japanese. Frequently told by white men that Japanese, Chinese, Filipina, Asian women are "better" than the "feminazis," "femic*nts" in the west and "know how to treat men"; we will cook and clean.

Told I look like a Russian-Mongolian rape baby . . . Then he pulled the skin around his eyes.

▸ I was walking on my university campus with my boyfriend, when we walked past a group of guys, one of whom shouted out "What did you pay for her then? Is she a mail order?" (My boyfriend is Chinese and I'm half Indian.)

Male strangers grinning at me and loudly inquiring "CHINA OR JAPAN?!" The worst thing is, I'm neither.

When I interviewed the writer Reni Eddo-Lodge, she explained:

Not all women experience incidents like street harassment in the same way. In particular it's helpful to consider how racism and exotification impacts into a black experience of sexual harassment. Often I've noticed a racialized dimension to the street harassment I've received—particularly since I cut off my relaxed hair, went natural and have a little afro. Calls in the street of "African queen," "ebony princess" and the like refer directly to my race as well as my gender. I think this is an

issue when navigating the first stages of any relationship as well (particularly if it's a mixed-race relationship), you find a considerable amount of your time being eaten up by wondering whether you're being taken seriously as a human being or being viewed as a novelty, or an exotic entity. The very idea of this makes me feel uneasy.

I think the exotification of black women can be traced back to the days of empire and colonialism, particularly the Hottentot Venus Saartjie Baartman. There's particular fascination with African women's bodies and because of the likes of hip-hop videos—the production of which is controlled by black men in a heavily male-dominated industry—our bodies are rarely equated with innocence and piety and instead are deemed as permanently sexually available. An added dimension of this is that these African body features are celebrated and considered mainstream beautiful in lighter-skinned women such as Jennifer Lopez, but seen as tacky and trashy in darker-skinned women like Nicki Minaj.

In fact, I can't tell you about the amount of times I've opted not to wear a miniskirt or short shorts on a hot day because (1) I know how my hips and thighs will look in them and (2) I know what conclusions people will draw about me because of this.

This idea of black women as "exotic," hypersexualized creatures can be seen again and again in cultural stereotypes. Type "pretty" into Google image search and you are greeted with pages and pages and pages of white women's faces (the fashion industry is notoriously white; of the seventy-five British *Vogue* covers from the beginning of 2008 to the time of writing, black women have featured on just three, while Kate Moss *alone* has graced nine). Now type in "sexy," and suddenly far more women of color appear—though they do remain far less represented than white women. Many project entries described the impact of this stereotype on real women's lives:

People attach this hyper-sexualized image to me because of my skin color and talk about how spicy and exotic I am.

But often this racialized aspect is overlooked because the sexism is more obvious and in your face. This case is strongly argued by Ikamara Larasi of the black-feminist organization Imkaan, who gives the example of the music video for the Major Lazer song "Bubble Butt." This starts with three white women dancing listlessly in their bedroom, when a giant black woman flies through the sky (implying exoticization to the extent that she isn't even from the same planet) wearing a costume that leaves her bottom completely exposed. She lands, and snakelike pipes come writhing out of her mouth (as a Medusa-like mythological creature, othered again to an extreme degree). The pipes slither through the bedroom window, "plug" into the white women's bottoms, and pump them up to huge, caricatured balloons. The rest of the video consists almost entirely of "twerking"—a dance move that involves energetic shaking and wobbling of the buttocks and is associated with black culture. But (because of the exposed bottoms of the women in the video, and lyrics like "Damn, bitch, talk much . . . I'm trying to get into you"), the inherent racism is often largely overlooked by those protesting the sexism of the song.

In fact, twerking itself is a perfect recent example of the hypersexualization of black women, having been famously and deliberately adopted, alongside other aspects of black culture, by the former Disney pop princess Miley Cyrus in her bid to shed her pure, good-girl image for something more "risky" and "sexy." But by consciously employing a dance move associated with black women (and indeed by using black women as literal objects and props, as she did during her notorious Video Music Awards performance), Cyrus has contributed to the idea of the appropriation of black culture, by a woman, as an immediate means to appear raunchy, oversexed, and vulgar. This is a tool that Cyrus, as a white woman, may pick up and put down again should she ever wish to lay her "risqué" persona to rest. The same cannot be said of the black women whose image she's helped to caricature and oversexualize.

I'm a barmaid—the white women behind the bar get standard sex/head jokes, I get asked to twerk.

But, as with the Major Lazer video, the mainstream outrage about Cyrus's transformation has focused almost exclusively on the nudity and sexualization it embraces, while its problematic racist implications have been ignored.

We know that sexism is not just a frustration, or a discomfort, but can actually have a huge impact on women's lives, careers, and success. When prejudices intersect, the same is doubly true. From education . . .

Known to be a lesbian by my boarding-school administration, I was forcibly set up on a prom date my last year at school. The guy would not keep his hands off me, and told me the faculty had said he had to kiss me to make it a "real date." (I am guessing they thought corrective kissing wasn't as serious, but just as effective, as corrective rape.) After I tried to end the "date" by returning to my single-sex dorm, he followed me across the campus. I eventually shoved him into the duckpond (still in his rented polyester tuxedo).

I was not allowed to graduate; he was.

To employment . . .

▸ When I sat down to be interviewed, all he spoke about was his strong desire for dark-skinned Black women. How he loves our skin. How his first wife or lover was Black. He kept looking me over and nodding his head in approval of my looks and whatever other fantasies he was playing out in his head. He hardly spoke about the job.

To personal safety . . .

▸ Told by a male acquaintance that he likes Chinese women as they "don't make a drama" over rape, and view date rape as just the guy being pushy. When I called him a disgusting prick the guy told me I don't count as Chinese because I was born in the UK.

And, as similarly demonstrated by accounts of other forms of sexism, these combined prejudices become evident at a tragically young age:

▸ I reported a boy at school who had been making racial and sexual remarks to me and other girls of ethnic minorities for about a year. Because, even though teachers and other students could hear the disgusting comments he was making about me being a "black whore who he wanted to put in a cage," a Pakistani girl being a "bomber" and stating the only attractive females were white, it was dismissed and nobody said a word.

As Joy Goh-Mah succinctly explained on the Media Diversity UK blog, when men approach her with phrases like "I love Asian women!" or "Asian women are so hot!" or "Japan, Korea, China?," "they aren't speaking to me, they're speaking to their idea of an Asian woman, their fantasy made flesh. They're speaking to every Asian woman they've ever seen in the media, every Asian porn actress they've ever leered at on their computer screens. My personality is rendered invisible, obscured by the lenses of racial stereotype."

The great effect of media stereotypes on the treatment of particular groups of people—especially those suffering various forms of "double discrimination"—is a vital part of the problem. The incredibly narrow media presentation of women as beautiful, sexualized objects is clearly detrimental and of great concern to feminism. Of equally great concern should be the overwhelming likelihood that the majority of women made visible to us in everyday media will be young, heterosexual, cisgender, middle or upper class, and nondisabled.

According to figures released in the UK in May 2013, just 18 percent of television presenters over the age of fifty are women. The percentage for older disabled women, LGBT women, and women of color is likely to be even lower. And in the United States, in prime-time television on broadcast networks in 2013–2014, only 17 percent of female characters were in their forties and only 3 percent over sixty.

The problem is exacerbated and inflamed by two key factors.

First, such women are so rarely portrayed on screen as to be considered strange and unusual. Second, when they *are* present, they have generally been molded into hackneyed caricatures that play to every stereotype in the book and exist solely to satisfy a specific storyline—*about* disability or lesbianism, for example. Which of course encourages the notion that certain characteristics are somehow all-consuming and utterly defining.

▸ I am a gay female and I often feel as though the media only seems to have one specific idea of what a female is/wants/desires. I often feel alienated and unseen/un-acknowledged. I would like to see the media become more complex and diverse including WOMEN in their audience, not just ONE specific TYPE of woman. I am made to feel like because I don't fit into a specific stereotype I am not worthy of being seen and I am ignored.

▸ The dearth of any women in the media anywhere near my size (I'm a UK 18 [U.S. 16]) who isn't (a) a pathetic lonely loser, or (b) the "before" shot on a weight-loss show.

▸ Can we talk about the lack of representation of WOC [women of color] in the media? When we are portrayed, it's usually as being "oppressed" and in need of saving.

▸ I very, very rarely see a woman on TV, fictional or real, who's my age *without children* and not depicted as either lonely and bitter, or a hard-driven career woman. Because reproduction has to be something we either tragically miss out on, or only choose to forego for huge financial gain.

▸ As a physically disabled woman, I feel invisible, both in the media and in real life, as it were. No one seems to think that I have a sexuality or even sensuality. There seem to be very few characters in films and TV shows who are incidentally disabled and/or queer. I'm going back a fair few years now but Dr Kerry Weaver from *ER* is the only one who springs to mind. A lot of the time, it seems as if disability or non-heterosexual sexuality is part of the plot rather than a character just so happening to be disabled/queer with no big deal made of their identity.

▸ The ideal woman lauded by the media is thin, conventionally attractive, perfectly groomed and shaved, an ideal that is hard to reach for many women, but impossible and out of question for women of color since beauty is linked to being white. You may try to be "pretty" when you're white, but you'll never be when you're not white.

▸ Next to no programs portray lesbians as just one of the characters, without being a story feature and portrayed to meet (hetero male?) viewer expectations. I'd note that we are a diverse bunch and don't have a "look" so much! As for the portrayal of lesbian families, except for high profile Australian people like Penny Wong, there are none that I know of. If that's demoralizing for us, I can't imagine it's good for our kids either . . .

▸ I'm fat. I've been heavy since my thyroid stopped working at 8. I've only very rarely seen positive images of women like me in the media. People my size are portrayed as stupid, weak willed, mean, annoying or worthless, despite the fact that most of the recent research into obesity contradicts the assumption that being fat is primarily a matter of will rather than genetics. Fat people can be brilliant, creative, strong, loyal, loving, and beautiful, but we're almost never shown that way.

▸ The media's complete failure to be able to cover trans folk in any way that considers them as people first and trans second—instead it is always made to be their entire identity, whether in the rare television shows when a trans person features (either as part of an episode specifically focusing on being trans, or as the butt of every joke, with the frequent suggestion on shows like "How I Met Your Mother" that accidentally kissing a "chick with a dick" is the worst, most embarrassing thing that could ever happen to anyone) or in the papers, where they insist on referring to people like Chelsea Manning as "Bradley" and "he" irrespective of her own wishes.

▸ Working-class women are rarely portrayed in a good light in the media, and equality of opportunity rather than focusing on women at the top is something feminism needs more of.

▸ As a 40-year-old woman, I find myself, often subconsciously, questioning whether what I am wearing is "appropriate" for my age—but why should I? Why should my age dictate my wardrobe? The media shaming of women who are "mutton-dressed-as-lamb" has instilled in me a terrible fear of looking "ridiculous." Most of the time I actively resist it and wear what I like, but sometimes I get scared and buckle.

▸ I'm bisexual. That in and of itself has so many negative stereotypes attached to it in terms of media representation . . . Bi men are often typecast as being effeminate and weak. Their bisexuality is just a cover for coming out as gay later on. And for bisexual women—well, my sexuality is for the entertainment of men only . . . We are portrayed [kissing] other women to get men to buy us a drink, or, of course, in pornography. I can't discuss bisexuality without some guy thinking I'll be up for a threesome. Like my sexuality is the only thing about me, instead of just another aspect of a human being. If I have a male partner, then people think it was just a phase, and if I have a female partner then I'm "experimenting." There is no legitimate representation of bisexuality in the media at all—so forget about older bisexual men and women!

It is easy to see how such media stereotypes leak into the general public's perceptions and consequently their behavior.

▸ Another bi woman here, sick of all the misconceptions. For me, people seem to not be able to believe that I can even be bisexual because I haven't had sexual experience with another person at all. Well, straight people can say they're straight with no experience and no one is skeptical of that!

The battle can feel endless—because it is a far more complex issue than just achieving representation in itself. It's also about the *way* people are represented. It's about the fact that, even when they are finally acknowledged and included, women facing complex discrimination are so frequently used as tokenistic representatives of a particular group rather than being viewed as a voice or an expert in their own right. It's about their voices being silenced in mainstream debates. Because when, say, one disabled woman sits on a panel of experts discussing a wide and varied topic, such as local politics, she might easily find every question about minority or women's issues directed to her while the general political questions go to the nondisabled men sitting in every other chair. It's about the co-opting of their achievements, as when Jeanne Socrates completed a nine-month round-the-world sailing trip and headlines omitted her name altogether, instead defining her by her age and childbearing status: "A British grandmother has become the oldest woman to sail solo around the world non-stop."

And always the ongoing othering makes every battle harder to fight—because, it is often implied, shouldn't women be grateful just to be included? How uppity and churlish it would be to complain about such a thing when one has "made it" into the hallowed inner ring in the first place. Similarly, when these women are fighting for their inclusion in the feminist movement—fighting just to establish what needs to be on the table—they have that much less breath and energy and momentum left when the real battles finally begin.

Before trans people can even begin to fight for equality, for instance, they have to overcome enormous ignorance and lack of understanding about their experience:

▸ A close friend of mine is a trans man and has been told many times by people who knew him before his transition (which began toward the end of his time at high school) or have seen pictures of him as a child that "it's a shame such a pretty girl wants to look like a guy," implying that his gender identity is a choice and deliberately neglecting the duty of anyone born with female organs to look "feminine."

Before disabled people can even start working toward equal rights, they have to contend with a society within which most people still subscribe to the medical model of disability, which holds that a person is disabled by his or her impairment (i.e., a mental-health issue prevents him from getting a job, or a physical condition restricts her ability to access certain venues) rather than the social model, which suggests that it is not the impairment in itself but the lack of accessibility created by our disablist society that makes a person disabled (i.e., our stigma around mental-health issues prevents that person from getting a job, or a lack of adequate measures to make a venue fully accessible prevents certain people being able to enter).

And women like Tulisa Contostavlos, despite huge achievements and enormous creative success, still find themselves having to overcome prejudice, again and again, on the basis of their perceived class, as if it is an insult or embarrassing slur they can never escape. It is kept in reserve to shame them and immediately put them down in any situation.

Meanwhile, this intersection of prejudice can also make it even harder for women experiencing multiple forms of abuse and discrimination to make progress against inequality. While Native American and Alaska Native women report rates of sexual assault more than twice the national average, the problem is often either ignored or compounded by racism—there is little awareness, for example, that at least 86 percent of the assaults are perpetrated by non-Native men, according to the U.S. Department of Justice. Such assaults recall and compound the brutal assault of colonization, which included the rape of indigenous peoples and, according to Amnesty International's "Maze of Injustice" report, "The attitudes toward Indigenous peoples that underpin such human rights abuses continue to be present in the USA today. They contribute to the present high rates of sexual violence perpetrated against indigenous women and help to shield their attackers from justice." Yet despite such shocking statistics, these multiple forms of discrimination are rarely prioritized by legislators—so, for example, 2012–2013 saw fierce opposition to the reauthorization of the Violence Against Women Act due to proposed amendments designed to give tribal courts jurisdiction to prosecute in cases of sexual violence involving non-Native perpetrators.

Other elements of the bill that were also stringently resisted proposed greater protections against sexual violence for victims in same-sex relationships and undocumented immigrants—more groups that don't fit the one-size-fits-all approach. House Republicans even created their own version of the measure, stripping it of the suggested amendment. It was an enormous struggle, even in 2013, for marginalized and vulnerable groups to be afforded the same protections against violence as white, heterosexual, middle-class women. Even in the eyes of the law, it seems that some people are considered more human than others.

This lack of awareness of multiple, intersecting forms of discrimination at a structural and authority level was also exemplified in 2014, when the U.S. army tried to implement new restrictions on acceptable hairstyles, apparently not realizing that banning styles such as twists, dreadlocks, and large cornrows would have a disproportionate impact on African American women who chose natural hair care.

Creating rules and protections for "women" will continue to see many marginalized and forgotten if, when we think of "women," we are really referring to white, middle-aged, heterosexual, nondisabled, cisgender, middle-class women.

One of the reasons it is so important to let members of oppressed groups tell their own stories in their own ways is that it's so easy to think you're getting it when you're not. (For example, U.S. *Vogue*'s proclamation: "We're in the era of the big booty," in an article that purported to celebrate curvier women but was criticized by black feminists for erasing black women's history and appropriating what has always been a part of their identity as something to be celebrated only after it has been adopted by white women.)

Many of the men writing to the project said they thought they knew about sexism when they imagined a catcall or a wolf whistle but had no concept of how it actually affected women's lives, living it every day, influencing every choice and thought.

Because it isn't just about the individual incidents; it's about the collective impact on everything else—the way you think about yourself, the way you approach public spaces and human interaction, the limits you place on your own aspirations, and the things you stop yourself from doing before you even try because of bitter learned experience.

As the writer John Scalzi brilliantly and simply put it on his blog, *Whatever*: "In the role playing game known as The Real World, 'Straight White Male' is the lowest difficulty setting there is." It is not a collection of individual moments but a constant setting that influences everything. Of course, this doesn't preclude individual circumstances from impacting negatively on people's lives—it's not to discount the difficulties faced by, for example, heterosexual white men from disadvantaged socioeconomic backgrounds—but it's a ballpark starting point that helps us get the general idea.

For many of these women, the relentless prejudice they experience has an enormous impact on their whole lives that is far greater than the sum of the individual incidents they experience, and is aggravated by living in a world that sends them constant messages about how they should expect to be treated.

Jasmine, a trans woman, told me:

I remember my dad saying those fateful words, "Don't ever come home and tell me you're gay"; how then would he react to the news that I wasn't actually his son, but his daughter?

Fear kept me in the closet for a very long time; fear of violence, of being rejected by my family and friends, and of losing my job (I've met several trans-women who lost their jobs when they came out, or were disowned by their parents, spouses, or children).

She was forced to endure seven years' waiting before she could transition, because of a prolonged period of job training during which "it would only have needed one of my instructors taking exception to me to make life extremely hard." For those who haven't experienced it, spending seven years hiding your true identity because of a very real fear that the world would reject you so violently that your entire career might be jeopardized is difficult even to begin to imagine.

She strikingly explains the extent of the stigma and lack of acceptance experienced by people who are othered in our society:

Many people have told me that I'm brave for undergoing all the surgery I have (five surgeries so far—one lasting eleven hours—with

more to come), but in fact the hardest and most terrifying thing by far was telling everyone. Not only did I risk estrangement from family and friends, but my employers are the only company in the whole of the country to provide the service that I'm trained for. If they or my co-workers reacted badly, I could [have lost] a very high-paying job, which I enjoyed very much, and which I'd spent seven years training for.

For many women who face multiple discrimination, even carrying out the simplest everyday activities that most of us take for granted can be fraught and painful. As Dee Emm Elms, a trans woman and brilliant writer, explains on her blog, *Four-Color Princesses*:

I notice that a lot of trans women don't put pictures of themselves on the internet. I've asked a lot of them why, and I get a variety of reasons. Unsurprisingly, a lot of it has to do with danger. I've been told that it's fear, but it's not the same kind of fear for everyone who feels it. For some, it's the fear of stigmatization. For others, it's the fear of recognition. For many, it's the fear of becoming the victim of the very real threat of physical violence and/or sexual assault. Since starting this blog, I've gotten death threats. I've gotten rape threats. I've gotten threats about everything in-between. I've been told I'm not really a woman. I've been told I'm not really a man. I've been told I'm not worth the air I "waste" by breathing. I've been told I'm the root cause of hurricanes and tornados. I've been told I'm fat. I've been told I'm ugly. I've been told I'm going to Hell.

This sense of instantly being judged and condemned purely as a result of others' preconceptions also comes across painfully clearly in the entries we have received from disabled women.

Strangers saying: "You're hot . . . for a girl in a wheelchair."

I have a long term illness that causes chronic exhaustion and means I need quite a lot of help from my family. I've been told I'm selfish for not having children.

I'm physically disabled, and live in chronic pain. There is no cure for my condition and it will only worsen with time. On days when I feel up to walking rather than using a wheelchair, I frequently have to stop and rest and am frequently grimacing with pain when walking. Every single time, without fail, I am told by men to "smile, it might never happen" or "cheer up, it'll get better."

I was once assaulted by an older man twice my size getting onto a bus because he thought I looked too young to be using a walking stick so I had to be a "scrounging lazy little bitch."

Seriously: I DO need my mobility aids, I AM genuinely disabled, yes, at my age (27), and NO, if I want your help I will ASK you. STOP touching me!

Every now and then in the thousands of stories we have collected comes a recurring word or description that echoes through the pages, used by woman after woman after woman to describe her lived experience. In the case of older women, that word is "invisible."

You really do become invisible when you hit middle age. Look around at all the middle-aged women you see wearing red coats or bright colors. It's so that people don't bump into us in the street because we're physically invisible.

▸ I'm now 51 and I definitely am beginning to feel invisible.

▸ I'm 43 and disappearing . . .

▸ As a grandmother of 3 and in my mid-50s, I find I am invisible everywhere!

▸ Not so long ago, my mum and I were talking, and she said something which is going to stick with me forever: "When you're a woman over forty, you disappear."

▸ I just turned 60. Have had trouble getting jobs for ages due to being invisible. But, hey, the upside is I don't get sexually harassed anymore either.

▸ I am 60 years old on Thursday but have been invisible for at least 10 years. Older people, women especially, just live on the sidelines of society, that's how it feels anyway. We are under-represented in every area.

▸ Society seems to expect women to disappear. And certainly we become a joke as far as being thought attractive is concerned. I have achieved much of value in my life and much to be proud of. It is insulting I am only considered worth noticing during my supposed childbearing years and after that am not worth anything.

▸ I am sick of being invisible—in the media, the supermarket queue, and most definitely the power tool shop. Turn 50 and become invisible to the world.

As men approach the late middle age at which their experience and knowledge, their skill and talent are most respected and in demand, the same characteristic is used utterly to dismiss their female peers from consideration—whether as professionals, members of society, or sexual beings.

For some women, what becomes oppressive in itself is, ironically, the invisibility of the characteristic that sets them apart. One woman with a chronic illness explains:

▸ Being unable to work, date, have a social life, looking "odd" because I'm ill and exhausted—those things make me feel invisible. There are a lot of illnesses which have no visible symptoms, and a lot of illnesses that men (and, sadly, some women) don't want to discuss publicly. Anything related to bladder/bowels/reproductive system isn't "polite" to talk about, I'm learning. I've encountered people who'd like me to be invisible AND silent.

For other women, the issue is complicated and exacerbated by further factors, such as receiving different kinds of discrimination from different angles. Nimko Ali is of Somali heritage; she's the director of Daughters of Eve, a not-for-profit organization that works with young people affected by or at risk of FGM (female genital mutilation), with a UK focus. She told me:

Because I live in two different worlds I kind of walk this tightrope between living in the UK and being from a certain community or

heritage. I kind of get it twofold, so it's basically being objectified by men in the West because of the way I dress and then being told, in another way, I shouldn't be dressing like that—again being objectified by men from the same community with the heritage that I have . . .

I was 13 years old, I was coming back from the dentist with my mother and the local cleric was talking at my mother about me about the skirt that I was wearing—because the grammar school that I went to had a specific length skirt which was too short in his eyes, and I remember being really, really angry that this man talked to my mother like that just because she was a woman and talked about me as if I didn't exist . . . that was the first time I stood up and said, "This is unacceptable. And just because I am a woman, I won't be spoken to like that."

Growing up I was very athletic as a teenager, so there were stereotypes of what girls should look like and me not looking like that—and then in another kind of population where I was from, because I didn't wear a headscarf again I never truly belonged, because it was this whole thing of everybody had a view of what women should be and that wasn't me. For me it was like being the black sheep of two different worlds.

I don't accept that there should be a cut out picture of how women should look like—whatever culture or color or heritage they're from.

Other women described similar experiences of suffering prejudice both from within their own communities and from outside:

I have been called an "uppity slag" & "coconut" by hardline traditionalists—just because I'm educated.

Ex told me white guys'll only date me to annoy their parents.

It's exhausting just to read about. Imagine what it's like to live it every day. And all this is before considering the stigma and double discrimination faced by women with mental-health issues . . .

Have been told I'm lucky to have found someone who'd marry me, because of mental illness/disability.

"What have *you* got to be depressed about, you silly girl?" "What's *wrong* with you? Stop crying and pull yourself together."

Or larger women . . .

Fat girls can get away with it if they've a pretty face like you.

Or those suffering even more intersections of prejudice . . .

Because I'm blind & disabled, guy tried convincing me blowing him would be good for me. Not that desperate!

There are far too many complex issues and experiences that fit into this area of multiple prejudice ever to be able to do them justice in a single chapter. Multiple entire books could be dedicated to each of these types of double discrimination, and it is the women who experience them who are best qualified to present and analyze the problem. I hope I've given an introductory sense of the enormity of the issues here while being acutely aware that there is so much more to say.

Nevertheless, two things are certain about the issues faced by each of these groups. First, as Ali eloquently explains, they all have extremely similar roots:

One of the main reasons inequalities exist is because we're scared and one of the things we have to overcome is the fear of "what do I have to lose if someone is as equal as I am?"

Second is the importance of working, as feminists, to include these varied priorities and experiences within the movement for equality.

Dee Emm Elms described this with beautiful simplicity:

It baffles me when I see people saying, "I don't focus on racism. I focus on sexism." It leaves me saddened when I hear people saying, "You're OK, but you're not." It makes people, in my opinion, guilty of the same crimes of thoughtlessness that lead to these problems . . .

Because that person on the bus being harassed is still being harassed whether she's being harassed for being religious or for being an atheist or being black or being a woman or because of her clothing or because of her body-language or because of her appearance or because of her handbag or because of her accent. That's all the same problem.

It's not recognizing the basic humanity of a person . . . That's the problem.

Chapter 10

What About the Men?

Firstly as a man of 28 why is it that I'm incapable of washing my own clothes? Secondly, why should my wife be expected to do it?

Everyday Sexism Project entry

Vital Statistics

Male suicide rates are 4 times higher than female rates.

–Centers for Disease Control and Prevention (CDC), Data & Statistics, Fatal Injury Report, 2012

Of those who died by suicide in 2012, 78 percent were male.

–CDC, Fatal Injury Report, 2012

In the past three decades, male body image concerns have increased from 15 percent to 43 percent of men being dissatisfied with their bodies.

–David Garner, "Body Image Poll Results," 1997; G. S. Goldfield, A. G. Blouin, and D. B. Woodside, "Body Image, Binge Eating, and Bulimia Nervosa in Male Bodybuilders," 2006; Deborah Schooler and L. Monique Ward, "Average Joes: Men's Relationships with Media, Real Bodies, and Sexuality," 2006

63 percent of men think their arms or chests are not muscular enough.

–University of the West of England, 2012

More than 1 in 10 men said they would trade a year of their life for the ideal body weight and shape.

–University of the West of England, 2012

A quarter of men age eighteen to twenty-four are worried about the amount of porn they are watching on the Internet.

–BBC/TNS, 2011

A guy sat me down to explain why feminism has no relevance in 2013 while stroking my leg the whole time.

I find the #ShoutingBack timeline is like being at the window onto a previously unknown world that's happening all around under my radar.

My husband is taking paternity leave and his colleagues mock him for it.

Mother to toddler son at nursery this morn, "Don't cry, you're not a girl are you?"

I became a single parent . . . [when] my youngest was 5. Often people were shocked I had custody. Men can raise children too!

Guys like me get an insight into what women have to put up with. I had no idea it was so bad.

Some people tweet using the hashtag #KillAllMen. I hate it. It's offensive, distasteful, and not conducive to progress, particularly when used by those who identify themselves as feminists. It doesn't matter if they choose to describe it as "ironic"—we wouldn't accept that as an excuse for a trending

#KillAllWomen hashtag. It's frustrating when people bring up this hashtag in discussions about feminism and use it to criticize all feminists—like it's "proof" that we really do hate men, or are trying to take over the world, "mwah ha ha haaa"–style. It's annoying to be automatically discounted on the basis of something you'd never support or subscribe to. So I am, by the same token, extremely sensitive to the unproductive tarring of all men with a single brush. The idea that roughly half the world's population exhibits the same strengths and flaws, behaviors and beliefs is the ridiculous notion I spend most of my time debunking and combating on behalf of women. I'm certainly not going to advocate its application to men!

I say this because it's so important to make it clear that tackling sexism in no way translates to a suggestion that all men are sexist. Men have been some of the project's greatest supporters, and they have also used it to share their own experiences of sexism. Often the stories we receive relate to sexism as perpetrated by women, not men, or by a particular company, or by society at large. The project is by no means intended to vilify men in general. Against the wider backdrop of structural gender imbalance, however—economic, political, social, and historical—I feel it's important for the focus of this particular venture, at least, to remain on women's experiences as the disproportionate casualties of sexism. Hence the crowding of all these very different men, and male attitudes, into a single chapter. This is not to underplay the importance of men to the movement, nor to dismiss the problems disproportionately faced by men—which are many and varied.

Why are you ignoring men's experiences—isn't that sexism? Do you hate all men? Do you want women to rule the world?

Haven't you ever heard of the draft? Don't you know men can face sexism too? HAVE YOU SEEN THE DIET COKE ADVERTISEMENT? And so on.

I hear these questions a lot. One of the things that interests me most about them is that, when they're posed by men, there's almost invariably no personal story or evidence to support them. It's rarely a case of "I think you're wrong to focus on women's experiences of sexism because here are five things that have happened to me . . ." (or even "one thing that's happened to me"). Instead, it seems to be the concept of the project itself that theoretically offends. Those men who do write in about experiences of their own don't tend to be the ones who have any issue with the project's aims.

And, in a way, I think that might explain a lot of the issue here. And the hostility. This is the invisible problem rearing its head again. For some men—usually those who haven't experienced prejudice themselves—the idea of protecting women from sexism feels akin to offering "special treatment." If you honestly don't think men are treated any differently from women—if you consider a catcall such a rare and "inconsequential" event that it happens no more frequently than a man is called a "girl" for crying, say—then it sort of makes sense that focusing on women's experiences of sexism might seem biased and unfair. And, if you come to it from a very self-centered perspective, you might not be able to see the ironic truth that insulting a man by calling him a "girl" and many, many more examples of everyday sexism are actually equally offensive to both men and women.

Really, the first thing to say about men is that they're wonderful. They have been, in the main, fantastically, vocally supportive of the Everyday Sexism Project. This goes for my always supportive partner, whose nights and days for the last four years have been filled with endless Twitter shifts, and harrowing reading, and journalists' phone calls, and dealing with death threats, and taking over the Web site moderation so I wouldn't have to read those graphic threats, and genuinely making it possible for the project to exist at all. It goes for my wary-but-proud dad and my bravely-exploring-completely-new-ideas-he's-never-been-exposed-to-before little brother. It goes for our ever patient and supportive Web developer, Jim. It goes for the men who wrote in to say that they had no idea what women were dealing with . . .

Reading your Twitter feed has really opened my eyes. I knew sexism existed, but to this extent? It's like there's a world in which women are constantly threatened, and I've suddenly discovered not only that it exists . . . but that it's the world *I* live in too.

And the men who promised they'll be doing something about it from now on . . .

Definitely think the awareness is useful from a male point of view. Has definitely led to me thinking more about what I say and do.

And the men who've reported rethinking their own behavior, and those who've challenged that of others . . .

Without even realizing, some posts have helped me change my ways a little now to be more empathetic.

And the ones who've publicly championed us—like Simon Pegg, Hugo Rifkind, Chris Addison, Robert Webb, and James Corden. And the thousands who follow the project on Twitter, turn up to events, participate in the Facebook group, ask questions and provide insights and discuss and love and learn with and alongside women everywhere. And most of all, the exceptional men mentioned in project entries, who are standing up and fighting beside us . . .

▸ As a student nurse I get a lot from guys who are intoxicated. I was assisting the doctor stitch up a drunk guy's face and the patient started stroking my arms (he had also previously asked me for a kiss 'cause I was "a bit of all right"). I didn't know how to react, I'm a young girl and being in the professional capacity I wasn't sure how to deal with it professionally so I ignored it. The doctor however after a few minutes raised his voice and very firmly told the guy to stop and behave himself because I "was there to assist him, not to be cuddled." I was really shocked that the doctor addressed it, but thankful, I thought he would have just ignored it. The world needs more people like that doctor.

Group of drunk lads shouted "get yer tits out" to a woman a few yards ahead of me so I lifted my T-Shirt and showed them mine.

This is not a men-versus-women issue. It's about people versus prejudice.

So let's talk about the men. Can men experience sexism? I think they can. To me, sexism means treating someone differently or discriminating against them because of their sex. If a boy is laughed at for being "soft" or unmanly because he gets upset, or he chooses to rock a particularly awesome shade of nail polish, I'd consider that sexist (and here, of course, sexism often intersects with homophobia). If a man is penalized for taking paternity leave from work because his bosses don't consider it his role to play a central part in the care of his newborn, I think that counts as sexism too. If we're going to challenge sexism, we should acknowledge and stand up against those kinds of problems. And the Everyday Sexism Project does: We welcome men with open arms and share their experiences on both the Web site and Twitter feed.

People who don't trust my ability as a parent without my partner there just because I'm a man out with my daughter.

Colleague left work early to collect his son from child care b/c he was sick. Our boss asked him "Can't your wife go?"

Took 2 yr old son to barbers, "pls leave long but tidy up." Reply "hmm you don't want him to look like a girl."

I'm a male doctor. On numerous occasions I have received comments from female patients about my youth and good looks. One drunk patient said to her friend as I walked past "I'd love to f*** him." A few days ago I was in my office and a patient knocked on the door. A nurse opened the door and asked if the patient needed help and was told "no, I just wanted a better view of the nice young doctor."

My husband is never given the same consideration for family policies as female colleagues.

And many of the stories we have received from men suggest that they face an added stigma against reporting sexism, because of stereotypical norms about men being strong and manly and "not making a fuss."

As a male nurse I have received endless quips from my female colleagues and patients. From "show us your pelvic thrusts" while working with new mothers helping with pelvic-floor exercises after giving birth to slaps on the backside. Men dare not speak out due to ridicule from other men "what are you complaining about?" or losing their employment.

This is, of course, yet another form of silencing.

But it is also important to acknowledge three things that make men and women's experiences of sexism, in the main, different: frequency, severity, and context.

In the United States and around the world, most women face disproportionately far greater sexism than most men do—in terms of both individual incidents and the general cultural climate. The incidents themselves are (again, in general) more severe. And within the framework of a patriarchal social structure—that is, taking into account the wider context of social, economic, professional, and political gender imbalance—sexist incidents often have a far greater impact on women's lives than they have on men's, both individually and in combination.

Consider, for example, a "minor" sexist remark made in the workplace. A woman and a man both stay home sick for a week. When the man returns to work, jibes and comments are made about "man flu." This is sexist, but it is unlikely to have wider ramifications for his position within the company. When the woman returns to work, people speculate that she might be pregnant and have taken the time off because of morning sickness. They tease and joke about the possibility. This is sexist. And within the wider context of professional inequality and gender bias relating to women and motherhood, such a rumor—or even the fact that she is of childbearing age—could potentially have a serious long-term impact on her career.

Then there are other issues, closely related to sexism, like sexualization and objectification, about which we once again hear the cry of, "What about the men?" Take, for example, *that* Diet Coke advertisement. Yes, let's talk about it. It is tweeted to the Everyday Sexism Project Twitter account at least once a week. Yes, it objectifies men. It shows women tricking a man into taking his top off so they can enjoy looking at his physique. The nudity isn't related to the product. It gratuitously involves a man being sexualized and treated like a piece of meat by women. But in the broader context, the very fact that this ad is so often cited as a "Ha! Men get it too!" trump card during discussions on sexism is also, ironically, proof that it differs from ads objectifying women. Because actually it highlights the undeniable truth that such examples of the sexualization and objectification of men are much fewer and farther between than those involving women. And so, while the ad itself may demean and objectify men, its impact on most men is not equivalent to the impact on women of an entire lifetime's narrative of images in which they are dehumanized, objectified, and sexualized at every turn. The ad is the exception rather than the rule. Neither the cumulative impact on the individual nor the effect on social and cultural norms follows in the same way.

Compare the odd Diet Coke ad with the utter debasement of women in advertising. Consider the Belvedere vodka advertisement showing a shocked-looking woman being forcefully held from behind by a man with the caption, "Unlike some people, Belvedere always goes down smoothly." Consider the PlayStation Vita commercial featuring a woman with two pairs of breasts, one set in front, the other on her back, but no head—because, after all, once you've got double the tits, who needs a face or a brain or a mouth? (The caption is, "Touch both sides for added enjoyment.") Remember the ads showing women on their knees covered in shoes and bags, like clothes horses, or the reams of pseudoviolent ads showing them stumbling to the floor as their clothes rip, or bound and gagged in the trunk of a car, or wearing a neck brace to extol the great virtues of a high-energy diet for their boyfriend, or prone on the ground with a man's foot firmly on their throat? All real and recent examples.

Additionally, in a society that values men for their talents, and regards them as a politician or businessman first and as a man second, the sexual objectification or portrayal of a man in a nonprofessional light is less potent. Articles have been written about the sexual attractiveness of Barack Obama, for example.

But they would come very low on the reading list of anybody interested in his career. Articles about Julia Gillard's childlessness, on the other hand, are extrapolated and interpreted as direct indicators of her unsuitability as prime minister. Pieces about Harriet Harman's shoes often come *in place of* rather than in addition to column inches that might have been devoted to her policies. That female politicians are considered first as women and *then* as public figures means that the effect of similar puff pieces on their careers is far more severe than it is for their male peers.

The sexualization and objectification of men and women differ not just in frequency but also in the specific points at which they occur. Yes, many male actors have been hailed as "hunks" in steamy *Cosmo*-style centerfolds that leave little to the imagination and mention precious little of their filmography. But at the juncture when a prince of Hollywood becomes notable for his career, or receives an award for his craft, the attention tends to remain largely on his credentials. Compare this to the spectacular achievement of Anne Hathaway, taking home the 2013 Best Supporting Actress Oscar for her role in *Les Misérables*. Was the coverage the next day representative of her wide and varied career, or the talent she displayed in the part? No. It focused almost exclusively on her nipples, and the *burning* question of whether or not they'd been visible through her Oscars dress. They even got their own Twitter account, for God's sake. (The same dubious honor was granted to Angelina Jolie's leg after she wore a dress with *stop the press* a *slit* at the side. Can you see a pattern here?) See also Jessica Ennis's butt being the most discussed aspect of her

Sports Personality of the Year nomination and appearance. Or Marion Bartoli's great Wimbledon triumph, forever overshadowed both in memory and column inches by the commentator's proclamation that she'd "never be a looker." Yes, of course, as people clamored to point out at the time, hurtful things have been said about male athletes' appearance over the years too.

But not when they've just raised the championship trophy, or scored a match-winning goal. At those moments, their tactics, technique, and skill are quite rightly at the fore; they aren't reduced, at the very moment of their crowning glory, to their physical attractiveness and the sum of their body parts, viewed through a hetero-female lens.

The rule of frequency, severity, and context holds true for sexism in pretty much every form. Take street harassment, for example. Men have written in to the project to describe being harassed and assaulted by women:

I work in a bar, and I am constantly getting groped by women.

Girl walked up to me and groped me, then after I said what the hell she said take it like a man. Not cool.

A group of drunk women shouted "keep moving gorgeous" when I passed them in a train compartment. Followed by "he's going to go home and cry about that tonight."

That last experience is doubly frustrating because it combines harassment in a public space with a sarcastic, sexist jibe aimed at silencing objection. And of course such incidents are just as serious and just as deserving of action as anything comparable experienced by women.

But the overall problem of harassment in public spaces affects women far more regularly than it does men. Stop Street Harassment's national study found that 25 percent of men had been street-harassed, compared to 65 percent of women, and among those men who had experienced harassment, the most common form had been transphobic or homophobic slurs.

The severity of incidents is also likely to be worse when the victim is female (compared to a heterosexual, cisgender man). Project entries concerning such men's experiences most frequently describe comments on appearance and unwanted sexual attention, while women far more regularly report angry threats of violence, physically being grabbed, dragged, or picked up, or being pursued, followed or, in many cases, physically attacked when they refused to respond.

And, finally, context is important here too. Because we face, in the world, a pandemic of violence (both domestic and sexual) against women, so women's experiences in public spaces are colored by a very different background appraisal of their own safety, which may give them a greater impact. Women are more likely than men to feel seriously afraid for their welfare (or even their life) when a stranger shouts at them in the street. This doesn't mean that men don't also sometimes fear for their safety, or that those instances are in any way less important and awful. But if we're looking at tackling the wider picture, then yes: There are clear reasons to logically conclude that this is an issue affecting women disproportionately. And it is no coincidence that it fits within a power hierarchy that favors men. This is often recognized by men who report to the project, who contextualize their experiences within an awareness that these things happen to women all the time.

Had a girl in a van shout "hey there, sexy" as she drove by. Had no idea how to react. A glimpse into what women deal with.

Unfollowed @EverydaySexism, weary of the constant barrage of horror. Then it clicked. That's what it must be like being a woman. #refollowed

Sexism against men is not good. And it's not nonexistent. But it's also not the same thing.

There are, of course, exceptions. Some men are subjected to other forms of discrimination that combine with sexist attitudes and rigid gender norms to cause them to suffer deeply. Men too are subject to double discrimination: Male members of the LBGT community, for example, or disabled men, or men of color may experience sexism intersecting with other forms of prejudice—and consequently may suffer far worse sexism than some women face.

Being told I can't be trans because I'm "not manly enough" or I "don't act like enough of a guy."

My seven-year-old son likes nail varnish and frequently asks to wear it, I put it on him and my father-in-law said to me in front of my son "He'll get called a poof."

Of course, not all women face sexism. That is fantastic. And, yes, some women can be sexist, which is sad and frustrating—just as it is when men are sexist. Tackling sexism is no more about suggesting that all men are sexist than fighting homophobia means accusing every straight person of it. Nor is it about suggesting that all women are victims. Rather it is about giving a voice to victims who have never been heard before because their oppression has become so normalized as to be accepted.

Also, of course, there are some issues that affect men disproportionately. We know that rates of male suicide and workplace death and injury are far higher than those for women. We know that men are often not allowed the same amount of parental leave as women are. We know that fathers sometimes struggle to be awarded the same amount of contact with their children as mothers after a divorce.

At my place of employ: 6–16 weeks maternity leave. Paternity leave? 3 days. And management must be informed "well in advance."

I was going to fight for custody of my two kids but my lawyer told me I don't have a chance because I'm not a woman.

But these are not issues that feminists glory in, or don't care about. Far from it. Many of the issues impacting men are rooted in the very same gender imbalance that negatively affects women. The irony is that we are on the same side here. Feminists would *love* fair, shared parental leave; it would shift patriarchal assumptions about women's careers being the ones to be compromised by having children and create a much more equal professional playing field. Part of the reason why men are the victims of the majority of workplace accidents is that women have found it very difficult to break into professions requiring physical labor, which are considered stereotypically "male jobs." The fact that seeking help for depression and mental-health issues can be seen as a "weakness," and is therefore incredibly difficult for men to do (which perhaps accounts at least in part for the high male suicide rate), is an aspect of sexist gender norms that paint men as strong and manly and women as weak and in need of protection. We hate those norms! Men fighting harder for child custody or having to pay child support are issues rooted in the idea that women are the "natural" caregivers and domestic homemakers, while men must bring home the bacon. These are sexist assumptions that feminists are fighting every day.

One of the most frustrating things about trying to get on board with issues specifically affecting men is that so many men's rights activists (MRAs), with whom we should have so much in common, set themselves up stubbornly and angrily in direct opposition to feminism. That's a great shame, given that so many of the issues we are dealing with are simply different sides of the same coin.

It is difficult to understand the unmitigated hatred of feminism that flows from many men's rights groups—often to such an extent that their true aim seems to be not the righting of wrongs affecting men and boys at all, but rather the demonization and petty abuse of women's campaigners.

Looking at the Web sites of many "men's rights activists," the content seems to follow roughly a 10–90 split, with 10 percent of the articles mentioning specific issues impacting men and 90 percent devoted to trivial, spiteful attempts to insult and discredit feminists. Such attacks are based on everything from criticism of their looks to taking issue with their tone of voice. Rarely are the women's arguments constructively engaged with. One particularly imaginative piece about me attacks my future children on the basis that my name is Bates—cue childish sniggers about the potential for a son to be titled Master Bates. Aside from the pause this gave me to smile at the MRAs' uncharacteristic assumption of a matrilineal nomenclature, such pathetic pieces can hardly avoid undermining their entire movement.

Less funny is the impact these groups and Web sites can have on the men who stumble across them online, as evidenced by the MRA-type slogans used by mixed martial arts fighter Jonathan Koppenhaver (aka "War Machine"), who attacked his ex-partner Christy Mack so brutally that she was left with eighteen broken bones, a broken nose, a ruptured liver, a fractured rib, and missing teeth. Having repeatedly suggested he was "provoked" into the act by Mack's unfaithfulness (in fact, she said, they'd broken up months before he found her with another man and almost killed her), he later attempted suicide after being apprehended, leaving a note that told Mack, "I forgive you," implored his brother to "keep alpha male shit alive," and complained that "society has killed men."

Just months earlier, twenty-two-year-old Elliot Rodger had rampaged through Isla Vista, California, killing six people and seriously injuring seven, in an attack he described as "retribution" against women who had rejected him romantically. "I don't know why you girls aren't attracted to me but I will punish you all for it," he said in a video statement, outlining his plan to "slaughter every single spoiled, stuck-up, blond slut I see." Though it emerged that Rodger had been seeking psychiatric treatment, it was also widely reported that he had been involved with and closely following the men's rights movement through Web sites and YouTube videos.

Both Koppenhaver's repeated implications that the untrustworthy Mack provoked his masculine rage and Rodger's outraged sense of entitlement to his female peers were highly evocative of the tenor of MRA discourse, which tends to focus on making wildly abusive claims about feminists and perpetuating damaging myths about rape and domestic violence. This is by no means to suggest that exposure to MRA ideology was the sole driving factor in either case, but after a short visit to some of these Web sites it isn't difficult to imagine that their vitriol might have a catalyzing or radicalizing effect on some impressionable followers.

For those men genuinely suffering the impact of real social issues, it is easy to see how the promise of a community fighting in their corner might be attractive. But sadly for those who truly need support, the "leaders" of this so-called movement are far too busy attacking women and carrying out puerile stunts (like inserting handwritten notes in numerous copies of this book when it was first published, reading, "say no to feminism: women lie about rape") to take action on any real issues.

I asked Ally Fogg, a journalist who writes about gender

issues from a male perspective and has explored the men's rights movement considerably, why it is that so many of its "activists" focus so relentlessly on demonizing feminism. His assessment:

MRAs actually adhere to a fairly coherent and simple political ideology. It holds that a primary (or even *the* primary) political dynamic within society is between feminists and everyone else. They see feminist influence everywhere and as almost entirely negative. To ask why MRAs focus on feminism is rather tautological; the Men's Rights Movement would be more accurately named the Anti-Feminist Movement. Issues which affect men severely but which don't involve women and feminism are largely ignored—look at how the MRM focuses so heavily on male victims of female violence and female sexual abuse, when the overwhelming majority of violence committed against men is committed by other men. This is of zero interest to MRAs.

How wonderful it would be—given that feminism means not female supremacy but very simply equality for all regardless of sex—if feminists did indeed hold the immeasurable level of political and social influence MRAs so generously give us credit for! We might make some real progress.

Fogg continues:

The Men's Rights Movement has a lot in common with old-fashioned conspiracy theorists. They have constructed an apparently simple and seductive explanation for how the world works which depends upon joining disparate dots to create a pattern, while ignoring all evidence

to the contrary. In their minds, something like the Fawcett Society (or National Organization for Women in the U.S.) becomes a secretive cabal that is pulling the strings of government; and any time politicians introduce a policy that is vaguely pro-women, it is taken as proof of their domination. MRAs fail to recognize that there are hundreds of other lobby groups and interests with similar limited influence, and, more importantly, ignore that there are huge capitalist, corporate and financial lobbies with levels of influence that are, by any rational measure, vastly more powerful. And no, of course it is not productive!

Looking at men as a whole more widely, it is a sadly undeniable truth that there are some who feel either a deep and vitriolic rage or a genuine, unquestioned superiority toward women. I have received too many long, specific messages from men detailing their fantasy of my rape and murder to believe those who say that it's always just a bit of harmless fun. And many of them have clearly never read anything I've written about gender or the importance of including men in the movement before sending me messages like these:

▸ Fuck you stupid slut.

▸ You're just another delusional feminist who hates men.

▸ Fucking women should know their place, fucking skanks.

▸ If you'd just stuck to the kitchen, none of this shit would have happened.

▸ You experience sexism because women are inferior in every single way to men. The only reason you have been put on this planet is so we can fuck you. Please die.

Laura Bates will be raped tomorrow at 9 P.M. . . . I am serious.

Anyone involved in a feminist movement today needs to have a penis put in their mouth and shoved up their arse.

LAURA BATES . . . I am seriously going to RAPE and KILL you TODAY at 8 P.M. near your house . . . Are you ready to get FUCKED?

It is often suggested that these men are angry at something else—that they are probably unpopular teenage boys transcending the frustration of their own powerlessness by terrorizing innocent strangers across the Net. But this seems too convenient a theory to fit the coordinated gang attacks and entire message-board threads religiously devoted to persecuting female "targets" (quite apart from being inexcusably offensive to nice teenage boys). And, as Fogg points out:

It could be that some of this is general anger with their lives, relationships or circumstances which is then being redirected onto random women online, but that doesn't seem especially relevant to me—as even if that is true there is something leading them to focus it, primarily, on women.

Instead, he suspects:

. . . it comes down to defense of privilege. A lot of it seems to stem from the feeling that something which is rightfully theirs is at risk of

being snatched away—whether that is the right to see Page 3 or lads' mags, the right to make rape jokes, the right to sexually proposition women or whatever.

There is also a sense of tradition—of men's entitlement and expectations being handed down from one generation to the next—which is accepted unthinkingly as just the way that men are "supposed" to behave. This is an idea many project entries corroborate:

▶ It's been quite a hot summer here, and I was wearing a mid-thigh dress. I got on the bus on my way home from school, and, as I passed him, a man looked, pointedly, down my legs and back up again. Reckon his son was sitting next to him, and the teenager looked to be about my age. For the record, I'm 17.

▶ On the bus to a friend's house, father and son sat next to me . . . Father looks at son and points to me and says very loudly "Have you checked that THING out?" He repeats this statement 4 or 5 times with the son nodding and saying "Yeah, I've checked IT out."

This is important, because those vitriolic, hate-filled e-mails aside, the vast majority of those men who are occasionally sexist, just like the vast majority of women who sometimes are, are not deliberately, hatefully trying to hurt women or put them down. They've just grown up in a world that teaches them that this is the way things are. All the same tiny cultural signifiers and media messages and behavioral norms that affect young girls impact their male peers too. Teaching them that it is their job to be strong and macho and masculine, that women should be treated as objects, and that putting girls down, or harassing them, or making sexist jokes is a way for men to prove their manliness, particularly to one another. So if we are (rightly) to be aware of the huge impact of these subtle influences on women, we must also, fairly, acknowledge that some of men's sexist behavior is not intentional, or deliberately prejudiced, but simply the result of being immersed in a very patriarchal culture too.

This comes out strongly in many of the project entries, which paint a clear pattern of boys receiving these messages from a very young age. Like the father who told his son, when he threw a tantrum on the bus, "Would you stop behaving like a little girl already?" Or the mother who described this litany of sad restrictions and social "rules":

▸ At three my son couldn't play with a pushchair because it was for girls. My friend's five-year-old son was teased for wearing colorful wellies. At seven he couldn't have a pink water bottle or luminous-pink football socks. At eight he shouldn't go to dance because it's girly. My fourteen-year-old can't accept a hug or a kiss from his family especially in public.

Peer pressure and masculine expectations increase as boys get older, with countless stories of male culture and teenage sexism including heavy elements of coercion.

One female university student told me:

The over-the-top type of culture is particularly apparent in sports teams and with reference to lad culture I've noticed it mostly in the

rugby and football teams. An ex-boyfriend who played in a university rugby team often told me about the "banter" that flew around and it seemed that the worse you treated a female the louder the applause, whereas any respectful behavior or indeed any indication of liking a female as opposed to just using her body as a means to an end was met with ridicule. I was told about certain acts that earned "lad points" such as slapping your "conquest's" face with your penis. Other "games" like "pulling" the ugliest girl they could find were pretty commonplace and certainly not isolated incidents. There is a big emphasis put on humiliation.

It's important not to underestimate the degree to which our young men are affected by the cumulative force of normalized misogyny. Such pressure doesn't come only from friends and peers, as one heart-wrenching project entry revealed:

▸ I'm a 17-year-old boy and started following Everyday Sexism and was shocked by what women go through all the time. I started noticing it more and pointing it out. I think some friends listen but the most opposition I've had is at home. My mum tells me to "man up" when I try to discuss sexism and that there's "something wrong with me" when I pull up my older brother (who's very into all that lad culture) on sexism. She said I'll never get a girlfriend because they want "real men" not ones who "act like girls" and said I shouldn't be bothered about sexism because it doesn't affect me and to "stop being such a whining girl." My dad ENCOURAGES me and my brother to harass women on the street and so my brother now does all the time. I'm not letting it stop me because all the stories I've read are terrible and talking to girls at school they all say they experience sexism regularly, but I can't believe how much my family and especially my mum hates me caring about it.

It is absolutely right and important not to demonize men for learned behavior, or for the invisibility of a problem that they may genuinely have been oblivious of. But what we *can* hope is that once they are made aware of it, they might join the ranks of those other men who stand voluntarily alongside us in the fight for change. Already a vast number of men have written to the project to express their shock and anger upon reading about women's experiences. Their determination to help make a difference is clear:

As a guy this Twitter feed has definitely opened my eyes and changed my behavior.

When I was a teen I probably said a lot of sexist things. I remember telling and laughing at rape jokes. Looking back at it I see that it was abhorrent and that I was allowing rape culture to run rampant. I did not go to a normal college but film school in Canada, I then had the honor of meeting a bunch of women from all over the world, and that helped me and changed me for the better. As I grew close to these women as friends I heard countless stories about not just sexual harassment but assault. It filled me with rage, but made me realize that I was part of that culture. I wanted to be part of a solution; the Dad that tells his son "Don't rape" instead of putting the onus on women. I slowly got turned to feminist thought and I can now proudly say I am a Feminist.

And of course, with the support of those many wonderful men who are willing to assist the move toward equality, we are also far better equipped to tackle the issues that those truly concerned about men's well-being rightly raise. Fogg, interestingly, prefers not to describe these as "men's rights":

Because the issues are rarely or never about legal rights and entitlements. There is not a single legal or civil right that men, as a gender, are systematically or structurally denied. The closest one could get to that would be fathers' rights. Personally I don't use that term, I think family disputes should hinge upon children's rights and welfare, not parents'. That said, I do think children have the right to a sustained and ongoing relationship with the natural father, where appropriate, and I do have concerns about the ability and willingness of family courts to ensure this happens.

Most of the real issues, from my point of view, are not of men's rights but of men's welfare and wellbeing. There's a pretty long list of issues which disproportionately or exclusively impact upon men: socialization into violence (the willingness to both inflict and accept it); disproportionate suicide rates; different patterns of physical and mental-health problems; drug and alcohol abuse and addiction; underachievement in education; homelessness; criminal offending and the workings of the judicial and penal systems.

Many of those issues are connected, and I believe a lot of them can be traced back to a relative overemphasis on men (and especially boys') personal culpability and agency. We really struggle as a society to see men's problems as products of social forces, preferring to attribute them to individual failings. And yes, all of this is attributable to patriarchy, in feminist terms, but I don't think that means the victims shouldn't matter.

There are never any victims who don't matter, because this isn't about men versus women. It's not about taking away men's rights, or about failing to focus on the issues that affect them. It is about working, together, toward a more equal society in which *everybody* is free from stereotypes, rigid expectations, and discrimination, enabling them truly to fulfill their natural potential.

Chapter 11

Women Under Threat

I'm crying and it's not just for these women but for all of us women. It is so rare to know a woman who hasn't been abused in some way.

Everyday Sexism Project entry

Vital Statistics

Nearly 1 in 5 women in the United States has experienced rape or attempted rape at some time in her life.
—National Intimate Partner and Sexual Violence Survey (NIPSVS), 2011

1 in 6 women in the United States has experienced stalking victimization at some time in her life.
—NIPSVS, 2011

More than 1 in 3 women in the United States (36 percent) have experienced intimate partner violence (rape, physical violence, and/or stalking) in their lifetime.
—NIPSVS, 2010

On average, more than 3 women per day are killed in the United States by a current or former partner.
—U.S. Bureau of Justice Statistics, 2013

Women age fifteen to forty-four are more at risk from rape and domestic violence than from cancer, car accidents, war, and malaria.
—World Bank, 1994

603 million women live in countries where domestic violence is still not a crime, and more than 2.6 billion live in countries where marital rape is not a criminal offense.
—UN Women, 2003

1 in 3 women will be raped or beaten in her lifetime.
—UN, 2008

Laura Bates . . . YOU BETTER WATCH YOUR BACK . . . I'M GONNA RAPE YOUR ASS AT 8 PM AND PUT THE VIDEO ALL OVER THE INTERNET.

My neighbour raped me when I was 16—he said I was a slut and was asking for it and no one would believe me if I told anyone.

I was told by a school support worker to "just sleep with" the boyfriend who was pressuring me for sex that I didn't want.

I walk with my keys between my knuckles, even in broad day light. I am scared to be in a city alone. I should not have to feel this way.

14 yrs old: Boys liked to play the "rape" game when we were at friends' houses for parties. Would take girls in turn and dry hump and grope them for fun—despite the screaming.

I don't want to live in a society that told ME not to get raped, but when it does happen, don't expect to get much help for it. I think that's the worst part.

The first thing is that there are two different worlds. I've talked to girls who are not yet sixteen but already understand a woman's place. They're used to being groped and grabbed on their daily commute in their uniform to school. I've spoken to teenagers who all know a girl who has been raped, or assaulted, or had intimate photographs of herself circulated until she feels desperate and suicidal. I've listened to women who have been assaulted and abused and then rejected by an asylum system that—irony of all ironies—refuses to believe their stories because they are too awful to countenance. I've heard from elderly women who are grateful for the invisibility of age in a society that deems them worthless because at least it is better than their earlier life full of harassment and assault.

The effect of living in a world where people of one sex are treated—in myriad tiny, indistinguishable, invisible ways—completely and utterly differently from people of another sex is enormous. You don't need to directly experience each individual component for this level of combined violence and oppression and prejudice to have a huge impact on you—on your life and your lifestyle, your ideas and ideals, and your fundamental perception of yourself and of the world around you.

Men and women inhabit two entirely different worlds.

At a recent meeting, I was seated next to a brilliant and inspiring teacher. She pointed out to me that it would be a natural cause for concern if, when they lined up for lunch, the young children in her class ordered themselves in groups by race—this would be something she'd take action to resolve. And yet, she said, every day, in classrooms across the country, children are lining up in strictly segregated groups of boys and girls and nobody bats an eye. In her classroom, for example, she told me there's a free-play area for "golden time"—when the boys go without fail to one corner, complete with toy cars and sports equipment and trucks, and the girls go to another, a pink procession of dolls and miniature shopping carts and pretend plastic cooking sets. And so it begins.

And just as surely as millions of tiny messages such as these shape and mold our children's earliest perceptions, so thousands of tiny pinpricks also serve, as our girls become women, to initiate them into a world in which their understanding of their own freedom and safety is completely different from that of men.

▸ Male friends do not understand the problem and do not understand the way I hold keys in my hand as a weapon when walking alone just in case.

We think of men and women as living and working in the same world and experiencing it similarly. But in very many ways the manifestation of an identical event or activity by one can be unrecognizable to the other.

▸ On nights out it has become the norm to have my ass grabbed, but the worst is when they grab for my crotch then disappear into the crowd so I don't even know who has done it (yes this has happened more than once and it hurts). I've also been threatened by men and pushed into walls for resisting or for standing up for friends they were trying to grope.

For many women, a night out means hassle and harassment, groping and unwanted advances, wolf whistles and catcalls. Most men's experience of going to a club or bar is manifestly different—though physically they are in the same space. This results in a difference in our own behaviors. For many men, the many routine steps women take to protect themselves—going out in groups and keeping tabs on one another, taking taxis to avoid badly lit routes, holding keys between their fingers on darkened pavements, standing protectively together to avoid groping—are difficult to conceive of.

My experience of walking down the street on which I live is completely different from my partner's, even though we live together, have similar schedules, and travel the route daily.

He doesn't tense at the approach of a car in a distinctive shade of dark green, because it once slowed to a crawl while the driver told him, in chilling detail, how he'd noticed exactly which streets he regularly walked down and at what time. He doesn't cross the road to avoid the fishmonger's, where the men stand in the doorway making comments under their breath about his body as he walks past. He doesn't have to go to the coffee place that's a bit farther away and without convenient Wi-Fi because the waiters at the closer place harassed him and asked him for his number and made bets about who would get it the last time he went in. He doesn't duck into a shop doorway when he spots the man who followed him off the bus that time and down the street asking insistently and aggressively whether he knew how beautiful he was until he ran into the supermarket to get away. None of this crosses my partner's radar. When he walks down the street, he just walks down the street. But my experience of the same exact journey is colored by every one of these experiences and more, not just on the day they happen but every day after that.

When men write online, they might experience hostility, opposition, and arguments. They're unlikely to experience a torrent of death and rape threats detailing exactly how they should be abused and disemboweled. The first flood of these messages I received were such a shock that I just sat very, very still and quiet for a while. The impact of reading something so personal, so invasive, and so very violent while sitting in your own living room makes it feel as if something terrifying is hovering directly overhead; your first instinct is not to move a muscle in case it drops. Not to rock the boat in case you attract that kind of vitriol again. When the words go around in your head at night and the images of what they describe dance against your closed eyelids, you start to think seriously about how to avoid this happening again. Then the police say there's nothing they can do and your twitchy jumps at every movement become so great that you actually leave home for a while. That's when you start to consider whether it's really worth writing any more articles, or continuing to talk about the issues you care about anymore. And you find yourself in a late-night bar writing your book with your laptop perched on your knees because there was a noise in the garden and your partner was out and you suddenly felt a choking terror thinking of all the threats and wondering . . . just wondering. Worst of all, they eventually decide the rape threats aren't getting to you enough and start threatening your family instead. It's a trade-off between your mental health and personal safety versus your ideals and career that most men never have to consider.

Different worlds. It's what lets half the population laugh at something the other half lives in constant fear of.

▸ **A coworker who I considered a good friend at a new workplace came up behind me, wrapped his arms around my waist, and whispered in my ear "Hey, mate, you know how I know we're having** sex tonight? Because I'm stronger than you." And fell over laughing because I instantly burst into tears.

▸ I was raped by my father as a child. When I first told this to someone I felt comfortable with, my current boyfriend, he made a rape joke and said, "Well, you shouldn't have led him on." This just shows that rape is not taken seriously in today's society.

▸ He raped me. I was a virgin. He thought that was hilarious. His friend . . . told me I'd be a nymphomaniac after. That was 20 years ago. Sometimes, while I'm doing dishes, or waiting for a train . . . I think about it. Why I wasn't strong enough to try to leave . . . What I'd do in the situation if it happened again. Trying to remind myself it wasn't my fault. I'm still really angry. And not just at him, but at me.

All these differences in perception and behavior also shape our more basic, foundational ideas of our own human rights and boundaries—our fear of assault, our assessment of our safety, and our judgment of our own culpability.

▸ Until I heard you on Woman's Hour just now I thought it was all my fault. I have had experiences of sexual harassment all my life—the uncle who fondled my breasts as he comforted me when my father was dying in the next room; the supermarket manager who commented on my short skirt during my Saturday job and who said "You shouldn't wear a short skirt if you don't want comments."

▸ As an 18-year-old civil servant, I was pushed against a wall and kissed and groped. And all this time I thought it was my fault for sending out the wrong signals.

The world around us sends us messages about ourselves as women—about our guilt, our difference, our accountability, and our flaws. It gives us endless reminders of our vulnerability and victimization. It lets us know that it is normal and common for women to experience assault and harassment and rape. It tells us that we deserve it. And all the while we are conditioned to be passive and pleasant, not to make a fuss—to be ladylike and compliant and socially acceptable. Before we ever experience violence we are conditioned to expect it—and to accept it.

▸ After a row with an ex-boyfriend about standing me up as he was still in the pub with his mates, he told me "You should be thankful that I treat you the way I do. Loads of men are at home beating their partners."

You want to know how early it starts?

▸ I was first molested when I was 8 years old. The same man waited until I was 9 to rape me. He raped me every morning before school for my whole 3rd grade year. I didn't tell anyone. He forced his son to do things to me. It was the most awful and brutal thing that has ever happened to me. But it wasn't the last.

▸ My first experience of groping was when I was 11 years old and was at a baseball game with my best friend and her dad. I was walking up a crowded staircase and someone behind me or beside me, not sure who, goosed me. It was horrifying feeling some strange man's finger groping my entire private region from my vagina to my anus. I was in shock and I felt very violated. That experience was the

beginning of my indoctrination into sexism and the idea that because I am female my body does not belong to me.

Vitally, it is impossible to separate these shocking accounts of violent assault from the stories we have received of harassment and verbal sexism, or those of abuse and rape. One does not necessarily lead directly to another, but they are composite parts of the same problem. The daily, normalized suggestion that women are "other," second-class, inferior beings; the overwhelming sexualization and objectification of them; and the structural sexism that means that news, politics, and crime alike are all seen through a default male gaze—these are all contributing factors to the crisis of sexual violence we face.

I don't mean to alarm you, but we are in the middle of an international *epidemic.* One in three women will be raped or beaten in her lifetime. According to the World Health Organization, 38 percent of all women murdered are killed by their partners. Around the world, women are subjected to forced marriage, stoning, trafficking, female genital mutilation, childhood pregnancy, acid attacks, "honor" killings, "corrective" rape, lives of slavery and servitude because of their second-class citizenship. In some countries they are pushed toward enlarging their breasts to satisfy male demand. In others their breasts are painfully flattened with hot stones to deter male lust. In some places their vaginas are painfully stuffed with dry cotton to make them swell with discomfort so they will tighten for men's pleasure. In others their sexual organs are decimated to control women's sexuality.

Actually, I do think you should be alarmed. I think we should all be alarmed.

This is by no means a "foreign" problem.

U.S. Department of Justice Statistics data released in 2013 revealed that more than three women *every day* are killed by a current or former partner.

According to the 2011 National Intimate Partner and Sexual Violence Survey, carried out by the U.S. Centers for Disease Control and Prevention, an estimated one in five women (19.3 percent) in the United States have experienced rape or attempted rape during their lifetimes. An estimated 1.6 percent of women reported experiencing a rape or attempted rape in the twelve months preceding the survey. Taking the most recent available census figures for women over the age of eighteen, that adds up to around 1.9 million women. Or more than 5,000 women per day. Or 3.6 women per minute. One in six women reported experiencing stalking victimization at some point in their lives.

An enormous 36 percent of women in the United States experience intimate partner violence at some point in their lives.

In 2000, the African Women's Health Center at Brigham and Women's Hospital in Boston estimated that 227,887 women and girls had been at risk of being subjected to female genital mutilation (FGM) in the United States that year. Activists estimate that the figure is likely to have increased since.

In 2012, the UK government Forced Marriage Unit dealt with nearly fifteen hundred cases, of which 82 percent involved female victims, though the number of unreported cases is likely to be much higher.

The UK-based charity Women for Refugee Women reported that of female asylum seekers in the UK, "48 percent had experienced rape, and two-thirds had experienced gender-related persecution, including sexual violence, forced marriage, and female genital mutilation. Almost all of the women had been refused asylum."

Were any other crisis to cost the lives of more than three U.S. citizens every day—or to threaten *one-third* of the entire world's population—it would be considered an international emergency. But the rape, assault, and murder of women by men is enshrined in our international history. It is so common that it has become an accepted part of the wallpaper.

Women are under threat from this epidemic of sexual violence and equally endangered by public attitudes toward it, which enable and encourage perpetrators, blame and silence victims, and even have a serious, damaging impact on the justice system designed to tackle the problem.

There is a massive anomaly inherent in the public and media perception of victims of rape, domestic violence, and sexual assault. What was she doing there? What was she wearing? Had she led him on? Didn't she know what she was getting herself into? Maybe she was winding him up. Men can't get raped—what's he talking about? Had they been drinking? Have you heard how many people she's slept with before? And so on.

Each of these horribly common reactions relates to the misapprehension that a victim can somehow influence her own assault or be partially to blame for what happens to her. And most are steadily reinforced by the myths and misconceptions about rape and assault that flow through our culture.

Myths about the responsibility of the victim make women and girls feel unable to report:

▸ I was 16. We had spoken on the internet several times before I agreed to meet him, and he persuaded me to go to his home, where he proceeded to rape me and take my virginity . . . But because of things I have read on the internet about how you "can't change your mind," I have never talked about this before.

Hence, according to U.S. Department of Justice Statistics, only 35 percent of rapes or sexual assaults were reported to the police in 2013. Hence, according to UK government statistics released in January 2013, 28 percent of women who are victims of the most serious sexual offenses never tell anybody about it at all.

Myths about what a rapist looks like blur the boundaries of consent:

▸ I'm 38 and reckon between the ages of 11 to the present day I've been sexually assaulted at least 20–30 times. Of course, never thought about going to the police. I had never been held at knifepoint in a dark alley after all . . .

▸ I was raped by a girl. When I told my friends, they said it didn't really count because girls can't rape each other.

Myths about female vulnerability and male strength discourage male victims from coming forward or receiving support:

▸ Been put in a situation where saying "No" to a Lady who was older, bigger and stronger than myself didn't count for anything. But of course being that I'm a guy you wouldn't class that as rape would you now?

Myths about dark, shadowy strangers make girls think they "owe" their boyfriends sex, and boys think it's not possible to rape a girl you know, even if she's drunk or semiconscious. They make men think it's not "abuse" if it's your own wife:

▸ 6 years of rape, sexual assault, physical, and emotional abuse because "I can do what I want to you—you are my wife."

▸ My boyfriend raped me . . . He got drunk and I tried to leave, but he pinned me down and forced me to have sex. Then he acted like nothing happened . . . He said boyfriends couldn't rape girlfriends. He told me that no one would believe me because I was a big slut.

Myths about women asking for it—secretly enjoying rape—lead to blame and excuses:

▸ My rapist blamed me for his violence: "You are a slut, you want it!" and later I blamed myself.

▸ At 16 I was raped, and at 17 I was raped. To this day even though I'm 20 now I get told that I probably liked it.

Myths that a rape victim must have struggled and shouted and screamed in order for the rape to have been "real" leave the many victims who freeze in fear feeling doubted and blamed. Like the rape survivor who told me of her rape at the hands of a housemate, who had entered her room as she slept in the middle of the night. She was told her case wouldn't be taken to court because there was no evidence of a struggle that was likely to convince a jury. In the weeks that followed, when she went out and had her drink spiked and was raped again—a proper, legitimate, believable, official, respectable STRANGER rape—she never dreamed of going back to report it to the police. Because, she asked, "What was the point?"

And cultural myths are used to sweep violence against women under the carpet, as Nimko Ali explains:

FGM for me is the same as any other form of oppression that women face . . . these things happen to girls because they're female—because they're girls, not because of the color of their skin or their faith—it's patriarchy that's actually the foundation of all these things.

FGM has been overlooked, and we've put it in this cultural cul-de-sac, because we're uncomfortable talking about what it actually is [which is] a form of violence against women that happens because women are unequal in the society in which they live. I remember it quite vividly . . . I was 7 and we were on holiday in Djibouti and I had the FGM—I remember the whole thing very clearly and for me it just did not make sense. And what did not make sense was everybody pretending it didn't happen the day after . . . And then I came back to the UK and I went to my teacher and I said, "Why did this happen? It's really silly, it's really stupid." And she said, "That's part of your culture."

Worst of all, these myths are peddled not only by misinformed individuals but also by our national and international press and even our own judiciary, members of government, and police forces. And this is where you start to see the real impact they have on justice and on perpetuating the whole violent cycle.

While running for governor of Texas in 1990, Clayton Williams compared rape to bad weather: "If it's inevitable, just lie back and enjoy it." In 2008, while sentencing a rapist, Orange County, California, superior court judge Derek Johnson dismissed the prosecutor's call for a sixteen-year sentence and instead sentenced the now convicted felon to just six years. He said, "I'm not a gynecologist, but I can tell you something: if someone doesn't want to have sexual intercourse, the body shuts down. The body will not permit that to happen unless a lot of damage is inflicted, and we heard nothing about that in this case."

In 2010, Colorado district attorney Ken Buck, who would later be elected to the U.S. House of Representatives, declined to prosecute an alleged rapist because the victim had invited the perpetrator to her room. He told her it sounded like a case of "buyer's remorse."

When CBS reporter and journalist Lara Logan was raped by a gang of men in Tahrir Square in Cairo while covering the Egyptian revolution, some U.S. media pundits criticized her for taking such high-risk assignments and for daring to do her job when she had a young family at home. In a newspaper article titled "Women with young kids shouldn't be in war zones," one (male) writer asked, "Should women journalists with small children at home be covering violent stories or putting themselves at risk? It's a form of self-indulgence and abdication of a higher responsibility to family." Another commentator asked, "Why did this attractive blonde female reporter wander into Tahrir Square last Friday? What was she thinking?" As if to imply that Logan were a silly tourist out on shopping jaunt, not an experienced, trained journalist doing her job under extremely difficult conditions. (To add insult to injury, compare this with the rightly adulatory coverage of male journalists injured on assignment.)

In March 2011, the *New York Times* reported on the gang rape by eighteen young men of an eleven-year-old girl in Cleveland, Texas. Neighbors reported that the child victim "dressed older than her age, wearing makeup and fashions more appropriate to a woman in her 20s. She would hang out with teenage boys at a playground." The article suggested that local residents would be left asking, "How could their young men have been drawn into such an act?" One member of the community was quoted saying, "These boys have to live with this the rest of their lives."

At Caernarfon Crown Court in December 2012, a forty-nine-year-old man was found guilty of raping a teenage girl. As he jailed the rapist, the judge said, "She let herself down badly. She consumed far too much alcohol and took drugs, but she also had the misfortune of meeting you." The implication was clear: The silly girl put herself in harm's way. The rapist was a "misfortune"—something natural, something to protect yourself from, something that just happens. The agency was all hers.

After the conviction of nine men for the systematic grooming and sexual abuse of a group of young girls in Rochdale in 2012, one of the victims told BBC's *Woman's Hour,* "Quite a few people rang social services: school, the police . . . even my own dad . . . basically they told my mum and dad that I was a prostitute and it was a lifestyle choice. And because I was only six months off turning sixteen they wasn't going to do anything."

In October 2012, a former Metropolitan Police detective constable was jailed for sixteen months for his failings relating to rape cases, which included falsely claiming that a rape victim had dropped charges. In February 2013, an investigation by the Independent Police Complaints Commission revealed that the Metropolitan Police's specialist Sapphire Unit, which investigates rape and other serious sexual violence, had "encouraged" rape victims to withdraw allegations in order to boost detection rates.

In 2012, Republican Senate candidate Todd Akin said that in cases of "legitimate rape" women rarely fall pregnant, because "the female body has ways of shutting that whole thing down."

Stating that abortion should be illegal even in cases of rape or incest, Republican presidential candidate Rick Santorum said in 2012 that rape victims must "accept what God has given to you" and "make the best of a bad situation."

In August 2012, UK MP George Galloway publicly said that the allegations against Julian Assange, who was accused of raping a sleeping woman who had previously consented, were simply "bad sexual etiquette . . . not rape as anyone with any sense can possibly recognize it."

In Italy in 2012, a priest posted a notice at his church about domestic violence and the murder of women by men. It read: "The core of the problem is in the fact that women are more and more provocative, they yield to arrogance, they believe they can do everything themselves and they end up exacerbating tension . . . How often do we see girls and even mature women walking on the streets in provocative and tight clothing?"

When two boys were convicted in the Steubenville rape case, the CNN reporter covering the story said, "I've never experienced anything like it . . . It was incredibly emotional, incredibly difficult even for an outsider like me to watch what happened as these two young men that had such promising futures, star football players, very good students literally watched as they believe their lives fell apart."

In December 2012, in the aftermath of the Delhi gang-rape case, Botsa Satyanarayana, transport minister and State Congress chief in the southern state of Andhra Pradesh, told reporters, "It would have been better if the girl did not travel by a private bus at that time."

In the wake of the Egyptian revolution, as female protesters took to the streets alongside their male peers, they experienced wave after wave of sexual violence, sexual harassment, groping, serious assault, and rape. But as the problem persisted, in August 2013, the *Egypt Independent* newspaper reported that the human rights committee of the Shura Council, part of Egypt's Parliament, declared that female protesters were responsible for the harassment and attacks. One member of the committee was reported to have said, "By getting herself involved in such circumstances, the woman has 100 percent responsibility."

At Snaresbrook Crown Court in 2013, a forty-one-year-old man admitted engaging in sexual activity with a thirteen-year-old girl. The judge spared him jail time, instead handing down an eight-month suspended sentence. He said, "I have taken in to account that even though the girl was thirteen, the prosecution say she looked and behaved a little bit older . . . On these facts, the girl was predatory and was egging you on."

In August 2013, a Montana judge handed a sentence of just one-month imprisonment to a man who raped a fourteen-year-old girl. The girl later committed suicide. The judge said that the girl was "older than her chronological age" and declared her "as much in control of the situation" as her rapist.

Does this list of situations in which women and girls are blamed for their own assaults seem endless? Then it mirrors the reality.

In 2012, Alison Saunders, head of the UK Crown Prosecution Service, warned in an interview with the *Guardian* that "myths and stereotypes" about rape victims may give jurors "preconceived ideas" that could affect their decisions in court. When victims are "demonized in the media," she said, "you can see how juries would bring their preconceptions to bear."

And yet—while even the head of the Crown Prosecution Service is able to see the connections between a culture awash with victim blaming and the potential miscarriage of justice—it is incredibly difficult to talk about the connections between other forms of latent misogyny within our culture and the epidemic of sexual violence faced by women on a daily basis. This is often because of the enormous imbalance of power in this scenario, between the music moguls and media magnates profiting from our misogyny-drenched culture and its vulnerable, silenced victims.

Talk about dehumanized, objectifying images of naked women in advertising and mainstream media and you're immediately asked to provide evidence that they lead men to rape, or you're banned from mentioning the rates of sexual assault and domestic violence in the context of your argument. Criticize Robin Thicke's "Blurred Lines" video, with its references to splitting a girl in two, and you're shut down because the song is "ironic" and therefore beyond reproach. But why *can't* we have an open, serious, mainstream conversation about this? Why can't we discuss the fact that we have a society in which one in five women will experience rape or attempted rape, while our culture—from music and magazines to advertisements and films—constantly blares out the crystal-clear message that women are submissive, disposable sex objects? Why can't we have a conversation that doesn't suggest a direct cause but nonetheless takes into account the context that inextricably links them?

In Australia (where one in five women over the age of fifteen has experienced sexual violence), police commissioners recently spoke out about the relationship between a society that belittles and demeans women and a high incidence of violence against them. Ken Lay, chief commissioner of Victoria, told *Guardian Australia,* "I place family violence in a wider culture where vulgar and violent attitudes to women are common . . . These attitudes show that we perceive women differently than men and by differently I mean we perceive them as less valuable. In order to stop a problem we have to tackle the cause."

A 2009 study of ten thousand Australians found that only 53 percent considered "slapping or pushing a partner to cause harm or fear" to constitute "very serious" behavior and that one in five believe domestic and sexual violence can be excused "if it results from people getting so angry that they temporarily lose control." The study described a "powerful association between attitudes toward violence against women and attitudes toward gender . . . the more that people maintain egalitarian gender attitudes, the less acceptance of violence against women."

In other words, when we talk about sexual and domestic violence, wider cultural attitudes matter very much.

In December 2012, the *Daily Mail* journalist Richard Littlejohn wrote an article about a primary-school teacher who was transgender, with little apparent reason why the case merited national news attention. Repeatedly referring to the woman as "he," Littlejohn claimed to have sympathy with those who required gender-reassignment surgery—yet said "his" transition would have a "devastating effect" on the children at the school where "he" taught. Littlejohn even attacked the school for its supportive stance, in a paragraph dripping with sarcasm: "The school is 'proud of our commitment to equality and diversity.' Of course they are." But when Lucy Meadows, the teacher at the center of the article, committed suicide three months later after being hounded by the press, the *Daily Mail* slammed anybody who dared to mention the article. As they told the *Huffington Post,* "Those criticizing Littlejohn might do well to consider today's words of media commentator Roy Greenslade: 'it is important to note that there is no clear link—indeed any link—between what Littlejohn wrote and the death of Lucy Meadows.' " That is perfectly true. (Though the *Daily Mail* immediately removed the article from its Web site, which seems a strange step if it genuinely considered it to be utterly unrelated to Meadows's death.) But in any case, why should this preclude us from considering the article, and the wider press bias in reporting on stories involving trans people, within the context of this important debate?

A woman died not in isolation, not in a bubble, but within a world that was utterly hostile to her, unable to respect her personal choices. At the inquest, the coroner exclaimed, "And to you the press, I say shame, shame on all of you." But for goodness' sake, let's not risk hurting the feelings of the privileged acid-tongued reporter who made money from mocking and turning the world's eyes on this vulnerable woman at the most difficult period in her life, because there's no reason to think he had anything *directly* to do with her decision.

Women are being raped, assaulted, and murdered every day, but let's not upset anybody by worrying too much about what might be contributing to it in an "indirect way." Let's not worry about connecting these cases, though the murder of a five-year-old girl and the abduction of a teenager and the sexual assault of another teenager and the rape and imprisonment of three women for more than a decade are reported consecutively, one after the other, on the evening news. We don't want to make anybody feel *uncomfortable*.

Let's focus on the importance of freedom of speech above all else, without stopping for inconvenient questions like, "Hang on, does it actually include the right to threaten to kill or rape someone online?" (It doesn't). Or "What about the freedom of speech of the women silenced and driven from online spaces as we fall all over ourselves to protect the speech of their abusers?" Just get off the Internet if you don't like it.

Criticize gaming at your peril, because video games don't force people to emulate them, and developers have every right to showcase balloon-size jiggling breasts and chopstick waists on characters designed more often as window dressing than heroines. And if you want to point this out in a considered analysis, you're attacking the industry, bitch. You're not a "real" gamer. Tits or GTFO. There is no problem with misogyny in gaming, and those arguing as much have proved their point clearly over and again, by harassing and abusing female gamers and journalists who dare to disagree.

Wait . . .

Best not to talk about porn, either, since that's another freedom-of-speech issue. Although ironically the issue isn't necessarily the medium itself—the idea of sharing filmed sex—but rather the violent misogyny inherent in so much of the mainstream porn available. Can we have a conversation about that? Are we allowed to ask not why there's porn online, or why it's available, but simply what it says about the world that so much of its most accessible presence focuses on humiliating and degrading women, making them hurt and cry, forcing them to submit and ejaculating over their faces? Can we ask why little girls are writing to me in tears because they've seen it and they think that's what sex is and they're afraid? Just as a necessary discussion about the deep misogyny in many men's magazines isn't an attack on all print journalism, so the issue with porn isn't the medium but the way it's being used.

Can we look at life from the point of view of a thirteen-year-old girl and stop to acknowledge that it looks like a fucking obstacle course? Can we ask why her every move is a tactical maneuver as she navigates sexting and porn and body image? Because those girls are the ones who lose out when we tie ourselves in knots trying not to say anything that might force some multimillionaire media mogul to pause for five minutes and defend the extent to which his empire is built on the backs of naked teenage girls.

Better for us women to put up and shut up than to risk offending anybody. Better we stop going for runs, like the 24 percent of American women surveyed by Stop Street Harassment in 2008 who choose not to exercise outside for fear of harassment or assault. Better we just reconsider our route home, or buy a car, or change our outfits than piss people off by saying how unsafe we are made to feel on our own neighborhood streets. Better we teach our teenage girls to carry whistles and alarms, and travel in packs than question why the world allows them to be walking, talking prey.

Because after all, this is normal. This is the world we live in. This isn't something that's gone wrong; it's just the way things already are—it's the point we started from. Don't forget that "women are equal now, more or less."

We immerse young people in a world of sex and sexualization, but we don't stop to talk about consent, or relationships, or their right not to be touched or coerced or assaulted.

▸ I didn't know any of it was wrong until when I was 17, about six months after I was raped. I almost reported it but didn't, because I thought it was my fault and I shouldn't have talked to the guy who did it.

When we end up justifying and normalizing and getting used to everything, telling young women that this is the world they will have to navigate and the way they should expect to be treated, we leave them with nowhere to go. When we tell them that everything they are is what they look like—that their bodies and their sexuality and their sexiness comprise their sum value—and then bully, repress, criticize, and censure them *for* their bodies and their sexuality, we create a society that has no place for them in it.

When we introduce them to a world in which they're seen as sexual prey and have a one-in-three chance of being raped or beaten, without stopping to question that status quo or trying to fix the culture that enables it to continue, we have already robbed them of their right to belong. And so we lose them.

I was raped when I was 14. My partner was raped all throughout elementary school. My friend was raped when she was 14. Another friend was raped at 12. Another friend was raped when she was 15. And so on, and so forth . . .

We lost Amanda Todd, pressured into exposing her teenage breasts to a stranger on the Internet and blackmailed and bullied for the photographs for the rest of her short life until she hanged herself at age fifteen.

We lost teenager Rehtaeh Parsons, who hanged herself after police declined to bring charges against those she reported had gang-raped her and posted the photographs online. We lost twelve-year-old Gabrielle Molina, who committed suicide after being taunted by school bullies who called her a slut and a whore.

We lost Felicia Garcia, fifteen, who jumped in front of a train after enduring bullying and taunts about being a slut because of sexual activity at a party.

We lost nineteen-year-old Lizzy Seeberg because when she tried to report that she had been raped she received threatening texts from his friend telling her, "Don't do anything you would regret," and campus security failed to interview the alleged perpetrator for ten days, by which time she had committed suicide.

We lost Audrie Pott, fifteen, who hanged herself after her brutal sexual assault was photographed and shared online and led to vicious sexual bullying.

We lost Rachel Ehmke when she committed suicide, age thirteen, after she was taunted by bullies who called her a slut and scrawled the word across her locker.

We lose them. And we will keep losing them as long as we're prepared to continue living—as if this is simply *normal*—in a world where the threat of rape or beating hangs over one-third of women's heads.

Chapter 12

People Standing Up

I don't feel intimidated anymore. I feel strong.

Feminist interviewee

"I said have a nice day BITCH!!" Wow thank you SO much, genuine gentlemen on the streets of NYC.

You have to wonder what a guy who is quietly cat calling women in a Starbucks at 6 A.M. is doing with his life.

Man called me an Opinionated Lesbian Cunt! Thank you I'm proud of being Opinionated, Lesbian & having a Cunt.

Thank you for telling me I'm beautiful, 14-year-old boy, but no, I won't be sucking your cock.

I never realized I could speak out against these daily experiences. I haven't even discussed these with my boyfriend of 10 years.

Had an experience a few years ago I've never told a soul about. Your video made me realize I'm not alone. Thank you.

Women everywhere have had enough. We've reached our tipping point and we're not afraid to say it. We're not afraid to be dismissed, or belittled, or laughed at anymore, because there are too many of us. There's no silencing someone who has tens of thousands of others standing right behind her. We can't be silenced when we're all saying the same thing.

A storm is coming. It didn't start out as a full-blown hurricane. It started with almost imperceptible whispers of, "Is it just me?" and "Hang on a minute . . ." and "Maybe I'm overreacting, but . . ."

But those whispers became a voice, fueled by the bravery of Malala Yousafzai, underpinned by the solidarity of social media, sharpened by the wit of *Jezebel,* spurred on by the incorrigible positivity of the SPARK Movement, the wry humor of Jessica Williams and Amy Poehler, the outrage of Julia Gillard, the legacy of Jyoti Singh Pandey, the strength of Zerlina Maxwell and Anita Sarkeesian, the fearlessness of Janet Mock, the courage of Mona Eltahawy and Nihal Saad Zaghloul. This is the voice of thousands and thousands of women, and it's saying: **Enough is enough.**

But if you think the storm has reached its peak, you haven't seen anything yet. This is just the beginning. The video of Australia's prime minister Julia Gillard decrying the misogyny she suffered in office swept virally across the globe. In India, protesters lined the streets after the horrifying gang rape and murder of Jyoti Singh Pandey and the subsequent death of a five-year-old rape victim. In Bangladesh, protest swelled into a human chain after the rape of a teenager by four men, the latest in a series of violent rapes of young women to which another victim lost her life. In Nepal, demonstrators swarmed Kathmandu after a gang rape case involving police and immigration officials. In Sri Lanka, protests in solidarity with the Delhi rape victim intensified after details of another gang rape near Colombo emerged. In Spain, thousands of women successfully marched to protest plans to decrease access to abortion. In Iran, women took to the streets in the thousands to protest a spate of acid attacks. And in America, at the peak of the war on women's bodies, Texas state senator Wendy Davis stood for eleven hours to filibuster a Republican bill that would severely limit access to abortion.

Feminism being, purely and simply, the notion that people of all sexes deserve to be treated equally, this movement looks very different in different countries—it has widely varied goals and aims, and diverse means of achieving them. But thanks to the rise of social media, there is a sense of cohesion and solidarity that is growing ever stronger among women across borders and boundaries that enables us to stand alongside our sisters and solicit for them as never before.

It's got power, this storm, and its power is in its immediacy, its vitality, and its pragmatism, as women around the world are united with the force of pressure that has been building for centuries. Enough is enough. It's the power of a generation of young women coming to the world and finding it wanting, and a generation of women who've fought this fight already rolling their sleeves back up to return to the fray and finish the job for good. It's the power of a movement that is spreading like an epidemic, that sees injustice in its path and will not be silenced as it has been silenced before. A movement so strong that its international outrage provoked a commitment from Pakistan's president to work with the United Nations to ensure education for all children after sixteen-year-old Malala Yousafzai was shot in the head by the Taliban for no greater crime than making the journey to school. Enough is enough. A movement that stood up and screamed when Egyptian protesters were assaulted and raped in Tahrir Square just for fighting for their freedom alongside their brothers. A movement that threatened to devastate the Maldives tourist industry when a fifteen-year-old rape victim was sentenced to one hundred lashes, until the president stepped in to overturn the court sentence. A movement that demanded justice and pardon for Marte Deborah Dalelv when the Norwegian national was jailed for extramarital sex after being raped in Dubai. It is a movement that would not stand by in silence when the devastating case of the teenage girl raped in Steubenville, Ohio, was reported by CNN in a way that expressed sympathy for the perpetrators rather than for the victim. A movement that forced one of the biggest social-networking sites in the world to admit that it was wrong about rape and domestic violence. Enough is enough.

Davis's legendary filibuster was able to proceed in part because of the stories from real women that poured in from around the world, enabling her to keep talking and stay on topic as the hours wore on. It was a feat of unity that wouldn't have been possible before social media and this new digital wave of feminism. Women from Texas, from other U.S. states, and from around the world began sending their stories, like ammunition passed along the lines as she stood, fighting a fight that was coming to represent so much more than opposition to a single bill.

But we haven't won yet. For the sentence of a fifteen-year-old rape victim to be overturned only because of international pressure remains a travesty for the hundreds of thousands of nameless, faceless victims whose fate is not elevated into the spotlight. A public outcry to help to raise awareness of certain human-rights abuses for the first time cannot be glibly interpreted as a happy solution for their victims.

Of course there are millions of women for whom the tools to directly access the online elements of this burgeoning movement are not available. But protest is happening offline too, from schools to streets to courthouses. There is great power in collective action, and in collective awareness, and every judgment or decision that incites international condemnation decreases the likelihood of such a decision being taken again in the future. This is not the end of the line—it is the beginning of change. The old systems that have oppressed and belittled and dismissed women for so long are under attack, and their archaic joints and scaffolding are creaking in the heat of the battle. Enough is enough..

This is a battle that we will win. Because women are wittier, brighter, stronger, and braver than a misogynistic and patriarchal world has given us credit for. The mass of tens of thousands of stories that we've collected does not represent a cluster of cowering victims. It is an outpouring of passion, borne of the frustration of being silenced for too long. And it is strong.

These women's voices are funny, mocking, shrewd, and wise. Do they sound like victims to you?

I'm tired of debating comfy mid-class white guys about what sexual oppression is. I talk facts, they talk unicorns.

"NICE, nice," said the man just behind me, nodding his head approvingly. "I like the way you walk. Boyfriend?" It took all the strength I had to keep my clothes on, I was so flattered and aroused.

Massive thanks to the guys who just yelled from a car that I have nice tits! I had NO idea until you pointed them out!

Thought I'd torn my coat when "lady got a hole" was shouted at me. No, just one man's shrewd observation that I have a vagina.

I'm a mechanical engineer, got told at an industry function "you don't look like an engineer." I asked him if it was the breasts.

"But what's in it for me?" is what I just asked the kind man who said he'd be willing to shag me if I lost some weight.

Modern feminism is strong. It's not a movement that has to apologize for its priorities but one that is marching forward, tackling every obstacle in its path one by one and not taking any crap about which jobs are too small or irrelevant, or which issues too "lightweight." People of all ages are rallying: schoolgirls who've had enough of being told to "get back in the kitchen," graduates finding themselves a step behind their male peers before they've even begun to scale the career ladder, mothers sick of the rigid categorization of their children, grandmothers not ready to disappear. The husbands and boyfriends and fathers and brothers, the bosses and colleagues, the friends and the lovers. The victims of sexism and assault and the perpetrators who've realized the impact of their actions; the boys who've been as bullied and bruised by societal norms and expectations as our girls.

As Hayley Devlin, a nineteen-year-old student and feminist campaigner, brilliantly puts it:

Women are bored of it. Bored of being told to "get our tits out for the lads," bored of double standards and bored of being belittled by the media. It's 2016! We should be equal by now and won't give up until we are.

It's that simple.

Women's activism around the world is marked by its sense of purposeful pragmatism—from Samira Ibrahim taking the Egyptian military to court to successfully ban the barbaric process of forced "virginity testing," to the World Courts of Women, started by the Asian Women's Human Rights Council to provide an outlet for women's experiences to be acknowledged, subverting patriarchal forms of traditional justice. In the Democratic Republic of Congo, tens of thousands took part in a mass march for women and peace. In India, rural women in pink saris came together to form the Gulabi Gang, which intervenes and publicly shames perpetrators of abuse and sexual violence. In the United States, you can see this pragmatism in escort programs providing volunteers to walk with women into abortion clinics and support them against the vitriolic abuse from protestors. Powerful online awareness-raising campaigns like #YesAllWomen and #GirlsLikeUs have given a voice to daily, normalized, often invisible experiences of misogyny, discrimination, and transphobia. The Stop Rush campaign mobilized to target Limbaugh's advertisers, refusing to take his misogynistic vitriol lying down, and the high-profile stunts of FORCE: Upsetting Rape Culture have provoked national conversations about rape and consent. Organizations like the Women's Media Center keep the spotlight relentlessly on media inequality. Campaigns like Ready to Run and She Should Run drive women into politics. Organizations like 2020 Women on Boards support them in business. And initiatives like Know Your IX fight back against campus assault by informing students and supporting victims. Then there are international initiatives, like Take Back the Night and Slutwalk marches, International Anti-Street Harassment Week, 16 Days of Activism, and more. It's a movement in which anyone and everyone is welcome, whether or not they want to wear lipstick and high heels, whether they choose to crack jokes or debate the issues, with leagues of supportive men and boys standing alongside. Given that feminism simply means thinking everybody should be treated equally, regardless of sex, the entry criteria are refreshingly wide.

We can tackle sexism any way we like. Sometimes we'll get angry about it; sometimes we'll demand legislative change, or lobby the government; sometimes we'll write a poem, or go on a march; sometimes we'll sing, or scream, or shout; and sometimes . . . Well, sometimes, we'll just laugh . . .

A guy kept harassing me for my phone number so I gave him the number of another sexist, figured they'd have a lot in common.

Man: "Nice tits." Me: "If you're going to be a sexist pig at least be accurate. I have fantastic breasts." Silence . . .

Managed to stop white van full of men mid-catcall by shoving a big powdery donut into my mouth then smiling with mouth full.

People often try to put down some forms of feminist activism, branding online campaigns "clicktivism" or "slacktivism" and arguing that they have no real offline impact. But in the twenty-first century, it is laughably naïve to think that the online world has no impact on the offline, when we live with a foot in each, commuting and reading e-mails, consuming an online article over lunch, tweeting our way through films and football matches. Awareness raised online doesn't stay online; people take it with them into the workplace and onto the street and into their homes. And what starts online can have enormous and far-reaching offline impact too. What began as an awareness-raising campaign in Everyday Sexism has become so much more as we've taken thousands of the stories offline, into schools and universities, using them to start vital conversations about consent, relationships, and gender stereotypes; or showing entries from women in the workplace to politicians so that their policy might be directly informed by the realities of what women are facing on the ground. The thousands of women who shared their stories of sexual offenses on public transport contributed directly to the retraining of the British Transport Police for Project Guardian, resulting in a massive surge in the reporting of sexual offenses and the detection of offenders. Men have written to explain how much the project has opened their eyes and changed their behavior, and huge numbers of women have written to say that they reported an assault as a result of the project, often not having realized that they had the right to do so before. And perhaps most important of all, online feminism has enabled a huge number of women to feel connected, for the first time, to a movement they otherwise might never have discovered at all. As one interviewee told me:

Seeing Page 3 in the newspaper, being shouted at by builders, men saying sexist things when I worked in bars . . . it used to make me feel vulnerable, upset, weak. I don't feel like that anymore. Now there are so many amazing and supportive social networks where we can discuss all this stuff, so many brilliant women coming together and looking out for each other that I don't feel intimidated anymore. I feel strong. Women are taking ownership of the internet and using it as a platform to stand up to sexism. This has been the turning point for me.

She is right about women using the Internet to take control. When Jaclyn Friedman, Soraya Chemaly, and I decided to take on Facebook over graphic content depicting and encouraging rape and domestic violence, people told us we were crazy. Others had tried before—there had been high-profile campaigns and a two-hundred-thousand-signature petition. Yet images of women bloody, battered, and beaten remained live on the site, alongside groups about killing "sluts" and forcing women to miscarry by punching them or throwing them down flights of stairs. Facebook had refused to budge. We knew it was a long shot, but we also knew that we could draw on this incredible burgeoning feminist spirit around the world. Instead of taking on Facebook directly, we launched a campaign aimed at the companies whose vast coffers were financing its content and, crucially, whose logos and advertisements were appearing emblazoned alongside the rape jokes and images of women's bruised, bleeding faces.

The sheer, international energy of digital feminists sent the campaign viral, using our #FBrape hashtag sixty thousand times in the first day alone and clocking up six thousand e-mails to advertisers as the international press picked up the story.

But what was most surprising and moving was the outpouring of creativity and effort from women and men around the world, who had their own ideas to offer and their own talents to help drive the campaign forward. It got personal. One woman began to make an art form out of what she called "brandalism." She took the famously recognizable advertisements and logos of companies that had refused to respond to the campaign or declined to withdraw their advertising from Facebook, and digitally altered them to include components of the horrific images their logos had appeared alongside.

While Dove scrambled to make placatory statements after refusing to withdraw its ads from Facebook, global followers of our campaign made their feelings about the company—supposedly built on an ethos of female empowerment—very clear indeed. When Dove posted inane pictures on its Facebook page asking women, "What do you dedicate most of your getting ready time to? A. Hair B. Nails C. Skin Care D. Makeup?" protesters answered with witty, angry replies, visible to all on the viral images:

I dedicate most of my time to hoping that one day women will be treated as equals in society.

Dear Dove, I spent most of my "getting ready time" this morning wondering why you are comfortable with your ads showing up next to pictures of women getting raped.

None of the above. I spend most of my time NOT patronizing companies that allow their ads to be shown on Facebook pages that make fun of violence against women.

Another artist created a composite version of one of the awful images Facebook had refused to remove—a picture of a little girl with two black eyes—using the avatars of Dove's own Twitter followers. He sent it back to them with the simple message: "Dove, these are your customers."

Messages demonstrating the strength of public feeling began to pour in, as small businesses around the world threw their hats into the ring. Completely unbidden, companies we never targeted or contacted as part of the campaign voluntarily joined us, withdrawing their ads from Facebook in solidarity with our cause. Granted, their ad budgets were peanuts compared to the big fish we were focusing on, but the gesture was incredibly powerful and it brought me to tears in those fraught twenty-four-hour days of trawling through images and messages of misogynistic hate that were so graphic and abusive I felt like I wouldn't ever be quite the same again.

Their messages summed up something much wider than their own small acts: They encapsulated the spirit of the whole campaign and of this new wave of feminism.

A small sweetshop said: "We understand we're a small company at the moment and that our stance will have little impact on this subject singly, but we hope that we might encourage others to do the same and that together we may be able to stop this from happening." Another tiny start-up, Down Easy Brewing, wrote: "Our measly few dollars a month will not make a dent in the Facebook bottom line, but our conscience as a corporation and as human beings will rest a little easier . . . Stand up to the bullies. Stand up for those who cannot or will not stand for themselves. We may never rid the world of hate, but we sure as hell should try."

And that was the moment that I knew we were going to win. Not just this campaign but the battle for hearts and minds that would take us toward wider gender equality too.

In a landmark victory, Facebook responded to the campaign within a week. The company promised to update its policies and guidelines on rape and domestic violence, and to train its moderators to recognize and remove images of violence against women. The battle had been won. The media hailed it as a triumph for online campaigning and social media. But really it was a testament to the growing strength of feminist feeling around the world.

Now, because of that strength of feeling, every one of the thousands and thousands of people who might post an image of a battered woman on Facebook just for "lolz," will receive a simple message from a platform that is such a large part of their culture that it serves to frame the world around them. They'll get the message that it's not okay.

The success of that campaign exemplified why this movement is so strong. It is because of the bond women form, across countries and cultures and borders—the incredible moving, heartwarming, strengthening solidarity of the feminist community. This is a community that lets women know they're not alone. That lets them realize they don't have to put up with prejudice—and that if they choose to take a stand, there will be others right behind them, every step of the way.

▸ I've never told anyone this story before, and it feels amazing to finally let it out.

A schoolgirl wrote to tell me that previously when the boys in her year had shouted sexist jibes and told her to get back in the kitchen, she'd never felt able to say anything—she'd felt so alone. It was just the way things were. But after discovering the project, she showed it to several of her female friends and, with each other's support, they started to stand up to the sexist bullying. Later, together, they showed it to the boys.

One of the seventeen-year-old girls I interviewed said it was hard to talk to her family about how she felt, because every time she mentioned women, or feminism, they would immediately cry, "Oh, she's off on one again!" But now she has the strength that comes with knowing that hundreds of thousands of women feel exactly the way she does, and she's less likely to be silenced.

To others it has given the courage to report a crime they had suffered the consequences of for years. One woman wrote:

▸ I was violently raped by a boy that I knew when I was 13 years old (he was 17). I told my parents and we went to the doctors the next day. My recollection is that I was so shamed by what had happened, particularly as it was my first "sexual" encounter, that I didn't want to either name the boy or go to the police. Years later I read the doctor's notes from the appointment: he had written that I had "gone a bit too far with a boyfriend" and I was pretending that I had been raped. He didn't even examine me, even though I was bruised quite badly.

I am going to make an appointment with the surgery manager when I feel strong enough and demand a formal apology for their appalling and criminal mismanagement. I will possibly also go along legal channels. Thanks to this site, I know I have a mass of women who support me and understand why this can't be left.

For still others, the kindness of strangers and the sense of belonging to a worldwide community are invaluable. A woman in Mexico tweeting us her experience might receive hundreds of responses from people she has never met, from Canada and Pakistan and Singapore, expressing their sympathies and concern, sharing stories of their own, and exchanging tips and advice: simply letting her know that she's not overreacting and she's not alone.

The few times I've offered my experiences to @EverydaySexism I've found myself crying with gratitude from people's kindness. I needed that.

I just found out about @EverydaySexism and I am so thankful that I am not alone in this journey. That all women are not alone.

And, simple though it sounds, for many girls and women the project is their first exposure to the idea that they have the right not to be subjected to prejudice because of their sex.

I think we're all taught subconsciously to be sexist to ourselves. Wish I'd stumbled upon this site earlier in life. It would have saved me all the hard lessons I had to learn on my own to realize what is right. When unpleasant things have happened to me, I'd always find me blaming myself first—not the man who's at fault. Always making up some sort of excuse thinking "maybe it's me" and "it probably is me." Or upon hearing something sexist I'd laugh it off . . . but really, it's not funny.

One woman wrote to me after hearing about the project online and seeing the *Chime for Change* video:

I went to your Twitter page, and started reading the tweets that women were posting, and I couldn't believe it. I've been experiencing

these exact same things ever since I was a child, really. I was so moved by the bravery of these women to speak out like this . . .

I feel like FINALLY someone is recognizing this and doing something about it, and openly acknowledging that it really *is* sexual harassment, and that it's *NOT* okay.

And then she took the single, simple step that has become the hallmark of today's feminism: She told everybody she knew.

I felt so moved by this 9 minute video, that I sent this e-mail out to everyone I know. It's very personal, but somehow after watching your video I felt like I needed to share my story and yours, and to let people know about this important movement and that we no longer have to live in silence. I'm 29 years old, and I suffer from PTSD from early childhood trauma and abuse. This movement has started a healing process in me already that I can't explain. And I only learned about this a couple of hours ago.

That single e-mail made me aware, suddenly and overwhelmingly, of the power of individual, grassroots activism. Because when the message comes from your friend or your sister, your loved one or your child, it has such powerful impact. And normal women and men being the ones stopping, thinking about this, and then taking the time to chat with their friends and families about it, to let them know what a big problem it is and ask them to help stop it—this is possibly the most effective way we can make real change.

When we worked on the *Chime for Change* film, a young guy in his twenties was part of the film crew. Attending the early meetings, he listened to the story of the project and the women's experiences I related, clearly understood the issue, and was extremely supportive. But when I saw him a week later, his face was ashen as he told me he'd been asking his female friends about their experiences. "Every one of them has so many stories," he said. "*Four* of them have been *ejaculated* on . . ." He trailed off, aghast. Even though I'd told him all this, even though he'd heard and cared, it took the harsh reality check of realizing that it was happening to those he loved to really make him grasp the true horror of what was happening. It got personal.

And just like the problem that caused it, this revolution *is* personal. Across the country and around the world, women and men are standing up to sexism in their own personal, dignified, and beautifully unique ways:

Tired of cold callers asking to speak to the "man of the house," now I put them on to my 6-year-old son . . . he sings them "Sexy and I Know It."

You don't *look* like a lesbian . . . "But since I am a lesbian, I *must* look like one!" is my answer.

I used to purposefully jam the copier so people would stop asking me to make photocopies for their meetings. I'm an engineer.

A woman working in an office wrote to tell us that after experiencing sexist jibes and insults at work she simply printed off her employer's sexual-harassment policy and firmly placed a copy on every desk in the workplace.

A waitress found her own way to get around the boss who turned a blind eye every time the chef groped her at work. She took a loaded tray full of glasses next time she walked past him and dropped them, shattering all over the floor, forcing the manager to come over and take note of what had happened.

An engineer realized a TV repairman was trying to take advantage of her presumed lack of technical knowledge when he told her, "TV needs a new tube, love, pricey." Quick as a flash, she replied, "That's a split capacitor; fix it for free or I'll report you." He fixed it for free and threw in an apology too.

A man described running after another guy who was shouting at two women in the street. He tapped him on the shoulder and asked him, simply, "Why did you do that?"

It's personal. Change is happening in a million different ways. Strong women are providing thousands of kick-ass role models for a new generation of fearless girls:

Aged 10: mocked mercilessly at school cos I said I was going to be a scientist with a lab with loads of cool stuff in it.

Aged 41: I'm actually an engineer (semiconductor failure analysis), and I DO have a lab with loads of cool stuff in it :)

Careers teacher said he'd eat my indentures if I became engineer. Took them & salt to school 5 years later.

One mother told me we should not underestimate a burgeoning tribe of fierce parents who will not let their daughters grow up to be cowed by sexism:

My daughter is clever, inquisitive, determined, strong, confident, imaginative, understanding, exuberant and bursting with the promise of all the achievements and experiences that await her. She could rule the world. Yet already and daily from here on in she will be slowly, gradually, insidiously told that she should be good, not make a fuss, make way for men, not expect too much from a career, have children, get married, look after a man and be thin and pretty.

I see it as my maternal duty to guard her against all of this. If it takes my last breath I will use it to tell her that she can be as great as she wants to be, that she should never accept less because she is female and that she is equal to any man that she ever meets.

I will not allow her glorious nature to suffer because the world cannot accept that she is a girl and a woman.

So this is it. It's happening everywhere. Don't think that you can hide, because you can't. Don't think you can opt out. You're either with us or you're against us. There is no in-between, because it's the in-between that has been the problem for so long. The people who discriminate against us, who scream at us in the street, who grope us at work, who attack us and abuse us and assault us—they're bullies. And bullies flourish only in an environment where their victims are weakened by isolation, where there's no supporting ourselves because there's no support to be had. But a bully loses his strength like a candle being snuffed out when the rest of the school stands up and links arms with the victim. There's no sitting on the fence, because sitting on the fence is turning a blind eye—even if you don't mean to or didn't realize you were until now. It doesn't make you bad or wrong if you just hadn't noticed sexism before. It doesn't mean that you're part of the problem. It means that now you can be part of the solution. We need you. We need you to stand with us. We can't do it without you. You can't achieve a victory that requires a culture shift from a whole society without half of that society on board. But more: This is for you too! It's for everybody who wants to live in a fair society—for the men who want fair paternity leave and hate the Diet Coke ad and the aunts and uncles and mothers and brothers and grandpas of all those little girls who deserve to grow up in a world where their horizons aren't limited and stunted and constrained to the number of inches around their stomachs. It's for the boys who deserve to cry when they need to, without being reprimanded and masculinized and forced into muscular, angry straitjackets.

The thing about sexism is that it is an eminently solvable problem. Unlike so many of the other major issues facing our society, which demand huge amounts of money, or medical research, or legislation to fix, the answer to this is already within our reach. The Everyday Sexism Project set out not to resolve the problem but to force people to recognize that it is real. I can't point to a single practical political change or a missing law that will make everything right, because it's not that clear-cut. But again and again in the past four years, I've seen change happen. I've seen what success looks like. And it's really very simple. Because all the different issues that the project has exposed—sexism, harassment, assault, rape—are so closely connected, so too are the methods of resolving them. By creating a cultural shift in attitudes and behaviors toward women, we would take a huge step toward tackling each of those problems. Whether it's in the professional, media, domestic, or social sphere, by making it unacceptable to disrespect and belittle and dehumanize women in one world, we immediately shift their status in another. But it truly does have to be a team effort. It's a bit like recycling—it's something every single person can make an active, practical contribution to, starting today, if they choose. But just like recycling, a few well-meaning people going all out and doing everything in their power to make it work won't make a jot of difference overall if everybody else carries on shrugging their shoulders and tossing the milk carton into the bin.

So be the person in the meeting who objects to an applicant being dismissed because she is a "maternity risk." Be the aunt or uncle who buys his niece a chemistry set and her nephew a toy stove. Be the picture editor who doesn't illustrate every article with a pair of women's legs. Be the teenager who challenges his friends when they're calling girls sluts. Be the colleague who points out inappropriate behavior when it occurs. Be the TV exec who commissions a program with five female leads. Be the guy who tells his friend it's not cool to shout at women in the street. Be the advertising director who thinks outside the box. Be the person at the bus stop who steps in to stop harassment. Be the parent who teaches their son about consent.

What we need is a change in ideas and inherited assumptions. And that is something everybody can contribute to. Enough is enough.

▸ Prior to reading the posts/tweets from the Everyday Sexism project, I would have been filled with doubt about whether I was making a mountain out of a molehill . . . I probably would have left it alone and thought, "Well, that's just how it is. There's nothing we can do." Fortunately, the E.S. project shows us all that it is the insidious nature

of small, everyday occurrences which erode an individual's confidence and freedom, and society's integrity and fairness; and that it IS worth rearranging even the smallest stone in order to re-direct the flow of the river.

For me, that one entry sums up what's happening with feminism now, and with this simple pragmatic, welcoming wave of activism. We might be moving small stones. People might sometimes find it hard to accept. They might point out that there are boulders elsewhere, or remark that they're used to seeing the bed of the stream littered with pebbles—that's just the way it is. But it doesn't have to be. And if you will pick up just one stone, then together we *will* redirect the flow of the river.

A Note on Statistics

The Vital Statistics sections included at the beginning of each chapter of this book are intended as a statistical snapshot of the inequalities referred to in each section, but they by no means represent the beginning and end of the available data on any given issue. I am aware that readers might have questions about the methodology and selection criteria of different studies, and while I have made every effort to include statistics only from reliable sources, I absolutely acknowledge that there may be other, occasionally conflicting data to be considered elsewhere. These statistics do not directly inform the conclusions of each chapter but nonetheless might provide a helpful general idea of the available research in each area.

Resources

This list is by no means exhaustive, but it's a good place to start!

For Information and Getting Involved

American Association of University Women: www.aauw.org
Amy Poehler's Smart Girls: http://amysmartgirls.com
Audre Lorde Project: http://alp.org
Black Women United for Action: www.bwufa.com
Canadian Women's Foundation: www.candadianwomen.org
Collective Action for Safe Spaces: www.collectiveactiondc.org
Crunk Feminist Collective: www/crunkfeministcollective.com
DisAbled Women's Network Canada: www.dawncanada.net
End Rape On Campus: http://endrapeoncampus.org
Equality Now: www.equalitynow.org
Feminist Alliance for International Action: ww.fafaia-afai.org
Feministing: http://feministing.com
Feminist Majority Foundation: www.feminist.org
Gay & Lesbian Alliance Against Defamation: www.glaad.org
Girls Action Foundation: http://girlsactionfoundation.ca.en
Girls for Gender Equity: www.ggenyc.org
Girls Inc.: www.girlsinc.org
Girls Leadership: http://girlsleadership.org
Grrrl Zine Network: http://grrrlzines.net
HeForShe: www.heforshe.org
Hollaback!: www.ihollaback.org
INCITE! Women, Gender Non-Conforming and Trans People of Color Against Violence: www.incite-national.org

Know Your IX: http://knowyourix.org
Latinitas: http://laslatinitas.com
Men Can Stop Rape: www.mencanstoprape.org
Mobility International USA: www.miusa.org
Ms. Foundation for Women: http://forwomen.org
National Asian Pacific American Women's Forum: http://napawf.org
National Council of Women of Canada: www.ncwcanada.com
National Indigenous Women's Resource Center: www.niwrc.org
National Latina Institute for Reproductive Health: www.latinainstitute.org/en
National LGBTQ Taskforce: www.thetaskforce.org
National Organization for Men Against Sexism: www.nomas.org
National Organization for Women: http://now.org
Native Women's Association of Canada: www.nwac.ca
OWL—National Older Women's League: www.owl-national.org
Raging Grannies: http://raginggrannies.org/philosophy
Representation Project: http://therepresentationproject.org
SisterSong Women of Color Reproductive Justice Collective: www.sistersong.net
SPARK Movement: www.sparksummit.com
Stop Street Harassment: www.stopstreetharassment.org
UN Women: www.unwomen.org
White Ribbon: www.whiteribbon.ca
Women Action and the Media: WAM!: www.womenactionmedia.org
Women's Media Center: www.womensmediacenter.com

For Help and Support

1 in 6 Support for Men: http://1in6.org
AHA Foundation (Honor Violence): www.theahafoundation.org/honor-violence
Canadian Association of Sexual Assault Centres: www.casca.ca
GLBT National Help Center: www.glbtnationalhelpcenter.org
International Sexual Assault Resources: www.rainn.org/get-help/sexual-asault-and-rape-international-resoures
National Domestic Violence Hotline: 1-800-799-7233 | 1-800-787-3224 (TTY); www.thehotline.org
Rape, Abuse & Incest National Network: www.rainn.org

Acknowledgments

This book would not exist without the thousands of people who found the strength to speak out about often deeply personal and painful experiences. I am immensely grateful for their courage.

Enormous thanks are due to so many people without whom it wouldn't have been possible to begin at all.

To Elinor Cooper, who truly "got it" from the start and was the best guide and friend I could have hoped for, and everybody at Rochelle Stevens. To Georgia Garrett and everybody at Rogers, Coleridge and White for their kindness, enthusiasm, and support. To Melanie Jackson, for her invaluable guidance and expertise. To Marcia Markland, for sharing my passion and excitement and being such a staunch supporter, and the whole fantastic team at Thomas Dunne Books, including Quressa Robinson, Joanie Martinez, Staci Burt, Laura Clark, and Tracey Guest. To Abigail Bergstrom, for her infectious enthusiasm about the project and her passion in championing it, and all the brilliant team at Simon & Schuster. To Monica Hope and Cynthia Merman, for being the most excellent, thoughtful, and meticulous copy editors I have been lucky enough to work with.

To each inspiring interviewee who gave so generously of her (and his!) time and energy, and to those, in particular Harriet Walter, whose insights were invaluable even if their words do not appear directly in this book. To each of the schools and universities that so kindly welcomed and accommodated me.

To James Bartlett, whose patience and charity enabled the project to come about in the first place; to every one of the incredible volunteers who keep it running; to Emer O'Toole, who was my saving grace at the exact moment when it all could have fallen apart; and Beryl-Joan Bonsu, for her tireless work and assistance. To Peter Florence, for his enormous generosity, kindness, and support of the project and this book. To Aisha Mirza, Lucy Anne Holmes, and Aileen Bintliff, for their compassionate and intelligent guidance as trustees.

To Natasha Walter, Chitra Nagarajan, Ceri Goddard, Holly Dustin, Sarah Green, Stella Creasy, Lauren Wolfe, Soraya Chemaly, Jaclyn Friedman, Josh Shahrayar, Nimko Ali, Leyla Hussein, and all the other people, too numerous to name, who welcomed me and the project into the feminist movement with open arms and made us at home. To Anna, who first showed me how to break gender boundaries and still inspires me daily, and to Nick, without whose tireless help, support, listening ear, and love none of it ever would have happened. And finally to my mom, who showed me what compassionate social justice looked like before I even knew what it meant.